CONCISE COLL

GILL: THE LAW OF ARBITRATION

OTHER BOOKS IN THIS SERIES

Tort, by C. D. Baker
Law for Retailers, by Jennifer Brave
"O" Level Law, by W. J. Brown
Contract, by F. R. Davies
Sale of Goods and Consumer Credit, by A. P. Dobson
Labour Law, by C. D. Drake
The English Legal System, by K. J. Eddey
Hotel and Catering Law in Britain, by David Field
Family Law, by Judge H. B. Grant and Jennifer Levin
Land Law, by W. Swinfen Green and N. Henderson
Shipping Law, by Robert Grime
Introduction to Commercial Law, by C. Hamblin and F. B. Wright
"A" Level Law, by B. Hogan, P. Seago and G. Bennett
The Law and Procedure of Meetings, by Matthew Moore
General Principles of Law, by C. R. Newton
Criminal Law, by P. Seago
Press Law, by Robin Callender Smith
Construction Law, by J. Uff
Patents, Trade Marks, Copyright and Industrial Designs, by T. A. Blanco White and Robin Jacob

W. Green & Son Ltd.'s *Concise College Texts—*

Questions and Answers on the Law of Scotland, by F. Bates and W. Coull
General Principles of Scots Law, by Enid A. Marshall

AUSTRALIA
The Law Book Company Ltd.
Sydney: Melbourne: Brisbane: Perth

CANADA
The Carswell Company Ltd.
Toronto: Calgary: Vancouver: Ottawa

INDIA
N. M. Tripathi Private Ltd.
Bombay
and
Eastern Law House Private Ltd.
Calcutta

M.P.P. House
Bangalore

ISRAEL
Steimatzky's Agency Ltd.
Jerusalem: Tel Aviv: Haifa

PAKISTAN
Pakistan Law House
Karachi

CONCISE COLLEGE TEXTS

GILL: THE LAW OF ARBITRATION

Third Edition

ENID A. MARSHALL, M.A., LL.B., Ph.D.
*Solicitor, Reader in Business Law
at the University of Stirling*

WITH A FOREWORD
BY
Anthony Walton Q.C.
Senior Editor of "Russell on Arbitration"

LONDON
SWEET & MAXWELL
1983

First Edition 1965
Second Edition 1975
Third Edition 1983
Reprinted 1985
Reprinted 1990
Reprinted 1994

Published by Sweet & Maxwell Limited now of
South Quay Plaza 183 Marsh Wall, London
Computerset by Promenade Graphics Limited, Cheltenham
Printed in Great Britain by
Hartnolls Limited, Bodmin, Cornwall.

British Library Cataloguing in Publication Data
Gill, William H.
    The law of arbitration.—3rd ed.—Concise
college texts
    1. Arbitration and award—England
    I. Title   II. Marshall, Enid A.
    344.207'9   KD7645

ISBN 0–421–25110–7

All rights reserved
No part of this publication may be
reproduced or transmitted, in any form or by
any means, electronic, mechanical, photocopying,
recording or otherwise, or stored in any retrieval
system of any nature, without the written permission
of the publisher, application for which shall be made
to the Publisher

©
William H. Gill
&
Enid A. Marshall
1983

FOREWORD

As the Preface to the latest (20th) edition of *Russell* points out, arbitration is in the future likely to become ever more popular. There are various reasons for this, but high amongst them is the growing realisation that arbitration does in truth afford the parties a choice of the law and a choice of the judges that they do want, and, more importantly, an opportunity to reject the law which, and to reject the particular judges whom, they do not want.

The opportunity is there. That is undoubted. But like any other opportunity it has to be grasped. What is more, it has to be grasped in time. A single wrong step and all advantage may be thrown aside. A "modern" amongst chess players once observed "As soon as White has played P-K4, his game is in its last throes." Whether that be so or not, it is clear that in the much more serious business of arbitration an initial step—an ill-thought-out arbitration clause in a contract—can have serious consequences in that the real advantages that could have been obtained have not been obtained, the wishes of at least one party have been thwarted and the opportunity has not been grasped.

How is this to be avoided? In one way only. Every party to a contract must take thought as to what he wishes to happen if there is a dispute, and, if he desires arbitration, provide exactly for the kind of arbitration that he wants, so that he can get the things he himself regards as advantageous. In short, he must at an early stage take effective steps to make a real choice.

But choice can only be made effectively in the light of knowledge of what arbitration can provide, how it works, and how it can go wrong if wrong steps are taken. Nothing in law is so heavily punished as ignorance.

That is where *Gill* comes in so handy. To start off with, it is concise. To obtain a copy and read it through from cover to cover before finalising the arbitration clause is merest prudence, and well within the time available even to a busy person.

Not that *Gill* is in any sense potted (though even potting, when the hands are as skilled as those of my old friend William Gill, and those of Dr. Enid Marshall upon whom his mantle has fallen, is most wholesome as well as being most useful). It is rather that *Gill* is that most indispensable of travel guides, the guide that tells you the essential things you want to know before you embark upon your journey.

And, as in the case of the best of such guides, all the directions are here given with the greatest clarity of style and are as full as necessary before the journey starts. This guide also has beautiful illustrations.

Dr. Marshall is much to be congratulated.

June 1983　　　　　　　　　　　　　　　　　　　　Anthony Walton

PREFACE

The object of this work as expressed by Mr. Gill in the prefaces to the first two editions, is "to give in simple language a general survey of the law and practice of arbitration."

As editor of this third edition I have not departed from Mr. Gill's objective, but have thought it desirable, if not essential, to find space for a number of innovations, while substantially retaining the pre-existing dimensions of the book.

First, there have been since 1974 many developments in the law of arbitration—both statutory (the Arbitration Acts of 1975 and 1979, with their associated subordinate legislation) and judicial; space had to be found to bring the text up to date in these respects.

Secondly, it seemed desirable, with students particularly in mind, to adopt an explanatory approach to decided cases. This involved abandoning the copious citation of authority given in the second edition and using the space thus saved to include short accounts, or at least brief indications of the facts, of selected important cases only. Full citation of authority and also fuller accounts of virtually all the cases mentioned in this book will be found in *Russell on Arbitration* (20th ed. by Anthony Walton and Mary Vitoria), on which this little book heavily relies; *Russell* will continue to be essential reading for any in-depth study of arbitration as well as an indispensable tool for practising arbitrators.

Thirdly, it seemed desirable, with practising arbitrators and advanced students not wholly excluded, to enlarge the appended material: whereas the Appendix in the second edition set out only Parts I and III of the Arbitration Act 1950, there are now eight appendices, which may be consulted for the whole of the Act of 1950 (as amended), and also for other statutes and for statutory instruments.

Fourthly, it seemed desirable to include a chapter giving an introduction to the law of arbitration in Scotland, where the Acts of 1950 and 1979 do not apply, and a chapter on some aspects of international arbitration.

I am grateful to the publishers for having given me the opportunity of undertaking this edition and for their work in the preparation of the Tables of Cases and Statutes and the Index.

The law is intended to be stated as at January 1, 1983, though it has been possible to add some material which became available to me not later than May 25, 1983.

June 10, 1983   Enid A. Marshall

CONTENTS

	page
Foreword	v
Preface	vii
Table of Cases	xv
Table of Statutes	xxiii

CHAPTER 1: THE NATURE OF AN ARBITRATION	1
Generally	1
The Arbitration Acts	1
Statutory arbitrations	2
Advantages of arbitration	3
The qualities of an arbitrator	3
Valuations and certifications	4
(1) *Sutcliffe* v. *Thackrah* (1974)	5
(2) *Arenson* v. *Arenson* (1977)	6
Limitations of time	8
(1) Limitations imposed by statute	8
(2) Limitations imposed by the arbitration agreement	10
CHAPTER 2: THE ARBITRATION AGREEMENT	14
Capacity of parties	14
The statutory definition	16
Incorporation of arbitration agreement from other contract	18
Terms of arbitration agreement	21
Scope of arbitration agreement	23
Enforcement of arbitration agreement	24
(1) When a party does not proceed to arbitration	24
(2) Legal proceedings have been commenced by one party in respect of a dispute contained in an arbitration agreement	25
Alteration and amendment of arbitration agreement	30
Revocation of arbitration agreement	31
Repudiation, frustration and abandonment of arbitration agreement	31
(1) *Bremer Vulkan*	31
(2) *The Hannah Blumenthal*	33

Chapter 3: Arbitrators and Umpires — 35

Generally — 35
Appointment by the parties — 35
   Reference to a sole arbitrator — 37
   Reference to two or more arbitrators — 38
   Reference to a fluctuating body — 40
Appointment by the court — 40
   Section 10 — 41
     (a) Failure in the appointment of a sole arbitrator — 41
     (b) Failure of an appointed arbitrator to act — 41
     (c) Failure in the appointment of an umpire or third arbitrator — 42
     (d) Failure of an umpire or third arbitrator to act — 42
   Section 25 — 43
Revocation of authority and removal — 43
   Section 1 — 44
   Section 2 — 45
   Section 7 — 45
   Section 13 (3) — 45
   Section 23 (1) — 46
   Section 24 (1) — 46
   Section 24 (2) — 47
   Section 25 — 47
Remuneration — 48

Chapter 4: Procedure Prior to the Hearing — 50

Notification to arbitrator of appointment — 50
First duties of arbitrator — 51
The preliminary meeting — 52
   Points of claim and defence — 52
   Particulars of claim or of counterclaim — 53
   Amendments — 53
   Discovery and inspection of documents — 53
   Inspection of property and things by arbitrator and parties — 53
   Fixing time and place for hearing — 54
   Proceeding *ex parte* — 55

Chapter 5: Procedure at the Hearing — 56

The rules of natural justice — 56
Private communications from parties — 57
Persons entitled to be present — 57
Conduct of the hearing — 57

Closing the case	59
Stamps on documents	60
Counsel's opinion	60
Legal adviser at the hearing	60
Joint arbitrators	61
Irregularities in procedure	61
Protest against irregularities	62
Waiver of procedural objections	62
Delegation of duties	64

CHAPTER 6: EVIDENCE — 66

Generally	66
Kinds of evidence	66
Admissibility of evidence	67
Arbitrator must hear all evidence	68
Decision must be made on the evidence	69
The taking of evidence	69
Attendance of witnesses	70
False evidence	71
Competence of witnesses	71
Examination of witnesses	72
(a) Examination-in-chief	72
(b) Cross-examination	73
(c) Re-examination	74
Arbitrator calling witnesses	74
Expert witnesses	74

CHAPTER 7: THE MAKING OF THE AWARD — 76

Time for making award	76
Enlargement of time	76
Formal requisites	77
Substantive requisites	79

CHAPTER 8: PROCEEDINGS SUBSEQUENT TO THE AWARD — 83

Effect of award	83
Award does not transfer property	84
Award as evidence	84
Interest in awards	84
Enforcement of award	86
Enforcement under section 26	86
Enforcement of award by action	88
Challenge of award	90
Appeal under arbitration agreement	90

Defence to action on award or action for declaration	90
Remission or setting aside	90
Appeal to court under Arbitration Act 1979	92
(1) Judicial review of award	92
(2) Determination of preliminary point of law	95
(3) Exclusion agreements	96

Chapter 9: Costs   99

Section 18	99
Extent of arbitrator's discretion	100

Chapter 10: Introduction to Scots Law of Arbitration   103

Terminology	103
Sources	103
The courts and arbitration	104
(1) Enforcement of arbitration agreement	104
(2) Questions of law	104
Appointment of arbiters and oversmen	106
(1) Arbitration (Scotland) Act 1894	106
(2) Law Reform (Miscellaneous Provisions) (Scotland) Act 1980, section 17	107
Procedure	108
Time-limits and prorogation	108
Enforcement of award	109
Challenge of award	109
(1) "Corruption, bribery, or falsehood"	109
(2) Excess of jurisdiction	111
(3) Improper procedure	111
(4) Defects in award	111
Judicial references	111

Chapter 11: Some Aspects of International Arbitration   113

Proper law of the contract and law governing the arbitration proceedings	113
Part II of the Arbitration Act 1950	114
Arbitration Act 1975	116
Recognition of arbitration agreements	116
Enforcement of awards	118
Arbitration Act 1979	119
UNCITRAL Arbitration Rules	119
I.C.C. arbitrations	119
Arbitration (International Investment Disputes) Act 1966	119

Appendices

1. Arbitration Act 1950	123
2. Arbitration Act 1979	141
3. The Arbitration (Commodity Contracts) Order 1979	148
4. Arbitration (Scotland) Act 1894	151
5. Administration of Justice (Scotland) Act 1972	153
6. Arbitration Act 1975	154
7. The Arbitration (Foreign Awards) Order 1978	158
8. The Arbitration (Foreign Awards) Order 1979	162
Index	165

TABLE OF CASES

ABU DHABI GAS LIQUEFACTION CO. LTD. v. Eastern Bechtel Corporation and
  Anor. [1982] 2 Lloyd's Rep. 425 43
Adams v. Catley (1892) 66 L.T. 687 28
—— v. Great North of Scotland Railway Co. [1891] A.C. 31; (1890) 18 R.
  (H.L.) 1 110
"Agroexport" Enterprise D'Etat pour le Commerce Extérieur v. N.V.
  Goorden Import Cy. S.A. [1956] 1 Lloyd's Rep. 319 .... 51, 68
Allen v. Francis (1845) 9 Jur. 691 70
Alfa Nord, The; A/S Gunnstein & Co. K/S v. Jensen, Krebs and Nielsen
  [1977] 2 Lloyd's Rep. 434 117
Amalgamated Metal Corporation v. Khoon Seng Co. Ltd. [1977] 2 Lloyd's
  Rep. 310 90
Angeliki, The [1973] 2 Lloyd's Rep. 226 12
Anglo-Newfoundland Development Co. v. R. [1920] 2 K.B. 214 28
Annefield, The [1971] P. 168 21
Anon. (1468) Jenk. 128 64
Arenson v. Arenson [1977] A.C. 405 .... 1, 6
Aspen Trader, The. See Libra Shipping and Trading Corporation Ltd. v.
  Northern Sales Ltd.
Associated Bulk Carriers Ltd. v. Koch Shipping Inc. [1978] 1 Lloyd's Rep.
  24 118
Astley and Tyldesley Coal Co., Re (1899) 68 L.J.Q.B. 252 8
Atlantic Shipping and Trading Co. v. Louis Dreyfus & Co. [1922] 2 A.C.
  250 .... 22, 23

BABANAFT INTERNATIONAL CO. S.A. v. Avant Petroleum Inc. [1982] 1 W.L.R.
  871 .... 13, 96
Baker v. Yorkshire Fire and Life Assurance Co. [1892] 1 Q.B. 144 18
Banks v. Banks (1835) 1 Gale 46 70
Barnes v. Hayward (1857) 1 H. & N. 742 49
Baron v. Sunderland Corporation [1966] 2 Q.B. 56 17
Batson, Re, ex p. Hastie (1894) 70 L.T. 382 71
Beck and Jackson, Re (1857) 1 C.B.(N.S.) 695 77
Bellshill and Mossend Co-operative Society Ltd. v. Dalziel Co-operative
  Society Ltd. [1960] A.C. 832; 1960 S.C. (H.L.) 64 89
Belsfield Court Construction Co. Ltd. v. Pywell [1970] 2 Q.B. 47 84
Bignall v. Gale (1841) 2 M. & G. 830 62
Birchall v. Bullough [1896] 1 Q.B. 325 73
Blackett v. Bates (1865) L.R. 1 Ch. 117 88
Blundell v. Brettargh (1810) 17 Ves. 232 78
Boks & Co. and Peters, Rushton & Co. Ltd., Re [1919] 1 K.B. 491 87
Bonnin v. Neame [1910] 1 Ch. 732 29
Borthwick (Thomas) (Glasgow) Ltd. v. Faure Fairclough Ltd. [1968] 1 Lloyd's
  Rep. 16 46
Bremer Vulkan Schiffbau und Maschinenfabrik v. South India Shipping
  Corporation [1981] A.C. 909 .... 31, 32

xv

TABLE OF CASES

Brighton Marine Palace Ltd. v. Woodhouse [1893] 2 Ch. 486 28
Bristol Corporation v. Aird [1913] A.C. 241 29
British Celanese Ltd. v. Courtaulds Ltd. (1935) 152 L.T. 537 74
British Westinghouse Electric and Manufacturing Co. Ltd. v. Provost, etc., of Aberdeen (1906) 14 S.L.T. 391 (O.H.) 107
Brook and Delcomyn, Re (1864) 16 C.B.(N.S.) 403 62
Brown (Christopher) Ltd. v. Genossenschaft Oesterreichischer Waldbesitzer R. GmbH [1954] 1 Q.B. 8 .... 51, 63, 80, 88
Bruce Ltd. v. Strong [1951] 2 K.B. 447 28
Buckingham v. Daily News Ltd. [1956] 2 Q.B. 534 54
Burton v. Plummer (1834) 2 A. & E. 341 73

CALEDONIAN RAILWAY v. Lockhart (1860) 3 Macq. 808; (1860) 22 D. (H.L.) 8.... 63
Cassidy (Peter) Seed Co. Ltd. v. Osuustukkukauppa I.L. [1957] 1 W.L.R. 273 3
Chandris v. Isbrandtsen-Moller Co. Inc. [1951] 1 K.B. 240 85
Chappell v. North [1891] 2 Q.B. 252 .... 27, 28
City of Calcutta, The (1898) 79 L.T. 517 15
Cleobulos Shipping Co. Ltd. v. Intertanker Ltd. (The Cleon) [1982] Com.L.R. 146 117
Cocks v. Macclefield (1562) Dyer 2186 77
Compagnie Financière pour le Commerce Extérieur S.A. v. Oy. Vehna A.B. [1963] 2 Lloyd's Rep. 178 76
Coombs, Re, (1850) 4 Ex. 839 48
Cottage Club Estates Ltd. v. Woodside Estates Co. (Amersham) Ltd. [1928] 2 K.B. 463 27
Crighton and Law Car and General Insurance Corporation Ltd., Re [1910] 2 K.B. 738 53
Czarnikow v. Roth, Schmidt & Co. [1922] 2 K.B. 478 .... 21, 104, 105

DALTON v. Clark and Fenn (1963) 107 S.J. 595 75
Darnley (Earl) v. London, Chatham & Dover Railway (1867) L.R. 2 H.L. 43 63
Davies v. Price (1864) 34 L.J.Q.B. 8 .... 36, 63
Denton v. Legge (1895) 72 L.T. 626 29
Dineen v. Walpole [1969] 1 Lloyd's Rep. 261 100
Dobson v. Groves (1844) 6 Q.B. 637 61
Docker v. Hyams [1969] 1 Lloyd's Rep. 341 30
Drew v. Drew (1855) 2 Macq. 1; (1855) 18 D. (H.L.) 4 .... 56, 62
Dreyfus (Louis) & Co. v. Arunachala Ayya (1930) L.R. 58 Ind.App. 381 60
Drummond v. Hamer [1942] 1 K.B. 352 .... 25, 37
Dunmore (Earl of) v. M'Inturner (1829) 7 S. 595 108

EADS v. Williams (1854) 24 L.J.Ch. 531 .... 69, 89
Eastern Bechtel Corporation and Anor. v. Ishikawajima-Harima Heavy Industries Ltd. See Abu Dhabi Gas Liquefaction Co. Ltd. v. Eastern Bechtel Corporation and Anor.
Ellison v. Bray (1864) 9 L.T.(N.S.) 730 61
Emanuel (Lewis) & Son Ltd. v. Sammut [1959] 2 Lloyd's Rep. 629 76
Emmanuel Colocotronis (No. 2), The [1982] 1 W.L.R. 1096 .... 20, 21
English Exporters (London) Ltd. v. Eldonwall Ltd. [1973] Ch. 415 75
Enoch and Zaretzky, Bock & Co., Re [1910] 1 K.B. 327 .... 54, 68, 74
Erich Schroeder, The, L. Figueiredo Navegacas S.A. v. Reederei Richard Schroeder K.G. [1974] 1 Lloyd's Rep. 192 100

TABLE OF CASES

European & American Steam Shipping Co. *v.* Crosskey & Co. (1860) 8 C.B.(N.S.) 397 44
European Grain and Shipping Ltd. *v.* R. Johnston [1982] 1 Lloyd's Rep. 414 77
Eyre and Leicester Corporation, *Re* [1892] 1 Q.B. 136 43

FAIRCLOUGH, DODD & JONES LTD. *v.* J. H. Vantol Ltd. [1957] 1 W.L.R. 136 3
Fairlie Yacht Slip Ltd. *v.* Lumsden, 1977 S.L.T. (Notes) 41 106
Falkingham *v.* Victorian Railways Commissioner [1900] A.C. 452 68
Fallon *v.* Calvert [1960] 2 Q.B. 201 74
Fehr (Frank) & Co. *v.* Kassam Jivraj & Co. Ltd. (1949) 82 Ll.L.Rep. 673 18
Finer *v.* Melgrave, *The Times*, June 4, 1959 30
Finzel, Berry & Co. *v.* Eastcheap Dried Fruit Co. [1962] 2 Lloyd's Rep. 11 41
Ford *v.* Clarksons Holidays Ltd. [1971] 1 W.L.R. 1412 29
Ford's Hotel Co. *v.* Bartlett [1896] A.C. 1 28
Fowler *v.* Fowler and Sine [1963] P. 311 73

GATLIFFE *v.* Dunn (1738) Barnes 55 77
Gerard (Lord) and London & North Western Railway, *Re* [1895] 1 Q.B. 459 .... 44, 45
Gilbert & Wright, *Re* (1904) 20 T.L.R. 164 48
Goodwins, Jardine & Co. Ltd. *v.* Brand & Son (1905) 7 F. 995 19
Greenough *v.* Eccles (1859) 28 L.J.C.P. 160 73
Gunton *v.* Nurse (1821) 5 Moore C.P. 259 84

HAGGER *v.* Baker (1845) 14 M. & W. 9 68
Haigh *v.* Haigh (1861) 31 L.J.Ch. 420 .... 57, 61, 62
Hamlyn *v.* Betteley (1880) 6 Q.B.D. 63 63
Hare and Milne, *Re* (1839) 6 Bing.N.C. 158 60
Harvey *v.* Shelton (1844) 7 Beav. 455 62
Heaven & Kesterton Ltd. *v.* Sven Widaeus A/B [1958] 1 Lloyd's Rep. 101 100
Henck (Gunter) *v.* Andre & Cie. S.A. [1970] 1 Lloyd's Rep. 235 .... 23, 46
Heyman *v.* Darwins Ltd. [1942] A.C. 356 .... 23, 26
Hicks *v.* Richardson (1797) 1 B. & P. 93 78
Hodson *v.* Railway Passengers' Assurance Co. [1904] 2 K.B. 833 28
Holt *v.* Meddowcroft (1816) 4 M. & S. 467 63
Hookway (F.E.) & Co. Ltd. *v.* Alfred Isaacs & Sons and Ors. [1954] 1 Lloyd's Rep. 491 58
Hopcraft *v.* Hickman (1824) 2 S. & S. 130 64

INTERNATIONAL SEA TANKERS INC. *v.* Hemisphere Shipping Co. Ltd. (The Wenjiang) [1982] 1 Lloyd's Rep. 128 95
Iossifoglu *v.* Coumantaros and Ors. [1941] 1 K.B. 396 50
Ives & Barker *v.* Willans [1894] 2 Ch. 478 .... 28, 29, 30

JOHNSON *v.* Lamb, 1981 S.L.T. 300 (O.H.) 107
—— *v.* Latham (1850) 91 L.J.Q.B. 329 77
Johnston *v.* Cheape (1817) 5 Dow. 247 .... 54, 69
Jugoslavenska Oceanska Plovidba *v.* Castle Investment Co. Inc. (The Kozara) [1974] Q.B. 292 81
Jungheim, Hopkins & Co. *v.* Foukelmann [1909] 2 K.B. 948 63

KAWASAKI KISEN KAISHA LTD. *v.* Government of Ceylon [1962] 1 Lloyd's Rep. 424 51

Keighley, Maxsted & Co. and Durant & Co., *Re* [1893] 1 Q.B. 405	40
Kirchner *v.* Gruban [1909] 1 Ch. 413	29
Kiril Mischeff Ltd. *v.* British Doughnut Co. Ltd. [1954] 1 Lloyd's Rep. 237	37
Kitchen *v.* Turnbull (1871) 20 W.R. 253	30
Knowles & Sons Ltd. *v.* Bolton Corporation [1900] 2 Q.B. 253	76
Kruger Townwear *v.* Northern Assurance Co. [1953] 1 W.L.R. 1049	30
LAING (JAMES), SON & Co. (M/C) LTD. *v.* Eastcheap Dried Fruit Co. [1962] 2 Lloyd's Rep. 15	53
Lane *v.* Herman [1939] 3 All E.R. 353	28
Lewis *v.* Haverfordwest R.D.C. [1953] 1 W.L.R. 1486	100
Liberian Shipping Corporation "Pegasus" *v.* A. King & Sons Ltd. [1967] 2 Q.B. 86	10, 11, 12
Libra Shipping and Trading Corporation Ltd. *v.* Northern Sales Ltd. (The Aspen Trader) [1981] 1 Lloyd's Rep. 273	11, 12
Lindsay (W.N.) & Co. *v.* European Grain & Shipping Agency Ltd. [1963] 1 Lloyd's Rep. 437	52
Lingood *v.* Eade (1742) 1 Atk. 501	64
Little *v.* Newton (1841) 9 Dowl. 437	64
Llandrindod Wells Water Co. *v.* Hawksley (1904) 20 T.L.R. 241	48
London General Omnibus Co. Ltd. *v.* Lavell [1901] 1 Ch. 135	54
Lovelock Ltd. *v.* Exportles [1968] 1 Lloyd's Rep. 163	17
M'LAREN *v.* Aikman, 1939 S.C. 222	111
M'Millan & Son Ltd. *v.* Rowan & Co. (1903) 5 F. 317	107
Macpherson Train & Co. Ltd. *v.* Milhem (J.) & Sons [1955] 2 Lloyd's Rep. 59	68
Mansell *v.* Burredge and Roberts (1797) 7 Term Rep. 352	16
Mansfield *v.* Robinson [1928] 2 K.B. 353	99
Marchon Products Ltd. *v.* Thornes (1954) 71 R.P.C. 445	29
Maritime Insurance Co. *v.* Assecuranz-Union von 1865 (1935) 52 Ll.L.R. 16	60
Marsh *v.* Bulteel (1822) 5 B. & Ald. 507	89
Martin *v.* Selsdon Fountain Pen Co. Ltd. (No. 2) (1950) 67 R.P.C. 64	29
Matson *v.* Trower (1824) Ry. & Moo. 17	62
Maunder, *Re* (1883) 49 L.T. 535	60
Mediterranean and Eastern Export Co. Ltd. *v.* Fortress Fabrics Ltd. (1948) 81 Ll.L.R. 401	69
Melgrave and Melgrave *v.* Finer. *See* Finer *v.* Melgrave.	
Merak, The [1965] P. 223	12, 20
Middlemiss & Gould (a Firm) *v.* Hartlepool Corporation [1972] 1 W.L.R. 1643	87
Miller (James) and Partners Ltd. *v.* Whitworth Street Estates (Manchester) Ltd. [1970] A.C. 583	105, 114
Milnes and Robertson, *Re* (1854) 15 C.B. 451	14
Minister of Materials *v.* Steel Bros. & Co. Ltd. [1952] 1 Lloyd's Rep. 87	29
Mitchell *v.* Cable (1848) 10 D. 1297	105
Mitchell Construction Kinnear Moodie Group *v.* East Anglia Regional Hospital Board [1971] C.L.Y. 375	53
Mitchell-Gill *v.* Buchan, 1921 S.C. 390	106
Modern Building Wales Ltd. *v.* Limmer & Trinidad Co. Ltd. [1975] 1 W.L.R. 1281	19
Moran *v.* Lloyd's [1983] 2 W.L.R. 672	91
Morphett, *Re* (1845) 14 L.J.Q.B. 259	30

TABLE OF CASES xix

Morriston Tinplate Co. v. Brooker, Dore & Co. [1908] 1 K.B. 403 24
Morton v. Hargreaves Motors (1963) 107 S.J. 513 75
Moscow V/O Exportkhleb v. Helmville Ltd. (The Jocelyne) [1977] 2 Lloyd's Rep. 121 .... 11, 12
Munday v. Black (1861) 30 L.J.C.P. 193 54

NATIONAL ENTERPRISES v. Racal Communications [1975] Ch. 397 25
Naumann v. Nathan (1930) 37 Ll.L.R. 249 56
Nea Agrex S.A. v. Baltic Shipping Co. Ltd. (The Aghios Lazaros) [1976] Q.B. 933 13
Neale v. Ledger (1812) 16 East. 51 40
Nema, The. *See* Pioneer Shipping v. B.T.P. Tioxide.
Nickels v. Hancock (1855) 7 De G.M. & G. 300 .... 88, 89
Nova (Jersey) Knit Ltd. v. Kammgarn Spinnerei GmbH [1977] 1 W.L.R. 713 117

OAKLAND METAL CO. LTD. v. Benaim (D.) & Co. [1953] 2 Q.B. 261 .... 62, 76
Olver v. Hillier [1959] 1 W.L.R. 551 30
Owen v. Nicholl [1948] 1 All E.R. 707 69

PAAL WILSON & Co. A/S v. Partenreederei Hannah Blumenthal (The Hannah Blumenthal) [1982] 3 W.L.R. 1149 .... 31, 33
Paczy (Janos) v. Haendler & Natermann GmbH [1981] 1 Lloyd's Rep. 302 118
Palgrave Gold Mining Co. v. McMillan [1892] A.C. 460 36
Parker, Gaines & Co. v. Turpin [1918] 1 K.B. 358 24
Partabmull Rameshar v. Sethia (K.C.) (1944) [1951] W.N. 389 29
Pegler v. Railway Executive [1948] A.C. 332 10
Perry v. Stopher [1959] 1 W.L.R. 415 100
Philipps v. Philipps (1878) 4 Q.B.D. 127 52
Phipps v. Ingram (1835) 3 Dowl. 669 68
Phoenix Timber Co. Ltd.'s Application, *Re* [1958] 2 Q.B. 1 3
Pioneer Shipping v. B.T.P. Tioxide [1981] 3 W.L.R. 292 94
Pitchers Ltd. v. Plaza (Queensbury) Ltd. (1940) 162 L.T. 213 28
Plews and Middleton, *Re* (1845) 6 Q.B. 845 62
Pollich v. Heatley, 1910 S.C. 469 111
Ponsford v. Swaine (1861) 1 J. & H. 433 48
Printing Machinery Co. Ltd. v. Linotype & Machinery Ltd. [1912] 1 Ch. 566 30
Proctor v. Williams or Williamson (1860) 29 L.J.C.P. 157 61

QUALCAST LTD. v. Haynes [1959] A.C. 743 30

R. v. Vreones [1891] 1 Q.B. 360 71
Racecourse Betting Control Board v. Secretary of State for Air [1944] Ch. 114 2
Ramsden (W.) & Co. v. Jacobs [1922] 1 K.B. 640 .... 61, 62
Randell & Co. v. Thompson (1876) 1 Q.B.D. 748 76
Rathven Parish v. Elgin Parish (1875) L.R. 2 H.L. Sc. and Div. 535; (1875) 2 R. (H.L.) 136 40
Rena K, The [1979] Q.B. 377 .... 20, 117
Renshaw v. Queen Anne Residential Mansions and Hotel Co. [1897] 1 Q.B. 662 29
Riddell v. Sutton (1828) 5 Bing. 200 68
Ridoat v. Pye (1797) 1 B. & P. 91 70

TABLE OF CASES

Ringland v. Lowndes (1864) 17 C.B.(N.S.) 514 51
Rolland v. Cassidy (1888) 13 App.Cas. 770 63
Rowe v. Crossley (1912) 108 L.T. 11 29

S., Re [1973] 1 W.L.R. 178 15
Salkeld and Slater, Re (1840) 12 A. & E. 767 64
Sanderson & Son v. Armour & Co. Ltd., 1922 S.C. (H.L.) 117 104
Scott v. Avery (1856) 5 H.L.Cas. 811 .... 10, 22
Selby v. Whitbread & Co. [1917] 1 K.B. 736 88
Services Europe Atlantique Sud (SEAS) v. Stockholms Rederiaktiebolag Svea
   (The Despina R., The Folias) [1979] A.C. 685 82
Sharpe v. Bickerdyke (1815) 3 Dow. 102 62
Shayler v. Woolf [1946] Ch. 320 27
Shelling v. Farmer (1726) 1 Stra. 646 84
Skips A/S Nordheim v. Syrian Petroleum Co. and Anor. (The Varenna) [1983]
   1 Lloyd's Rep. 416 21
Slade v. Metrodent [1953] 2 Q.B. 112 14
Smeaton Hanscomb & Co. v. Sassoon I. Setty, Son & Co. (No. 2) [1953] 1
   W.L.R. 1481 .... 99, 100
Smith v. Hartley (1851) 10 C.B. 800 79
Spence v. Eastern Counties Railway (1839) 3 Jur. 846 54
Stevenson v. Watson (1879) 48 L.J.C.P. 318 64
Sutcliffe v. Thackrah [1974] A.C. 727 .... 1, 5, 7

TANCRED, ARROL & Co. v. The Steel Co. of Scotland Ltd. (1890) 15 App.Cas.
   125; (1890) 17 R. (H.L.) 31 106
Taunton-Collins v. Cromie [1964] 1 W.L.R. 633 29
Tehno-Impex v. Gebr. van Weelde Scheepvaartkantoor B.V. [1981] 1 Q.B.
   648 85
Tew v. Harris (1847) 11 Q.B. 7 36
Thames Ironworks and Shipbuilding Co. v. R. (1869) 20 L.T. 318 64
Thomas v. Atherton (1878) 10 Ch.D. 185 16
—— v. Fredricks (1847) 10 Q.B. 775 36
Thomas (T.W.) & Co. Ltd. v. Portsea Steamship Co. Ltd. (The Portsmouth)
   [1912] A.C. 1 20
Thorburn v. Barnes (1867) L.R. 2 C.P. 384 89
Threlfall v. Fanshawe (1850) 19 L.J.Q.B. 334 61
Timber Shipping Co. S.A. v. London & Overseas Freighters Ltd. [1972] A.C.
   1 86
Tradax Export S.A. v. Volkswagenwerk A.G. [1970] 1 Q.B. 537 51
Tramountana Armadora S.A. v. Atlantic Shipping Co. S.A. [1978] 1 Lloyd's
   Rep. 391 102
Trew v. Burton (1833) 1 Cr. & M. 533 79
Tritonia Shipping Inc. v. South Nelson Forest Products [1966] 1 Lloyd's Rep.
   114 43
Tunno and Bird, Re (1833) 5 B. & Ad. 488 64
Turner v. Midland Railway [1911] 1 K.B. 832 9

UNDERWOOD AND BEDFORD AND CAMBRIDGE RY., Re (1861) 31 L.J.C.P. 10 .. 61, 77
Union of India v. Bharat Engineering Corporation [1977] I.L.R. Delhi Series,
   Vol. 2 17
Universal Cargo Carriers Corporation v. Citati [1957] 1 W.L.R. 979 91

VASSO, THE, *The Times*, April 6, 1983 54
Vawdrey v. Simpson [1896] 1 Ch. 166 26

Veritas Shipping Corporation v. Anglo-Canadian Cement Ltd. [1966] 1 Lloyd's Rep. 76	46
WAKEFIELD *v.* Llanelly Railway and Dock Co. (1864) 34 Beav. 245	70
Walford, Baker & Co. *v.* Macfie & Sons (1915) 84 L.J.K.B. 2221	51, 68
Walters *v.* Morgan (1792) 2 Cox 369	16, 89
Warinco A.G. *v.* Andre & Cie S.A. [1979] 2 Lloyd's Rep. 298	102
Waugh *v.* H. B. Clifford & Sons Ltd. [1982] 2 W.L.R. 679	15
Westminster Chemicals and Produce Ltd. *v.* Eicholz and Loeser [1954] 1 Lloyd's Rep. 99	64
Whatley *v.* Morland (1834) 2 Dowl. 249	58
Wilkie *v.* Scottish Aviation, 1956 S.C. 198	48
Willesden Local Board and Wright, *Re* [1896] 2 Q.B. 412	87
Willesford *v.* Watson (1873) L.R. 8 Ch. 473	27, 29
Williams *v.* Wallis and Cox [1914] 2 K.B. 478	68
Wilson and Son and Eastern Counties Navigation Co., *Re* [1892] 1 Q.B. 81	40
Wright *v.* Howson (1888) 4 T.L.R. 386	69

TABLE OF STATUTES

[References in **bold** type are to pages where the section is set out in full]

1677	Statute of Frauds (29 Car. 2, c. 3) 89		1934	Law Reform (Miscellaneous Provisions) Act (24 & 25 Geo. 5, c. 41)—
	s. 4 ...... 16, 18			s. 3(1) 85
1697	Arbitration Act (9 Will. 3, c. 15) 1		1938	Evidence Act (1 & 2 Geo. 6, c. 28) 66, 67
1854	Attendance of Witnesses Act (17 & 18 Vict., c. 34)—		1939	Limitation Act (2 & 3 Geo. 6, c. 21) 9
	ss. 3, 4 71		1948	Companies Act (11 & 12 Geo. 6, c. 38)—
	Common Law Procedure Act (17 & 18 Vict., c. 125) 1			s. 32 ...... 15 Agricultural Holdings Act (11 & 12 Geo. 6, c. 63) 2
1889	Arbitration Act (52 & 53 Vict., c. 49) 1, 2, 16, 18, 21, 23, 104		1949	Finance Act (12, 13 & 14 Geo. 6, c. 47)—
	s. 4 ...... 27, 28			s. 35, Sched. 8 78
	Interpretation Act (52 & 53 Vict., c. 63) 159		1950	Arbitration Act (14 Geo. 6, c. 27) 1, 2, 4, 32, 56
1891	Stamp Act (54 & 55 Vict. c. 39) 60			Pt. I 2, 87, 114
1894	Arbitration (Scotland) Act (57 & 58 Vict., c. 13) 103, 106			s. 1 ...... 44, 76, **125**
				s. 2 ...... 44, 45, **125**
	ss. 1–4 ...... 107, **151**			(1) 31
	ss. 5–7 ...... **152**			(2) 45
1908	Statute Law Revision Act (8 Edw. 7, c. 49) 151			(3) 31, 45
				s. 3 ...... **125**
	Agricultural Holdings (Scotland) Act (8 Edw. 7, c. 64) 106			(1)(2) 15
				s. 4 ...... **126**
1911	Perjury Act (1 & 2 Geo. 5, c. 6)—			(1) 16, 19, 25, 26, 27, 28, 30, 104, 117
	s. 1(1)(2) 71			s. 5 ...... **126**
1914	Bankruptcy Act (4 & 5 Geo. 5, c. 59)—			s. 6 ...... 36, 37, 41, 107, **126**
				s. 7 ...... 25, 37, 40, 44, 45, **126**
	s. 56 14			(a) 39, 45
1925	Trustee Act (15 & 16 Geo. 5, c. 19)—			(b) 37, 45
				s. 8 ...... **127**
	s. 15 15			(1) 39
	Law of Property Act (15 & 16 Geo. 5, c. 20)—			(3) 37, 38
				s. 9 ...... 39, 78, **127**
	s. 40 ...... 16, 18			s. 10 ...... 16, 37, 38, 40, 43, **127**
1934	Arbitration Act (24 & 25 Geo. 5, c. 14) 1			(1) 25, 36, 40
				(a) 38, 41
				(b) 38, 41, 42
				(c)(d) 42

1950 Arbitration Act—*cont.*
    s. 10(2) 25, 38, 41, 42
    s. 11 .... **128**
    s. 12 .... **128**
        (1) 52, 54
        (2) 69
        (4)(5) 71
        (6) 52
            (*c*) 70
            (*d*) 71
    s. 13 .... **130**
        (1)(2) 76
        (3) 42, 44, 45, 49, 76
    s. 14 ....59, 80, **130**
    s. 15 .... **130**
    s. 16 .... 83, **130**
    s. 17 ....78, 83, **130**
    s. 18 .... 99, 100, **131**
        (1) 99
        (2) 100
        (3) 99
        (4) 83, 99
    s. 19 .... 48, **131**
    s. 20 ....85, 86, **132**
    s. 21 ....21, 92, 104, 105, 106, 132
    s. 22 .... 90, **132**
    s. 23 ....90, 91, **132**
        (1) 44, 46
        (2) 100
    s. 24 .... **132**
        (1) 36, 44, 46, 47
        (2) 29, 30, 31, 44, 47, 97
        (3) 29, 47
    s. 25 .... 40, 43, 44, 47, **133**
        (1) 42, 43
        (2) 31, 37, 38, 43
        (4) 48
    s. 26 ...... 86, 87, 116, 119, **134**
        (1) 86, 88
        (2) 87
    s. 27 ....10–13, **134**
    s. 28 .... **134**
    s. 29 .... **134**
        (2) 9
    s. 30 .... **135**
    s. 31 .... **135**
        (1) 2
        (2) 2, 51
    s. 32 .... 16, 26, 87, 92, **136**
    s. 33 .... **136**
    s. 34 .... 103, **136**
    Pt. II 114, 115, 118, 161, 162

1950 Arbitration Act—*cont.*
    s. 35 .... **136**
        (1) 115, 158, 162
    s. 36 .... **137**
        (1) 87, 116
    s. 37 .... **137**
    ss. 38–40 .... **138**
    s. 41 .... 16, 114, **139**
        (3) 116
    s. 42 .... 114, **139**
    s. 43 139
    s. 44 .... **140**
    Sched. 2 .... 158, 161
1959 County Courts Act (7 & 8 Eliz. 2, c. 22)—
    s. 40 87
    Mental Health Act (7 & 8 Eliz. 2, c. 72)—
    ss. 102, 103 15
1960 Corporate Bodies' Contracts Act (8 & 9 Eliz. 2, c. 46) 15
1962 Building Societies Act (10 & 11 Eliz. 2, c. 37) 2
1965 Industrial and Provident Societies Act (c. 12) 2
1966 Law Reform (Miscellaneous Provisions) (Scotland) Act (c. 19)—
    s. 10, Sched., Pt. I 139
    Arbitration (International Investment Disputes) Act (c. 41) 119
1968 Civil Evidence Act (c. 64) 66, 67
    ss. 1–10 67
1970 Finance Act (c. 24)—
    s. 32, Sched. 7 60
    Administration of Justice Act (c. 31)—
    s. 4 35
1971 Carriage of Goods by Sea Act (c. 19) 13
1972 Civil Evidence Act (c. 30) 66
    Administration of Justice (Scotland) Act (c. 59)—
    s. 3 ..... 103, 105, 106, 114, **153**
1974 Friendly Societies Act (c. 46) 2
    Solicitors Act (c. 47)—
    s. 73 131

TABLE OF STATUTES

1974	Trade Union and Labour Relations Act (c. 52)— Sched. 3, para. 17, Sched. 5 153	1979	Arbitration Act—*cont.* s. 1(6A) 93 (7) 94
1975	Arbitration Act (c. 3)... 116, 161		s. 2....92, 95, 96, 104, **142**, 149
	s. 1 .... 117, **154**		(1)(2)(2A) 95
	(2)(4) 117		(3) 96
	s. 2 .... 118, **155**		(*b*) 96
	ss. 3–7 118		s. 3 .... 92, **143**
	s. 3 .... 119, **155**		(1) 96, 97
	(1) 87		(3) 29, 47, 133
	ss. 4, 5 156		(6)(7) 97
	s. 6 157		s. 4 .... 92, **144**, 148, 149
	s. 7 157		(1) 97
	(2) 162		(2) 97, 148
	s. 8 157		(3) 97
	(2)(*a*) 126		s. 5 .... 34, 52, 55, 59, **145**
	(*b*) 134		s. 6 146
	(*c*)(*d*) 135		(1) 127
	(*e*) 103, 136		(2) 78, 127
1977	Patents Act (c. 37) 2		(3)(4) 127
	Administration of Justice Act (c. 38) 86		s. 7 .... **146** (1) 92
	s. 17(2) 134		(2)(3) 135
1978	Oaths Act (c. 19)—		s. 8 .... **146**
	Pts. I, II 70		(3)(*a*) 127
	Judicature (Northern Ireland) Act (c. 23)—		(*b*) 132 (4) 103
	s. 55 138	1980	Law Reform (Miscellaneous Provisions) (Scotland) Act (c. 55) 103
	s. 122 139		
	Sched. 5, Pt. II 138		
	Sched. 7, Pt. I 139		
	Statute Law (Repeals) Act (c. 45)—		s. 17 .... 106, 107
	Sched. 1, Pt. I 139		(4) 152
1979	Arbitration Act (c. 42) 2, 25, 32, 38, 39, 41, 42, 56, 113, 117		Limitation Act (c. 58) .... 9 ss. 7, 8 .... 9, 89 Pts. II, III .... 9 s. 34 9
	s. 1 .... 92, 96, 104, **141**, 149	1981	Supreme Court Act (c. 54) 93, 95
	(1) 79, 91, 92		s. 84 138
	(2)–(4) 93		s. 148(2) 142
	(5) 79, 93		(3) 143
	(6) 79, 94		s. 152(1), Sched. 5.... 138, 143

Chapter 1

THE NATURE OF AN ARBITRATION

	page		page
Generally	1	(2) *Arenson* v. *Arenson* (1977)..........................	6
The Arbitration Acts	1	Limitations of time	8
Statutory arbitrations	2	(1) Limitations imposed by statute	8
Advantages of arbitration	3		
The qualities of an arbitrator	3	(2) Limitations imposed by the arbitration agreement	10
Valuations and certifications	4		
(1) *Sutcliffe* v. *Thackrah* (1974).........................	5		

Generally

An arbitration is the reference of a dispute or difference between not less than two persons for determination after hearing both sides in a judicial manner by another person or persons, other than a court of competent jurisdiction. Commonly the reference is to two arbitrators, one appointed by each side, and there will then usually be the additional provision that in the event of the two arbitrators failing to agree the ultimate decision will be taken by an umpire.

This book is concerned only with commercial arbitrations and not with industrial arbitrations which may be used to resolve disputes in the sphere of industrial relations (*e.g.* arbitrations under the aegis of A.C.A.S.).

The Arbitration Acts

Arbitrations are probably as old as legal history itself. The need to have some degree of control exercised by the courts over arbitration was recognised by the English legislature as far back as the Arbitration Act 1697. In later centuries several further Acts were passed culminating in the Common Law Procedure Act 1854. The advent of railways, tramways and other mechanical means of transport from the middle of the nineteenth century led to an enormous increase in the number of arbitrations, and as a result Parliament passed the Arbitration Act 1889, which codified the general law of arbitration as it then stood.

The Act of 1889 and its subsequent amendments, notably the Arbitration Act 1934, were consolidated by the Arbitration Act

1950. From the nature of the Act of 1950 as a consolidating Act, it follows that cases decided on provisions of the Act of 1889 remain authoritative in so far as these provisions have been carried forward unaltered into the Act of 1950.

The legislation now applicable to English arbitrations, with which this book is mainly concerned, consists of Part I of the Arbitration Act 1950, as amended by the Arbitration Act 1979. Only brief notice is taken of Scottish and international arbitrations (see Chapters 10 and 11, respectively).

The Arbitration Acts of 1950 and 1979 are comparatively short Acts (See Appendices 1 and 2). They do not by any means contain the whole law of arbitration. Further, many of their provisions may be excluded by agreement between the parties to an arbitration for the parties may themselves determine what procedure is to be followed, what powers are to be vested in the arbitrator and what type of constitution the tribunal itself is to have in the particular circumstances. What the Arbitration Acts mainly do is to set out a code which governs these matters in the absence of agreement to the contrary between the parties.

In this book references to sections of an Act are to sections of the Act of 1950 unless the context requires otherwise.

STATUTORY ARBITRATIONS

Arbitrations may be consensual (*i.e.* founded on the agreement of the parties) or statutory (*i.e.* arising out of a statute which provides for disputes of a particular class to be determined by arbitration). Examples of statutory arbitrations are to be found in the Agricultural Holdings Act 1948, the Building Societies Act 1962, the Friendly Societies Act 1974, the Industrial and Provident Societies Act 1965 and the Patents Act 1977.

The particular statute in question may expressly exclude the Act of 1950 or it may include special provisions as to the appointment of arbitrators and the conduct of the arbitration which are inconsistent with the provisions of the Act of 1950. On the other hand it may expressly stipulate that certain provisions of the Act of 1950 are to apply.

Apart from such special provisions the general rule is that Part I of the Act of 1950, with specified exceptions, applies to every arbitration under any other Act (s.31(1)). The specified exceptions are listed in section 31(2) as amended by the Act of 1975. For the Act of 1950 to apply, there must exist an arbitral tribunal, and each particular statute must be studied in order to see whether such a tribunal has been included in its provisions (*Racecourse Betting Control Board* v. *Secretary of State for Air* (1944)).

It is possible for two arbitrations to be held concurrently, one statutory and the other consensual, for there may be matters in the reference with which a statutory arbitrator cannot deal. In such a case there ought also to be two awards, one under the Act of 1950, and the other under the particular statute.

The tendency since 1945 has been for public Acts containing provisions for statutory arbitration to exclude the Act of 1950.

Any further study of statutory arbitrations as such is beyond the scope of this book.

ADVANTAGES OF ARBITRATION

There are several advantages, in certain instances, for the parties to a dispute to refer it to arbitration rather than to commence an action in the courts.

The principal advantages are:

(a) When the dispute concerns a technical matter such as a building contract, persons chosen to arbitrate generally possess the appropriate special qualifications.
(b) The process can be speedier than a court case.
(c) There can be a saving in costs.
(d) Unwanted publicity can be avoided.
(e) The convenience of the parties as to time and place has first consideration.
(f) The arbitrator can view the subject in dispute at any reasonable time.

However, where the substantial issue between the parties raises a question of law of general importance such as the interpretation of a commercial document in common use, it may be more prudent for the parties to commence an action in the courts, for the main advantage of arbitration over the normal process of law arises when the dispute involves principally differences of opinion on the issues of fact (*Fairclough, Dodd & Jones Ltd.* v. *J.H. Vantol Ltd.* (1957), *per* Viscount Simonds and Lord Tucker; *Peter Cassidy Seed Co. Ltd.* v. *Osuustukkukauppa I.L.* (1957), *per* Devlin J.; *Re Phoenix Timber Co. Ltd.'s Application* (1958), *per* Lord Evershed M.R.).

THE QUALITIES OF AN ARBITRATOR

The arbitrator should be carefully chosen because of his special knowledge of the subject-matter which is in dispute. He should be able to keep the atmosphere clear at the tribunal and free from forensic eloquence and to see that the evidence is given in the manner customary in the courts of law and equity. He should give his attention to the facts in the dispute placed before him, and his decision should be based on a practical, as well as an impartial, judgment. He should possess a first-class knowledge of civil procedure, and of the laws of evidence; a sound understanding of the law of contracts and torts, of equity, and, of course, the law of arbitrations itself, for the validity of awards is frequently disputed on the grounds that the procedure at the hearing was irregular, and that arbitrators have acted beyond their jurisdiction.

The Arbitration Act 1950 regards an arbitration as a judicial inquiry conducted for special reasons before a private, rather than before an official, tribunal. The arbitrator's findings should be such as the court may deem fit to confirm, and in his conduct no laxity should be permitted. Expert witnesses must be checked in any desire to dominate justice or legal precedent by their own opinions.

Valuations and Certifications

There have been many cases in which distinctions have been drawn between arbitration and valuation and between arbitration and certification.

The main difference between an arbitration and a valuation may be explained as follows: where a judicial inquiry is held on a dispute, and it is intended by the parties to it that the question in dispute is to be determined on the evidence of other parties, the inquiry is an arbitration; but where any questions of value are referred to a third party for his opinion solely on that point, and to which he applies his own skill and knowledge, the inquiry is a valuation. In other words, whereas an arbitration determines a dispute, a valuation is generally a means of preventing a dispute. Certification frequently occurs in building contracts. There is often a provision in such a contract that work is to be done to the satisfaction of the architect who will issue a certificate entitling the contractor to receive payment from the building owner. The question can arise of whether the architect in issuing certificates is acting in the role of arbitrator or is merely an agent for the building owner with no authority to function independently of his principal.

The main importance of distinguishing between arbitration on the one hand and valuation or certification on the other hand lies in the question of immunity from being sued for negligence. The view which had for many years been regarded as settled law was that arbitrators could not be sued for negligence: they had a judicial function to perform and were therefore entitled to the

VALUATIONS AND CERTIFICATIONS

same privilege of immunity from being sued as was unquestionably enjoyed by judges in the courts of law. Valuers and certifiers, on the other hand, had no such immunity.

The long series of court cases involving the distinction between arbitration and valuation or certification culminated in two decisions of the House of Lords in the 1970s and it will be sufficient for the purposes of this book to examine each of these cases in some detail:

(1) *Sutcliffe* v. *Thackrah (1974)*

S. employed T., an architect, to design a house for him. Subsequently S. entered into a contract with builders to build the house, and T. was appointed architect. During the carrying out of the work, T. issued interim certificates to the builders. Before the work was completed, S. turned the builders off the site and engaged others to complete the work. The original builders later went into liquidation.

S. brought an action against T. for damages for negligence and breach of duty in supervising the building of the house and in certifying the work not done or improperly done by the builders. The official referee to whom this dispute was referred held that S. had been justified in turning the builders off the site and that T. had negligently over-certified sums due to them. He awarded damages to S.

The Court of Appeal reversed his decision on the ground that T. was acting in an arbitral capacity and was therefore absolved from liability for negligence. S. appealed to the House of Lords.

Held, allowing the appeal, that in issuing interim certificates an architect did not, apart from special agreement, act as an arbitrator between the parties, and that he was under a duty to act fairly in making his valuation and was liable to an action in negligence at the suit of the building owner (S.). The damages were assessed at £2,000.

The test applied was whether the architect had been acting in a judicial capacity, and he was held not to have been acting in such a capacity.

The speeches in that case indicate that at the date of the case it was accepted as clear law "that persons who are appointed as arbitrators, or as it has been called quasi-arbitrators, to resolve a dispute which has arisen or which may arise cannot be sued for negligence" (*per* Viscount Dilhorne). It was because the architect had not been appointed as arbitrator to resolve disputes between the parties that he was held liable in damages. Lord Morris of Borth-y-Gest said: "The mere fact that an architect must act fairly as between a building owner and a contractor does not of itself involve that the architect is discharging arbitral functions."

No doubt was cast in this case on the traditional view that arbitrators enjoyed the same immunity from being sued for negligence as judges had: the question was whether that immunity extended to persons who were *not* arbitrators but were persons who as valuers of certifiers were in a somewhat similar position or appeared to be so. Lord Salmon said: "Since arbitrators are in much the same position as judges, in that they carry out more or less the same functions, the law has for generations recognised that public policy requires that they too shall be accorded the immunity to which I have referred. The question is—does this immunity extend beyond arbitrators properly so called, and if so, what are its limits?"

(2) *Arenson v. Arenson (1977)*

Archy Arenson was the controlling shareholder and chairman of a private company. He took his nephew, Ivor Arenson, into the business and Ivor was given a parcel of shares under an agreement that on termination of his employment he would sell his shares to his uncle at their fair value—defined as the value determined by the auditors of the company for the time being, "whose valuation acting as experts and not as arbitrators shall be final and binding on all parties."

In 1970 Ivor's employment terminated. The auditors valued the shares at £4916.13s.4d., and Ivor transferred them to his uncle at that price.

A few months later the company offered its shares to the public, and that involved a report by the auditors. The report showed that the shares were worth £29,500, *i.e.* six times their value as assessed for the transaction between Ivor and his uncle. Ivor brought an action against the auditors claiming damages for negligence.

The judge and the Court of Appeal held that since the auditors had been performing a function of an arbitral or quasi-judicial character they were immune from any liability for negligence. Ivor appealed to the House of Lords.

Held, allowing the appeal, that Ivor's statement of claim did disclose a cause of action against the auditors: the immunity of judges and of arbitrators was exceptional and other persons (including in this case the auditors who had been appointed expressly to act "as experts and not as arbitrators") were subject to the general rule that negligence made them liable in damages.

Five Law Lords took part in the case, and although they reached a unanimous conclusion on the actual issue which it was necessary for them to decide, they expressed amongst them three divergent views on the general aspects of arbitral immunity. These three views were as follows:

(a) The first view, shared by Lord Simon of Glaisdale and Lord Wheatley, was very much in line with the attitude expressed and implied by the House in *Sutcliffe* v. *Thackrah*. It may be thought of as the traditional view.

Lord Simon said:

> " . . . the essential prerequisite for [a valuer] to claim immunity as an arbitrator is that, by the time the matter is submitted to him for decision, there should be a formulated dispute between at least two parties which his decision is required to resolve. It is not enough that parties who may be affected by the decision have opposed interests—still less that the decision is on a matter which is not agreed between them."

Lord Wheatley listed the following as the indicia which serve as guide-lines in deciding whether a valuer is constituted an arbitrator (or quasi-arbitrator) and clothed with immunity:

> "(a) there is a dispute or a difference between the parties which has been formulated in some way or another; (b) the dispute or difference has been remitted by the parties to the person to resolve in such a manner that he is called upon to exercise a judicial function; (c) where appropriate, the parties must have been provided with an opportunity to present evidence and/or submissions in support of their respective claims in the dispute; and (d) the parties have agreed to accept his decision."

(b) Lord Kilbrandon's view was fundamentally at variance with the traditional view. He did not accept Lord Wheatley's indicia, and was of opinion "that arbitrators at common law or under the Acts have no immunity"; only judges had immunity.

(c) The view of Lord Salmon and Lord Fraser of Tullybelton was midway between the extremes of (a) and (b). It was to the effect that it might be that a person, even if formally appointed as an arbitrator, ought not in all cases to be accorded immunity (*e.g.* if he were appointed arbitrator in a dispute between buyer and seller as to whether goods sold corresponded with sample or were of merchantable quality).

Lord Salmon said:

> "An expert may be formally appointed as an arbitrator under the Arbitration Acts, notwithstanding that he is required

neither to hear nor read any submissions by the parties or any evidence and, in fact, has to rely on nothing but his examination of the goods and his own expertise. He, like the valuer in the present case, has a purely investigatory role; he is performing no function even remotely resembling the judicial function save that he finally decides a dispute or difference which has arisen between the parties . . .

I find it difficult to discern any sensible reason, on grounds of public policy or otherwise, why such an arbitrator with such a limited role, although formally appointed, should enjoy a judicial immunity which so called quasi-arbitrators in the position of the respondents certainly do not . . .

The question as to whether there may be circumstances in which a person, even if he is formally appointed as an arbitrator, may not be accorded immunity does not, however, arise for decision in the present case, but it may have to be examined in the future."

Lord Fraser said:

"It may be . . . that a person, even if he is formally appointed as an arbitrator, ought not in all cases to be accorded immunity. But, as both parties accepted the immunity of arbitrators, we heard no argument on that matter and I express no opinion upon it."

The tentative conclusion which may be drawn from these two House of Lords cases is that even in the short space of years which separate them there has been a move away from the traditional view that arbitrators necessarily enjoy the same immunity from being sued for negligence as judges do. It is clear that if the function is valuation or certification there is no immunity. What is now open to argument is whether there are not at least some arbitrations also where there is no immunity.

LIMITATIONS OF TIME

A person seeking to enforce a claim by means of arbitration proceedings may find that if he has delayed too long his right to do so is barred by some limitation of time imposed by statute or by the arbitration agreement.

(1) *Limitations imposed by statute*

The submission of a claim to arbitration after it has become statute-barred does not prevent the statute from being pleaded at the hearing (*Re Astley and Tyldesley Coal Co.* (1899)).

The main statute calling for consideration is the Limitation Act 1980, which consolidated the Limitation Acts 1939 to 1980. Part I of that Act sets out the ordinary time limits for different classes of action, including time limits for actions to enforce awards: by section 7 an action to enforce an award, where the submission is not by an instrument under seal, is barred after the expiration of six years from the date on which the "cause of action" accrued, and by section 8 an action upon a specialty (which includes a submission under seal) is barred after the expiration of 12 years from the date on which the "cause of action" accrued.

The meaning of "cause of action" in these provisions is open to some doubt. Is the date when the "cause of action" accrued the date of the accrual of the original cause of action or is it the date of the award itself? "Until all uncertainty is removed a prudent course in all arbitrations is to ensure that it is possible to take steps to enforce the award within six years (or 12 in the case of contracts under seal) of the date of the accrual of the original cause of arbitration" (A. Walton and M. Vitoria, *Russell on Arbitration* (20th ed., 1982), p. 9). It is clear that if a statute (as opposed to an arbitration agreement) provides that a cause of action does not accrue until the award is made, the period of limitation runs from the date of the award (*Turner* v. *Midland Ry.* (1911)).

Part II of the Act of 1980 deals with extension or exclusion of the ordinary time limits (*e.g.* extension of the limitation period in case of disability), and does not require special attention here.

Part III ("Miscellaneous and General"), however, includes an important section relating to the application of the Act and other statutory limitations to arbitrations. The section—section 34—provides that the Act and any other statutory limitation apply to arbitrations as they apply to actions in the High Court (s.34(1)).

Section 34 further provides that, for the purposes of the Act of 1980 and other statutory provisions imposing a limitation, an arbitration is treated as being commenced—

(*a*) when one party to the arbitration serves on the other party a notice requiring him to appoint an arbitrator or to agree to the appointment of an arbitrator; or
(*b*) (if the arbitration agreement provides that the reference is to be to a person named or designated in the agreement) when one party to the arbitration serves on the other party a notice requiring him to submit the dispute to the person named or designated (s.34(3): *cf.* Arbitration Act 1950, s.29(2)).

The period of limitation runs from the date on which the cause of arbitration accrued, *i.e.* from the date when the claimant first acquired either a right of action or a right to require that an arbitration take place on the particular dispute (*Pegler* v. *Railway Executive* (1948)). This applies even where the arbitration clause is in the "*Scott* v. *Avery*" form, *i.e.* even where there is a provision in the arbitration agreement that no cause of action is to accrue until an award is made, or, in other words, a provision that an award is to be a condition precedent to the bringing of any action in court: the cause of action is deemed to have accrued at the time when it would have accrued but for the "*Scott* v. *Avery*" term in the agreement (Limitation Act 1980, s.34(2)). On *Scott* v. *Avery* (1856) see p. 22, below.

(2) *Limitations imposed by the arbitration agreement*

The parties may in their arbitration agreement stipulate that the arbitration must commence within some shorter period than that allowed by statute. In that situation the court has power under section 27 of the Arbitration Act 1950 to extend the time fixed by the agreement if in the court's opinion "undue hardship" would otherwise be caused. The court may exercise this power even though the stipulated period has already expired. The extension which may be granted will be for such period as the court thinks proper.

There are many cases illustrating the interpretation of "undue hardship" within the meaning of section 27. Before 1967 there were some cases in which the words had been given a narrow meaning, so that the power to extend time was only to be used in a very restricted class of cases. A change to a much more liberal view came with the decision of the Court of Appeal in *Liberian Shipping Corporation "Pegasus"* v. *A. King & Sons Ltd.* (1967):

A charterparty included the clause "Any claim must be made in writing and claimant's arbitrator appointed within three months of final discharge, and where this provision is not complied with, the claim shall be deemed to be waived and absolutely barred."

During the charter a number of delays and disasters occurred including a fire by spontaneous combustion of the cargo. Finally discharge was completed on March 26, 1966. Over the next three months the parties were in touch concerning their respective claims, but the three-month period expired without any settlement being reached.

About 10 days later the owners, whose claim for damage to the vessel exceeded £30,000, applied under section 27 for an extension of time.

Held, by the majority of the Court of Appeal, that the owners should be allowed an extension of 14 days from the date of the Court's judgment.

Salmon L.J. said:

> "I cannot find anything in section 27 which in these circumstances compels me to say that it would not impose undue hardship on the claimants to hold they must forfeit their claim to some £33,000 because of this small delay which has had no effect at all on the respondents . . . I have no doubt at all that if two ordinary business men entering into this contract had been asked if it would cause undue hardship to refuse to extend the time should circumstances such as the present occur, they would both unhesitatingly have answered 'yes.' I am not prepared to hold that the court's powers under the section should be rarely exercised. Still less that they should be exercised freely. The question as to whether or not those powers should be exercised must turn exclusively on the particular facts of each case in which the question arises."

The Pegasus has been described as "the key authority on the way to approach applications" under section 27, and as "an important milestone in the development of the law in relation to these matters" (*per* Brandon L.J. in *The Aspen Trader* (1981)). The two most notable applications of *The Pegasus* are the judgment of Brandon J. in *Moscow V/O Exportkhleb* v. *Helmville Ltd.* (*The Jocelyne*) (1977) and the judgment of the Court of Appeal in *Libra Shipping and Trading Corporation Ltd.* v. *Northern Sales Ltd.* (*The Aspen Trader*) (1981):

The Jocelyne. In this case Brandon J., after careful consideration of the relevant circumstances, concluded that the case was not one in which the court should extend the plaintiffs' time on the ground of "undue hardship": his reasons were that there had been a very long delay, the bulk of it (some two years) was attributable to the fault of the plaintiffs, and it had seriously prejudiced the defendants.

Brandon J.'s judgment contains a memorable summary of the guidelines laid down in *The Pegasus*. The judge said:

> "(1) The words 'undue hardship' in s.27 should not be construed too narrowly.
>
> (2) Undue hardship means excessive hardship and, where the hardship is due to the fault of the claimant, it means hardship the consequences of which are put out of proportion to such a fault.
>
> (3) In deciding whether to extend time or not, the Court

should look at all the relevant circumstances of the particular case.

(4) In particular, the following matters should be considered:
- (a) the length of the delay;
- (b) the amount at stake;
- (c) whether the delay was due to the fault of the claimant or to circumstances outside his control;
- (d) if it was due to the fault of the claimant, the degree of such fault;
- (e) whether the claimant was misled by the other party;
- (f) whether the other party has been prejudiced by the delay, and, if so, the degree of such prejudice."

The Aspen Trader. Lloyd J. had refused to grant Libra an extension of time under section 27 for the appointment of an arbitrator in a dispute between Libra and Northern Sales concerning demurrage. The Court of Appeal allowed Libra's appeal, holding that Lloyd J. had failed to apply the principles stated in *The Pegasus* and *The Jocelyne* in that he had apparently disregarded the absence of predjudice to Northern Sales and so could not be said to have exercised his discretion in the proper way.

Brandon L.J. included in his judgment a full exposition of the application of the six guidelines quoted above, and he concluded:

"To lose the chance of prosecuting a claim for $300,000 because of some neglect or inefficiency in a firm's office does seem to me to be grave hardship. If the delay has caused no problems to the other side, then it seems to me that to shut a claimant out from such a claim would involve undue hardship within the meaning of that expression in section 27 of the Arbitration Act 1950."

Section 27 and the Hague Rules. A question which arose was whether section 27 applied to a case where the time bar was imposed by Article III, rule 6, of the Hague Rules, scheduled to the Carriage of Goods by Sea Act 1924. Rule 6 provided:

"In any event the carrier and the ship shall be discharged from all liability in respect of loss or damage unless suit is brought within one year after delivery of the goods."

In *The Merak* (1965) the Court of Appeal held that "suit" in that context included arbitration. In *The Angeliki* (1973) Kerr J. held that in the interests of uniformity section 27 would not be applied so as to enable the one-year time limit to be extended. The Court of Appeal, however, in *Nea Agrex S.A.* v. *Baltic Shipping Co. Ltd.* (*The Aghios Lazaros*) (1976) took a different view. The Court held that in the circumstances of the case a particular letter could be construed as a request for the difference to be submitted to arbitration and that that would be sufficient to commence the arbitration. However, the Court went on to hold that if the letter was insufficient to commence the arbitration, the charterers would be given an extension of time under section 27.

Article III, rule 6, of the Hague-Visby Rules, scheduled to the Carriage of Goods by Sea Act 1971, imposes a similar time-limit.

Restricted scope of section 27. Section 27 relates only to the situation "where the terms of an agreement to refer future disputes to arbitration provide that any claims to which the agreement applies shall be barred unless notice to appoint an arbitrator is given or an arbitrator is appointed or some other step to commence arbitration proceedings is taken within a time fixed by the agreement," *i.e.* it is restricted to steps which commence arbitration proceedings, and it does not extend to any other time limits. Thus in *Babanaft International Co. S.A.* v. *Avant Petroleum Inc.* (1982) the Court of Appeal held that section 27 did not empower the court to extend a time-bar clause in a charterparty which provided that charterers were to be discharged from all liability in respect of any claims which the owners might have under the charterparty unless a claim had been presented to the charterers within 90 days from completion of the discharge of the cargo; that clause, in the Court of Appeal's view, had no apparent connection with commencement of arbitration proceedings.

Further Reading: A. Walton and M. Vitoria, *Russell on Arbitration*, (20th ed., 1982), Chaps. 1, 2, 5 and 7.

Chapter 2

THE ARBITRATION AGREEMENT

	page		page
Capacity of parties	14	party in respect of a dispute contained in an arbitration agreement...........	25
The statutory definition	16		
Incorporation of arbitration agreement from other contract	18	Alteration and amendment of arbitration agreement...........	30
Terms of arbitration agreement .	21	Revocation of arbitration agreement................................	31
Scope of arbitration agreement ..	23		
Enforcement of arbitration agreement	24	Repudiation, frustration and abandonment of arbitration agreement	31
(1) When a party does not proceed to arbitration	24	(1) *Bremer Vulkan*	31
(2) Legal proceedings have been commenced by one		(2) *The Hannah Blumenthal* ..	33

Capacity of Parties

GENERALLY, a person who has a right of which he can dispose is competent to submit any questions which affect that right.

As in the general law of contract, there are certain exceptions to the rule that any person can make a binding arbitration agreement.

A minor is bound by an arbitration agreement made by him if it relates to the supply of necessities or to a reasonable contract of service or if it is (or is part of) a contract which is plainly for his benefit; in other cases the arbitration agreement is voidable. *Slade v. Metrodent* (1953) gives an example of an arbitration clause in an apprenticeship deed: the court held that even if the arbitration clause, taken by itself, were not beneficial to the minor, it was nevertheless binding on the minor since it formed part of an agreement which was as a whole for his benefit.

A bankrupt is not deprived of his capacity to submit a dispute to arbitration (*Re Milnes and Robertson* (1854)), but he can only bind himself personally to the agreement; his trustee in bankruptcy, with the consent of the committee of inspection, may be made a party to the agreement, in which case the estate of the bankrupt will be affected (Bankruptcy Act 1914, s.56).

When a trustee in bankruptcy adopts a bankrupt's contract

which contains an arbitration clause, such clause will be enforceable by or against the trustee (1950 Act, s.3(1)).

By section 3(2) of the same Act, where, before he becomes bankrupt, a party has entered into an arbitration agreement, and matters in it have to be settled in connection with the bankruptcy proceedings, then, even if there is no adoption, any party to the agreement, or the trustee in bankruptcy with the consent of the committee of inspection, may apply for such matters to be referred to arbitration. The court which has bankruptcy jurisdiction may then order an arbitration if it thinks fit.

In the case of a person of unsound mind, his guardian may enter into an arbitration agreement, which will bind the estate, provided that the consent of the judge has been obtained. See Mental Health Act 1959, ss.102 and 103, and *Re S.* (1973).

As regards corporations the rule of the common law was that unsealed contracts were unenforceable. The position as regards the most important category of corporations in commercial matters, *viz.* companies registered under the Companies Acts, is governed by section 32 of the Companies Act 1948. The effect of that section is that a company can in general contract in the same form as an individual: if the contract is one which by English law requires to be under seal when made by individuals, the company's common seal must be affixed, but if the contract is one which merely requires to be signed by the parties, then it may be signed on the company's behalf by any person acting under the company's express or implied authority. As regards corporations other than registered companies, the Corporate Bodies Contracts Act 1960 contains provisions similar to those of section 32 of the Companies Act 1948.

Trustees, executors and administrators may enter into agreements on behalf of a deceased person, or of a *cestui que trust*, under the provisions of section 15 of the Trustee Act 1925.

Agents may enter into arbitration agreements which bind their principals, but the question really turns on the scope of an agent's authority to bind his principal in each particular case. For example in *The City of Calcutta* (1898) there was doubt as to whether the master could bind the shipowners to arbitration. In order to avoid liability for breach of warranty of authority, an agent should ensure that he has the necessary authority to submit the dispute to arbitration. He should also take care to make the submission expressly as agent; otherwise he may be held to have bound himself personally.

As a solicitor has implied authority to compromise a claim (*Waugh* v. *H.B. Clifford & Sons Ltd.* (1982)), he probably has implied authority to bind his client to submit to arbitration.

In the case of a partnership, an agreement for arbitration signed by one partner will not be binding on the other partner or partners without their express consent, except in the case where in the carrying on of the business of the partnership it is customary to refer matters to arbitration. However, the other partners may adopt an unauthorised submission by a co-partner; for example in *Thomas* v. *Atherton* (1878) co-partners were held to have ratified a partner's unauthorised submission of a dispute to arbitration (although, for another reason, the ultimate decision was in favour of the co-partners).

Where parties hold a joint interest, one cannot bind the other without express authority, but if the parties agree jointly and severally to refer a dispute and jointly and severally promise to perform the award, each is liable to perform the whole award and not only the part of the award affecting his own interest. Thus in *Mansell* v. *Burredge and Roberts* (1797) where two several tenants in a dispute with a succeeding tenant had jointly and severally promised to perform the award and the arbitrator had awarded that each of the two should pay a certain sum to the successor, the two tenants were held jointly liable for the sums payable by each.

The Statutory Definition

An arbitration agreement was called a "submission" by the Arbitration Act 1889, which showed that the parties intended to submit their dispute to arbitration. But the Act of 1950 uses the term "arbitration agreement," and defines this term in section 32 as "a written agreement to submit present or future differences to arbitration, whether an arbitrator is named therein or not."

Thus, the first requisite of an arbitration agreement, if it is to come within the Act, is that it must be in writing.

If, however, it is not intended to be within the Act, any particular form of agreement would suffice; the only essential requirement in that case is that the parties should intend to make a submission to arbitration. Where, however, there is not a written agreement the parties would find themselves in some difficulty. In an oral agreement, they could not obtain the assistance of the court to stay legal proceedings under section 4(1) of the Act, nor could they apply under section 10 to the court to fill the vacant office of an arbitrator. Other disadvantages would be that there is no record of the dispute submitted, and in order to be enforced the agreement must be within the provisions of the Statute of Frauds 1677, s.4, or the Law of Property Act 1925, s.40: it must not only be in writing but also be signed by the party to be charged, or some person lawfully authorised thereunto; see *Walters* v. *Morgan*

(1792), in which a written award relating to land made upon a parol submission was held to be unenforceable because of the Statute of Frauds, since the parol submission and the written award constituted only one parol contract.

The statutory definition of "arbitration agreement" covers both an ad hoc submission (*i.e.* an actual submission of a particular dispute to a particular arbitrator) and an arbitration clause by which the parties to another—the main—contract agree that if disputes arise they will be referred to arbitration.

Because of the requirement for a "written *agreement*" the parties must be *ad idem* ("at one").

There are divergent views as to whether mutuality is an essential ingredient in arbitration. On the one hand in *Baron* v. *Sunderland Corporation* (1966), a case arising out of a claim by a schoolteacher for additional salary under the Burnham scale, the Court of Appeal held that it was necessary in an arbitration clause for *each* party to agree to refer disputes to arbitration, and that as there was no agreement by the schoolteacher in the case in question, there was no mutuality and so the employers were not granted the stay which they sought. Davies L.J. said: "It is necessary in an arbitration clause that each party shall agree to refer disputes to arbitration; and it is an essential ingredient of an arbitration clause that either party may, in the event of a dispute arising, refer it, in the provided manner, to arbitration. In other words the clause must give bilateral rights of reference." In a learned analysis of the problem in *Union of India* v. *Bharat Engineering Corporation* (1977) the High Court of Delhi accepted the principle in *Baron's* case that an arbitration clause must be mutual, and decided that a unilateral arbitration clause giving the contractor an option to refer a dispute to arbitration was not an arbitration agreement; and it was only on the exercise of the option that an arbitration agreement arose for the first time. On the other hand, *Russell on Arbitration* (pp. 38–46) finds deficiencies in *Baron's* case and does not accept the *Union of India* analysis. Russell's final submission is:

> "13. It is submitted that the *Union of India* clause is plainly an arbitration agreement, that it is valid, that it is completely unilateral, and that the only mutuality it confers on the non-privileged party is the inevitable one that once the privileged party has chosen to arbitrate the non-privileged party can and must *ipso facto* arbitrate also."

An arbitration agreement must be capable of being given a sensible meaning. An illustration of this requisite is *Lovelock Ltd.* v. *Exportles* (1968): a contract included a clause referring "any dispute and/or claim" to arbitration in England and then a clause referring "any other dispute" to arbitration in Russia; the Court of Appeal held that the whole arbitration clause was void on account of ambiguity.

The writing may take the form of a deed (*i.e.* a written instrument signed, sealed and delivered), but need not. Where the writing is informal, it need not be contained in any one document but may be, for instance, in two or more letters in the course of correspondence. In *Frank Fehr & Co.* v. *Kassam Jivraj & Co. Ltd.* (1949) there was held to be a "submission" within the meaning of the Act of 1889 where buyers sent to sellers a contract form, with printed terms including an arbitration clause and having attached to it a printed form of acceptance which was intended to be signed by, but which was not signed by, the sellers.

There is some doubt whether the arbitration agreement must be signed by the parties to it. If it is to be enforceable and is within the Statute of Frauds 1677, s.4, or the Law of Property Act 1925, s.40, it must be signed by the party to be charged or some person lawfully authorised thereunto. Where, however, there is no statutory provision requiring signature, the weight of authority seems to support the view that signature is not essential. For example in *Baker* v. *Yorkshire Fire and Life Assurance Co.* (1892) an insurance policy containing an arbitration clause was held to amount to a valid arbitration agreement although it had not been signed by the assured.

The definition of "arbitration agreement" requires that there must be "present or future differences." If there is no "difference" there will be nothing for the arbitrator to decide. His jurisdiction depends on the existence or emergence of a dispute. On the distinction between arbitration on the one hand (which is to be regarded as a means of settling a dispute) and valuation and certification on the other hand (which are to be regarded as means of preventing disputes), see pp. 4–8, above.

INCORPORATION OF ARBITRATION AGREEMENT FROM OTHER CONTRACT

Where two or more contracts are closely associated with each other, it is common to find that clauses are incorporated from one contract into the other or others, *e.g.* in the building industry a sub-contract is likely to incorporate terms from the main contract between the employer and the main contractor, and in shipping a bill of lading issued to a shipper is likely to incorporate terms from the charterparty between the shipowner and the charterer. One of the terms incorporated often is the arbitration clause.

INCORPORATION FROM OTHER CONTRACT

The incorporation of the arbitration clause may be effected by an express provision in the sub-contract or the bill of lading or other document as the case may be. However, difficulties arise where there is no express incorporation of the arbitration clause but incorporation of it is left to depend on some general words which are intended to incorporate many other provisions as well. The preliminary rule to be applied in such cases is that if any of the terms sought to be incorporated conflicts in any way with expressly agreed terms in the sub-contract, bill of lading or other document, the expressly agreed terms prevail over the term which would otherwise be incorporated.

An illustration from the building industry is *Modern Buildings Wales Ltd.* v. *Limmer & Trinidad Co. Ltd.* (1975). The head contractors for the construction of a building had placed a written order with nominated sub-contractors to supply adequate labour, plant and machinery for the completion of certain ceilings "in full accordance with the appropriate form for nominated sub-contractors." The Court of Appeal held that the words "in full accordance" were wide enough to import the arbitration clause from the main contract into the contract between the head contractors and the nominated sub-contractors, and so the latter were entitled to an order under section 4(1) of the Act of 1950 staying proceedings in an action commenced against them by the head contractors for damages for breach of contract. Doubt as to whether the arbitration clause was or was not imported was not a sufficient reason for the judge's exercising his discretion under section 4(1) in such a way as to allow the action to go on.

An arbitration clause incorporated from a main contract into a sub-contract may not be sufficiently wide in scope to cover disputes between the main contractor and the sub-contractor: it may be limited to making the results of an arbitration between the employer and the main contractor binding on the sub-contractor. Such a situation came before the Court of Session in *Goodwins, Jardine & Co. Ltd.* v. *Brand & Son* (1905). The general contractors for the formation of parts of a railway entered into a sub-contract for the execution of the bridge work. The sub-contract provided that the work was to be done according to plans and specifications which formed part of the general contract between the railway company and the general contractors. One of the specifications was an arbitration clause. A dispute arose between the general contractors and the sub-contractors as to payment of a balance of the price for the bridge work, and the sub-contractors brought an action against the general contractors, who pleaded that the claim should be submitted to arbitration. The arbitration clause was held not to have been incorporated into the sub-contract in relation to the rights *inter se* of the general contractors and the sub-contractors: it was incorporated only for the purpose of making the result of any arbitration between the railway company and the general contractors binding on the sub-contractors.

As regards incorporation of an arbitration clause from a charterparty into a bill of lading, a long series of authorities established that where a charterparty contained an arbitration clause providing for arbitration of disputes arising under it, general words in a bill of lading incorporating into it all the terms and conditions of the charterparty were not sufficient to bring the arbitration clause into the bill of lading so as to make its provisions applicable to disputes arising under that document.

The leading case in the long series was *T. W. Thomas & Co. Ltd.* v. *Portsea Steamship Co. Ltd.* (1912): the charterparty arbitration clause referred to "any dispute or claim arising out of any of the conditions of this charter," and in the bill of lading there were two incorporation clauses:

"(a) he or they paying freight for the said goods, with other conditions as per charterparty"; and

"(b) deck load at shipper's risk, and all other terms and conditions and exceptions of charter to be as per charterparty, including negligence clause."

The House of Lords unanimously held that the arbitration clause was not incorporated in the bill of lading: it was directed only at disputes arising out of the charterparty.

However, more recent cases demonstrate that the long-established rule, though still good law, must be kept strictly within its own bounds. Thus, the decision of Brandon J. in *The Rena K* (1979) made it clear that if the usual general words of incorporation in a bill of lading were followed by specific words such as "including the arbitration clause," then the charterparty arbitration clause would apply to disputes arising under the bill of lading. Further, if the arbitration clause in the charterparty expressly stipulates for arbitration of any dispute arising out of the charterparty or any bill of lading issued under it, general words in the bill of lading are sufficient to incorporate the arbitration clause (*The Merak* (1965), a decision of the Court of Appeal), and according to the judgment of Staughton J. in *The Emmanuel Colocotronis* (*No. 2*) (1982) the same consequence follows even if the charterparty does not expressly mention the bill of lading but uses the expression "this contract" in the sense of the bill of lading contract.

Where, however, the expression "this contract" in the charterparty arbitration clause is interpreted as meaning the charterparty contract, disputes arising under a bill of lading would not be within the scope of the charterparty arbitration clause even if it were incorporated into the bill of lading (*The Annefield* (1971)). Moreover, in *Skips A/S Nordheim* v. *Syrian Petroleum Co. and Another (The Varenna)* (1983) Hobhouse J., giving a narrow interpretation to the word "conditions" in a bill of lading charterparty incorporation clause, refused to follow Staughton J.'s judgment in *The Emmanuel Colocotronis (No. 2)*.

Terms of Arbitration Agreement

While it is generally understood that the parties to an arbitration agreement may insert into it such lawful terms as they wish, the terms of such an agreement must be stated with certainty. The powers of the arbitrators or umpire must be clearly stated, as must be the question to be determined by the arbitration. Any matters for exclusion from the reference should be set out, and any technical or legal bar to the parties should be inserted in the agreement.

Certain terms are implied in any arbitration agreement unless there is an express contrary exception. Also, all arbitrators have certain powers to deal with costs, which partly override any express terms in the agreement. The courts will normally imply that arbitrators decide the cases before them in accordance with the law of the realm.

Historically the parties' freedom to include the terms of their own choice in their arbitration agreement has been restricted by the attitude of the courts in seeking to reserve for themselves the right to adjudicate upon disputes. There was thus a conflict between two major principles—the principle that parties should be free to contract on whatever terms they chose and the principle that they were not permitted to oust the jurisdiction of the courts.

The most famous expression of the latter principle is that of Scrutton L.J. in *Czarnikow* v. *Roth, Schmidt & Co.* (1922). Prior to the Act of 1979 an important aspect of the supervisory role of the court over arbitration was the special case (1950 Act, s.21) by which the court might direct that (a) any question of law arising in the course of the reference or (b) an award or part of an award should be stated by the arbitrator or umpire in the form of a special case for the decision of the High Court. The facts of the last-mentioned case were that a contract for the sale of sugar provided that the contract was subject to the rules of the Refined Sugar Association, one of which stated: "Neither buyer, seller . . . nor any other person . . . shall require, nor shall they apply to the

Court to require, any arbitrators to state in the form of a special case for the opinion of the Court any question of law arising in the reference, but such question of law shall be determined in the arbitration in manner herein directed." The buyers applied to the court to set aside the award on the ground that the arbitrators were guilty of misconduct in not affording the buyers an opportunity to apply to the court for a special case. The court held that the rule quoted and the agreement embodying it were contrary to public policy and invalid, as involving an ouster of the statutory jurisdiction of the courts under the Arbitration Act 1889 and that the award had to be set aside. Scrutton L.J. said:

> [The Courts] "do not allow the agreement of private parties to oust the jurisdiction of the King's Courts. Arbitrators, unless expressly otherwise authorized, have to apply the laws of England. . . . There must be no Alsatia in England where the King's writ does not run."

Despite the existence of this principle against ousting the jurisdiction of the courts, arbitration has on the other hand been fostered by the courts as a result of their having sanctioned what have become known as "*Scott* v. *Avery*" clauses and "*Atlantic Shipping*" clauses in arbitration agreements.

The essence of a *Scott* v. *Avery* clause is that the making of an arbitration award is a condition precedent to the bringing of an action in the courts. It takes its name from the case *Scott* v. *Avery* (1856) in which the House of Lords decided that, though it is a principle of law that parties cannot by contract oust the jurisdiction of the courts, any person may covenant that no right of action shall accrue till a third person has decided on any difference that may arise between the two parties to the covenant. The case related to a marine insurance policy which provided that the insured was not entitled to "maintain any action at law or suit in equity on his policy" until the matter had been decided by arbitrators, and "then only for such sum as the arbitrators shall award," and obtaining the decision of the arbitrators was declared a condition precedent to the maintaining of an action.

Held that these conditions were lawful and that until an award had been made no action could be maintained.

A *Scott* v. *Avery* clause, however, is not absolute in its effect, because the court, if it orders that an arbitration agreement is to cease to have effect, may further order that the *Scott* v. *Avery* clause is also to cease to have effect (1950 Act, s.25(4)).

An *Atlantic Shipping* clause is to the effect that arbitration must be commenced within a certain time and that if it is not so commenced the claim concerned is barred. The case from which it took its name was *Atlantic Shipping and Trading Co.* v. *Louis Dreyfus & Co.* (1922), another decision of the House of Lords. A charterparty provided: "Any claim must be made in writing and claimants' arbitrator appointed within three months of final discharge and where this provision is not complied with the claim shall be deemed to be waived and absolutely barred."

Held that the arbitration clause was not open to objection on the ground that it ousted the jurisdiction of the court. (However, as the claim was based on breach of the implied condition of seaworthiness, the shipowners were not entitled to the benefit of the term and so the claim was not barred by the arbitration clause.)

Scope of Arbitration Agreement

The question of whether a particular matter is within the scope of the arbitrator's jurisdiction depends on the interpretation of the words used by the parties in their arbitration agreement.

The scope is wide where the words used are "all matters in difference" or "all matters in difference in a cause."

In *Gunter Henck* v. *Andre & Cie. S.A.* (1970), where the words of an arbitration clause were "all disputes from time to time arising out of or under this contract," Mocatta J. said that the words "arising out of" clearly extended the meaning that would otherwise have been applied to the clause had it been limited to "all disputes arising under this contract."

The House of Lords' decision in *Heyman* v. *Darwins Ltd.* (1942) firmly settled the point that an arbitration clause in a contract may be wide enough to cover a dispute as to whether the contract itself has been repudiated or frustrated:

D. Ltd., manufacturers of steel in Sheffield, by a written contract appointed H. to be their sole selling agent in certain territories. The contract contained an arbitration clause providing: "If any dispute shall arise between the parties hereto in respect of this agreement or any of the provisions herein contained or anything arising hereout the same shall be referred for arbitration in accordance with the provisions of the Arbitration Act 1889 or any then subsisting statutory modification thereof."

H. maintained that D. Ltd. had repudiated the contract and he brought an action of damages. D. Ltd. admitted the existence of the contract but denied that they had repudiated it, and they applied to have the action stayed in order that the matter might be dealt with under the arbitration clause.

Held that the arbitration clause applied.

The language of the arbitration clause in the contract was

described by Viscount Simon L.C. as being "as broad as can well be imagined." Questions as to whether the contract had been repudiated or frustrated were within such a clause. The Lord Chancellor also mentioned matters which the clause would not have covered: he said:

> "If the dispute is whether the contract which contains the clause has ever been entered into at all, that issue cannot go to arbitration under the clause, for the party who denies that he has ever entered into the contract is thereby denying that he has ever joined in the submission. Similarly, if one party to the alleged contract is contending that it is void ab initio (because, for example, the making of such a contract is illegal), the arbitration clause cannot operate, for on this view the clause itself also is void."

ENFORCEMENT OF ARBITRATION AGREEMENT

The necessity for the enforcement of an arbitration agreement generally arises when a party to it attempts to obstruct it. The remedy available to the other parties is then to request the arbitrator to proceed *ex parte*, and in the absence of the obstructing party. If the latter refuses to be bound by the award, he must bring the case before the court with a request that the award shall be set aside. The "court" in this context includes a county court (*Morriston Tinplate Co.* v. *Brooker, Dore & Co.* (1908); *Parker, Gaines & Co.* v. *Turpin* (1918)).

Where one party to the agreement obstructs its enforcement, the other party may either (1) compel him to proceed to arbitration, or (2) prevent him from taking the dispute in the agreement to the court. The court will not interfere with the parties in a direct manner, *e.g.* it will not compel the obstructing party to go to arbitration, neither will it order specific performance of the agreement to arbitrate or award damages (as opposed to legal costs) against a party who issues a writ in a dispute covered by the arbitration agreement. The indirect remedies available to the court will depend on the circumstances of the particular agreement. These different kinds of remedies will now be discussed in brief.

(1) *When a party does not proceed to arbitration*

(a) Where the parties are in disagreement as to whether or not there is an effective arbitration agreement relating to the dispute, the court may give a declaratory judgment to the effect that the dispute is within the scope of the arbitration agreement and so cannot be litigated. This is of rare occurrence.

(b) The arbitrator may proceed *ex parte* in the absence of the obstructing party. This is an effective remedy when the arbitrator has been nominated and one of the parties does not appear. The arbitrator should give the absent party definite notice of his intention to proceed *ex parte*, so that that party may have the opportunity of changing his mind.

(c) Where there is a reference to a sole arbitrator, who has not been nominated by the parties, either party can be granted a remedy by section 10(1) of the Act of 1950. This provides that if the parties do not concur in the appointment of the arbitrator, any party may serve the other parties with a written notice to concur in appointing the arbitrator, and if the appointment is not made within seven clear days after the service of the notice, the court may, on application by the party who gave the notice, appoint an arbitrator who shall have the like powers to act in the reference and make an award as if he had been appointed by consent of all parties.

Under section 10(2), added to the Act of 1950 by the Act of 1979, the court also has jurisdiction to appoint an arbitrator where the arbitration agreement provides for the appointment of the arbitrator to be made by a third party and that party refuses or fails to make the appointment within the time specified in the agreement or, if no time is specified, within a reasonable time. This additional provision closes the loophole which was evident in *National Enterprises* v. *Racal Communications* (1975).

(d) Where the arbitration agreement provides that the reference is to be to two arbitrators, one to be appointed by each party, and one party fails to appoint an arbitrator, the other party may appoint his own nominated arbitrator to proceed. The remedy is provided by section 7 of the Act of 1950. But in such cases, there must be an express appointment of one of the arbitrators to act as sole arbitrator. Also he must be appointed after seven days' notice has been given to the other party that the appointment will be made. The notice must be express in form, and a notice which merely demands of the other party to appoint an arbitrator is not sufficient. The sole arbitrator so appointed may proceed exactly as if he had been appointed by consent. See *Drummond* v. *Hamer* (1942) (invalid procedure in relation to an arbitration clause in a lease).

(2) *Legal proceedings have been commenced by one party in respect of a dispute contained in an arbitration agreement*

In such an instance, the other party has the remedy of making application to the court to stay the proceedings under section 4(1) of the Act of 1950. The party must, first of all, enter an appearance, but he must not yet have delivered any pleadings or taken any other steps in the proceedings. If he is to succeed in his application the court must be satisfied that there is no sufficient reason why the matter should not be referred to arbitration in accordance with the arbitration agreement and that he (the applicant) was, at the time when the proceedings were commenced, and still remains, ready and willing to do all things necessary to the proper conduct of the arbitration. Whether the court exercises its power to stay the court proceedings is a matter for the court's discretion.

Section 4(1) does not prevent the plaintiff bringing a court action, but it gives the other party an opportunity to make his opponent bring the matter to arbitration before resorting to the ordinary courts. When the defendant offers no objection to the reference being superseded by court proceedings, no application to the court need be made, and the dispute will be settled in court, and not by arbitration.

In exercising its discretion the court regards the onus of proof (to show that proceedings shall continue) as resting on the shoulders of the plaintiff. Once the defendant has satisfied the court that a valid agreement exists and that he is ready to refer the matters in the plaintiff's statement of claim to arbitration, it is for the plaintiff to show a contrary reason, and unless he can do so, prima facie a stay will be granted (*Vawdrey* v. *Simpson* (1896)).

The discretion of the court under section 4(1) to make an order for stay of proceedings depends on seven main provisions, *viz.*: (a) there exists a valid agreement to have the dispute settled by arbitration; (b) proceedings in court have been commenced; (c) proceedings have been commenced by a party to the agreement, or a person claiming through or under him, against another party to the agreement, or a person claiming through or under him; (d) proceedings are in respect of a dispute agreed to be referred; (e) application to stay has been made by a party to the proceedings; (f) application to stay is made after appearance, but before the applicant has delivered pleadings or taken any other "step in the proceedings"; and (g) the party applying for the stay was, and is, ready and willing to do all things necessary for the proper conduct of an arbitration.

(a) *Valid agreement.* If the court is to exercise its discretion under section 4(1), there must be a valid arbitration agreement within the meaning of section 32.

A party who has repudiated the contract containing the arbitration clause is not necessarily disqualified from applying to have an action stayed, for, as was decided in *Heyman* v. *Darwins Ltd.* (1942) (see p. 23, above), even where there is a total breach of contract by one party so as to relieve the other party of his obligations, an arbitration clause in the contract, if wide enough in its scope, still remains valid although the other party has accepted repudiation. The test has been said to be that if the contract is determined by something outside itself, then the arbitration clause is also determined with it (*Woolf* v. *Collis Removal Service* (1948)).

(b) *Court proceedings commenced.* Proceedings in court include presenting a counterclaim as well as a statement of claim; the former, therefore, may also be stayed when, on the application of the plaintiff, it refers to matters in dispute. See *Chappell* v. *North* (1891).

(c) *Persons claiming through or under party to agreement.* An arbitration clause will bind a valid assignee of the contract which contains it; generally the presence of the clause will not cause the court to hold that a contract cannot be assigned (*Shayler* v. *Woolf* (1946)). Will the benefit of such a clause pass to the assignee of a debt arising out of the contract which contains it? In *Cottage Club Estates Ltd.* v. *Woodside Estates Co. (Amersham) Ltd.* (1928), Wright J. held that the benefit of an arbitration clause was personal, and could not be assigned to the assignee of a debt. In *Shayler* v. *Woolf*, above, the Court of Appeal confined this statement of Wright J. to the particular facts before him. Some authorities regard the view of Wright J. to be inconsistent with section 4(1) of the Act of 1950 (s.4 of the Act of 1889).

Other persons who would seem to be covered by the phrase "persons claiming through or under a party to the agreement" are the personal representatives of a deceased party and the trustee in bankruptcy of a bankrupt party.

(d) *Dispute agreed to be referred.* The legal proceedings must be in respect of a matter which is within the scope of the arbitration agreement; otherwise there is no question of the exercise of the court's discretion in granting a stay.

(e) *Application by a party.* If there are several defendants any one of them can make the application for the stay; thus in *Willesford* v. *Watson* (1873) an application for a stay was granted where only two out of three defendants were willing to concur in the application.

(f) *"Step in the proceedings."* The application must be made before the defendant has delivered any pleadings or taken any other step in the proceedings. If he chooses to allow the action to continue, the court has no discretion to grant a stay under section 4(1).

The following have been held to be "steps in the proceedings": appearance before a master to ask leave to defend (*Pitchers Ltd.* v. *Plaza (Queensbury) Ltd.* (1940)); application for leave to interrogate on a counterclaim (*Chappell* v. *North*, above); application for a stay until security for costs was given (*Adams* v. *Catley* (1892)); taking out a summons and obtaining an order for further time to deliver a defence (*Ford's Hotel Co.* v. *Bartlett* (1896)).

The following have been held not to be "steps in the proceedings": the granting of a fiat on a petition of right (*Anglo-Newfoundland Development Co.* v. *R.* (1920)); defendant's solicitors writing for further time to deliver defence (*Brighton Marine Palace Co. Ltd.* v. *Woodhouse* (1893)); having a summons transferred from one list to another (*Lane* v. *Herman* (1939)); giving notice to the plaintiff requiring a statement of claim (*Ives & Barker* v. *Willans* (1894)).

The judgment of Lindley L.J. in the last-mentioned case gives a highly regarded description of the borderline between what is and what is not a "step in the proceedings":

> "The authorities shew that a step in the proceedings means something in the nature of an application to the Court, and not mere talk between solicitors or solicitors' clerks, nor the writing of letters, but the taking of some step, such as taking out a summons or something of that kind, which is, in the technical sense, a step in the proceedings."

(g) *Applicant "ready and willing" to arbitrate.* The applicant for a stay must, not only at the time of his application but also at the time when the proceedings were commenced, have been ready and willing to do all things necessary to the proper conduct of the arbitration.

An applicant may still qualify as "ready and willing" to arbitrate, despite the fact that the other party has allowed the time for arbitration to run out, thereby enabling the applicant to plead that the arbitration is out of time (*Bruce Ltd.* v. *Strong* (1951)).

An insurance company which objected to the arbitrator nominated by the policy-holder but took no further steps in the matter was held nevertheless to be "ready and willing" within the meaning of section 4 of the Act of 1889 (*Hodson* v. *Railway Passengers' Assurance Co.* (1904)).

The following are some of the more important cases where the courts have granted a stay:

(a) Where interpretation of documents involved a question of law, but the legal points could not be decided until certain facts had been ascertained (*Rowe* v. *Crossley* (1912)).
(b) Where the agreement referred the dispute to a tribunal abroad (*Kirchner* v. *Gruban* (1909)).
(c) Where a contract of employment included an arbitration clause and the employee brought an action for wrongful dismissal. (*Renshaw* v. *Queen Anne Residential Mansions and Hotel Co.* (1897)).

The following cases relate to grounds for refusal of stay by the court:
(1) Where relief is beyond the powers of the arbitrator (*Willesford* v. *Watson* (1873), *per* Lord Selborne L.C.).
(2) Where reference entails unnecessary expense, (*Denton* v. *Legge* (1895)); but see also *Ford* v. *Clarksons Holidays Ltd.* (1971), in which the Court of Appeal held that the possible extra cost of arbitration over a county court action was not a proper ground for refusing a stay.
(3) Where charges of a personal character are made (1950 Act, s.24(2) (3); 1979 Act, s.3(3)).
(4) Where the principal issue is a question of law (*Martin* v. *Selsdon (No. 2)* (1950); *Partabmull Rameshar* v. *Sethia (K.C.) (1944)* (1951); *Marchon Products Ltd.* v. *Thornes* (1954); *Minister of Materials* v. *Steel Bros. & Co. Ltd.* (1952)); however, each case is a matter for the discretion of the court (*e.g.* in *Martin* v. *Selsdon Fountain Pen Co. Ltd. (No. 2)*, above, a stay was granted where the dispute involved only the construction of one of the terms in "Heads of Agreement" made by the parties in relation to certain patents).
(5) Where there is multiplicity of proceedings, which would involve the risk of inconsistent findings (*e.g.* in *Taunton-Collins* v. *Cromie* (1964) a stay was refused to builders who had been joined as second defendants in an action brought by the building owner against the architect).
(6) Where there is misconduct, interest or bias on the part of the arbitrator; *e.g.* the arbitrators appointed may have become "advocates of the parties . . . and . . . have already expressed themselves in strong terms as to the merits" of the dispute (*Bonnin* v. *Neame* (1910)) or there may be a conflict of evidence between one party and the other party's engineer who is the arbitrator (*Bristol Corporation* v. *Aird* (1913)); however, an arbitration clause referring disputes to the engineer of one party cannot be disregarded on the ground that the engineer is in substance a judge in his own case unless there is sufficient reason to suspect that he will act unfairly (*Ives & Barker* v. *Willans*, above).

(7) Where arbitration is appropriate for only part of the dispute (*Printing Machinery Co. Ltd.* v. *Linotype & Machinery Ltd.* (1912), in which only one of two alternative claims made by a lessor was within the arbitration clause in the lease; *Docker* v. *Hyams* (1969), in which the arbitrator indicated that he would deal only with the disputes as to defects in a yacht and not with the disputes as to the construction of the contract for the sale of the yacht); however, the fact that a small portion of the relief claimed is not within the arbitration clause is not of itself a sufficient reason for refusing a stay where the main subject of the action is within the arbitration clause (*Ives & Barker* v. *Willans*, above).

(8) Where there is a claim to dissolve a partnership (*Qualcast Ltd.* v. *Haynes* (1959); *Melgrave and Melgrave* v. *Finer* (1959); *Olver* v. *Hillier* (1959)); but the mere fact that the dispute is more appropriate for trial in court is not a sufficient ground for refusing a stay (*e.g.* in *Kitchen* v. *Turnbull* (1871) a plaintiff partner's action to have the partnership wound up was stayed where his arbitrator had died and he refused to appoint another).

An application for a stay under section 4(1) of the Act of 1950 is made in the following ways:

(1) In an action in the Queen's Bench Division it is made by summons in chambers to a master or the Admiralty Registrar, who may exercise all the powers of a court or judge (R.S.C., Ord. 73, r. 3(1)).

(2) In an action in the Chancery Division the application is almost always made by motion in open court on notice to the plaintiff, but occasionally it is made in chambers.

The evidence upon the application is by affidavit.

An order for a stay under section 4(1) does not preclude the plaintiff's right to apply for an order under section 24(2) (power of court to give relief where the dispute involves a question of fraud). See *Kruger Townwear* v. *Northern Assurance Co.* (1953).

ALTERATION AND AMENDMENT OF ARBITRATION AGREEMENT

It must be remembered that an arbitration agreement, just like any other agreement, can only be altered or amended by the two or more parties to such an agreement. This may be done by their mutual consent at any time before an arbitrator makes his award. The arbitrator has no power to alter the terms of the agreement himself. See *Re Morphett* (1845), in which a memorandum, indorsed on the deed of submission after its execution and signed by the arbitrators but not by the parties, was held not to have the effect of introducing to the submission a time limit for the making of the award. All alterations and amendments must be recorded in writing signed by the parties to the agreement, and where an agreement is by deed, the amendments and alterations must be by deed also.

REVOCATION OF ARBITRATION AGREEMENT

An arbitration agreement is a contract and it is not possible for a sole party to revoke it. By section 2(1) of the Arbitration Act 1950 it is provided that the death of one party to an agreement shall not discharge it, and the agreement shall be enforceable by or against his personal representatives. This provision does not affect the operation of any rule of law by which the death would extinguish any right of action with which the arbitration may be concerned (s.2(3)).

The court, however, may assist a party to revoke an arbitration agreement if it sees fit in three instances. On an application by one of the parties, the court may order that an arbitration agreement shall cease to apply (1) where the appointment of an arbitrator is revoked by the court, (2) where an arbitrator or arbitrators or an umpire is or are removed by the court, and (3) where an agreement refers to future disputes, and there is a dispute relating to a charge of fraud against one party (1950 Act, ss.25(2) and 24(2)).

REPUDIATION, FRUSTRATION AND ABANDONMENT OF ARBITRATION AGREEMENT

These issues have featured prominently in several cases in the early 1980s, culminating in two decisions of the House of Lords: *Bremer Vulkan Schiffbau und Maschinenfabrik* v. *South India Shipping Corporation* (1981); and *Paal Wilson & Co. A/S* v. *Partenreederei Hannah Blumenthal* (*The Hannah Blumenthal*) (1982).

(1) *Bremer Vulkan*

The case concerned a shipbuilding dispute which arose out of a contract for the building by Bremer Vulkan of five bulk carriers for South India. The ships were delivered in 1965–66, but it was not until 1971 that South India gave notice of arbitration. A London arbitrator was appointed in 1972. Detailed points of claim were delivered by the claimants (South India) in 1976. Neither party applied to the arbitrator for directions, and nothing further happened until Bremer Vulkan in 1977 issued a writ seeking (a) an injunction restraining South India from proceeding with the arbitration or (b) a declaration that the arbitrator had power to dismiss South India's claim for want of prosecution.

Donaldson J. was satisfied that South India's inaction had been such as to repudiate the arbitration agreement and he granted Bremer Vulkan an injunction restraining South India from proceeding further with the arbitration. He also held that an arbitrator did have power to dismiss a claim for want of prosecution just as a court had power to dismiss an action on that ground.

The Court of Appeal held that the court, but not an arbitrator, had an inherent jurisdiction to restrain arbitration proceedings where it would be just to do so (as would be so where the claimant had been guilty of "such inexcusable and inordinate delay that a fair hearing is impossible"), *i.e.* the court could dismiss the claim for want of prosecution, just as it could dismiss an action; there had been delay amounting to frustration in this case and the judge had been right to grant an injunction.

This unanimous judgment of the Court of Appeal was reversed by the narrowest of majorities in the House of Lords: the analogy between dismissing an action in court for want of prosecution and granting an injunction to restrain a pending arbitration was, the House held, not sound in law; the court did not have an inherent jurisdiction to supervise arbitrators beyond its statutory powers under the Acts of 1950 and 1979; both parties to an arbitration were under a mutual obligation to one another to join in applying to the arbitrator for appropriate directions to put an end to a delay which would involve a substantial risk that justice could not be done and neither party could rely upon the other's breach as giving him a right to treat the arbitration agreement as at an end. "Respondents in private arbitrations are not entitled to let sleeping dogs lie and then complain that they did not bark" (*per* Lord Diplock). Bremer Vulkan, in letting South India continue with the preparation of detailed points of claim and in not applying to the arbitrator for directions until so much time had elapsed that there was a risk that a fair trial would not be possible, had been in breach of their contractual obligations to South India.

This decision was much criticised: it was a "lamentable gap in English jurisprudence" that there should be no means of preventing an arbitration from proceeding even where the delay had been such as to preclude the possibility of a fair trial (*per* Lord Fraser in his dissenting speech in *Bremer Vulkan*). Nor did the decision find favour with the lower courts in subsequent cases: there were several instances of *Bremer Vulkan* being "distinguished"—which left the court free to hold that there had been frustration.

(2) *The Hannah Blumenthal*

This case arose out of a contract for the sale of a ship entered into in 1969. The buyers complained of engine defects, and arbitrators were appointed in 1972. The buyers served points of claim and the sellers points of defence in 1974. From that year until 1980 there were various delays on both sides, but neither party applied to the arbitrators for directions. In 1980 the sellers issued a writ seeking a declaration that the arbitration agreement had been discharged by the buyers' repudiation of it accepted by the sellers, or, alternatively that it had been discharged by frustration or by mutual rescission arising out of a mutual agreement by the parties to abandon it.

Staughton J. held that (a) certain letters were inconsistent with an agreement to abandon the arbitration agreement, (b) the sellers could not treat the buyers as having repudiated the arbitration agreement because *Bremer Vulkan* placed the parties under a mutual obligation to each other to apply to the arbitrator for directions so as to prevent delay, and (c) since the delay had amounted to inordinate and inexcusable delay which made a fair hearing of the arbitration impossible, the arbitration agreement had been discharged by frustration.

The Court of Appeal by a majority, dismissing an appeal by the buyers, concurred in Staughton J.'s decision as to abandonment and repudiatory breach and held that in view of the long delay and the nature of the dispute it would be impossible for there to be a fair trial of the buyers' claim and that the arbitration agreement had therefore been frustrated because if an arbitration were to take place it would be radically different from what the parties had contemplated.

The buyers appealed to the House of Lords, and the sellers cross-appealed on the question of abandonment.

Allowing the buyers' appeal, the House of Lords held that because both parties had a mutual obligation to apply to the arbitrators for directions to prevent the delay, and because a failure to comply with the obligation was a "default" which excluded the operation of the doctrine of frustration, the arbitration agreement had not been frustrated: there were no special or unusual circumstances to justify the House in departing from its previous decision in *Bremer Vulkan*.

Lord Brandon, who gave the principal speech, said: " . . . there are two essential factors which must be present in order to frustrate a contract. The first essential factor is that there must be some outside event or extraneous change of situation, not foreseen or provided for by the parties at the time of contracting, which either makes it impossible for the contract to be performed at all, or at least renders its performance something radically different from what the parties contemplated when they entered into it. The second essential factor is that the outside event or extraneous change of situation concerned, and the consequences of either in relation to the performance of the contract, must have occurred without either the fault or the default of either party to the contract. . . . neither such factor is present. . . . the state of affairs relied on as causing frustration is delay by one or both of the parties of such a length as to make a fair, or as I prefer to call it satisfactory, trial of the dispute between the parties no longer possible. That delay, however, . . . was clearly itself caused by the failure of both parties to comply with what your Lordships' House in *Bremer Vulkan* decided was their mutual contractual obligation owed to one another, namely . . . , to apply to the full arbitral tribunal . . . for directions to prevent the very delay which is now sought to be relied on by the sellers as having frustrated the agreement to refer.

"Whatever may be the precise ambit of the expression 'default' in this context, . . . I entertain no doubt whatever that the conduct of the parties in the present case, in failing to comply with what this House has held to be their mutual contractual obligation to one another, comes fairly and squarely within such expression."

The sellers' cross-appeal was dismissed on the ground that, though the buyers' prolonged delays were such as to induce in the minds of the sellers a reasonable belief that the buyers had abandoned the arbitration agreement, the conduct of the sellers' solicitors in continuing to seek evidence from witnesses made it impossible for the sellers to say that they acted on any such belief or altered their position in reliance on it; there had therefore been no abandonment.

The arbitrations in these two cases commenced before the Act of 1979 had come into operation (on August 1, 1979: The Arbitration Act 1979 (Commencement) Order 1979 (S.I. 1979 No. 750)), and so were not affected by section 5 of that Act, which was designed to give "teeth" to orders of arbitrators and generally to counter delaying tactics. Section 5 enables the arbitrator or any party to the reference to apply to the court where there has been failure to comply timeously with an arbitrator's order, and the court may order that the arbitrator is to have the same power to continue with the proceedings as the court would have in a litigation.

Further Reading: *Russell on Arbitration*, Chaps. 4, 5, 6 and 11.

CHAPTER 3

ARBITRATORS AND UMPIRES

	page		page
Generally	35	ment of an umpire or third arbitrator	42
Appointment by the parties	35	(d) Failure of an umpire or third arbitrator to act ...	42
Reference to a sole arbitrator .	37	Section 25	43
Reference to two or more arbitrators	38	Revocation of authority and removal	43
Reference to a fluctuating body	40	Section 1	44
		Section 2	45
Appointment by the court	40	Section 7	45
Section 10	41	Section 13(3)	45
(a) Failure in the appointment of a sole arbitrator	41	Section 23(1)	46
		Section 24(1)	46
(b) Failure of an appointed arbitrator to act	41	Section 24(2)	47
		Section 25	47
(c) Failure in the appoint-		Remuneration	48

GENERALLY

ARBITRATORS may be appointed in several different manners: (a) by mutual consent of the parties to an arbitration agreement; (b) nominated under a clause in a contract by some third person such as the president of a professional institution; or (c) appointed by the court. Actually, the appointment of arbitrators may be said to be confined to those appointments made by the parties themselves, and appointments made by the court. Note that section 4 of the Administration of Justice Act 1970 empowers Her Majesty's Judges of the Commercial Court to take commercial arbitrations, and therefore they may be appointed as arbitrators.

The appointment need not be in any particular form but should be in writing, and should be generally defined in the arbitration agreement. The office does not commence until the arbitrator informs the parties, or their agents, that he accepts the duty. No stamp is required for the appointment unless made by deed, when a 50p stamp is required.

APPOINTMENT BY THE PARTIES

The constitution of an arbitral tribunal and the manner of appointment of its presiding officer are matters which should be determined by the clauses in an arbitration agreement.

As for the capacity of arbitrators to act, particular disabilities include lunacy, infancy, outlawry and some physical incapacity.

Where there is an express arbitration agreement there should be a reference to (a) a sole arbitrator; or (b) two or more arbitrators; or (c) two arbitrators with an umpire who shall decide any difference between them. The arbitrator may be expressly nominated in the agreement or the method of his appointment may be set out in the agreement. This latter method has been growing in favour in recent years, especially where there are printed standard contracts such as those used for the erection and completion of buildings, or civil engineering works. In such cases, the appointment of an arbitrator is left to the president of a particular professional institution, such as the Royal Institute of British Architects, or the Institution of Civil Engineers, or the Chartered Institute of Arbitrators. If the President of the Chartered Institute of Arbitrators nominates, the advantage is that a person of the relevant profession is appointed. In many instances, however, the agreement may leave the appointment of arbitrators indeterminate, or indeed make no provision at all. When an agreement is silent on these matters, then, by section 6 of the Act of 1950, there is read into the agreement a provision that the reference is to be to a single or sole arbitrator. If the parties cannot agree on this appointment, they may apply to the court for an appointment under section 10(1) of the same Act. The appointment of an arbitrator by one party is not complete without communication of the fact to the other party to the dispute; see *Thomas* v. *Fredricks* (1847), *per* Lord Denman, and *Tew* v. *Harris* (1847).

When the parties knowingly appoint an incompetent person as arbitrator, there may be a ground for complaint against his award. Section 24(1) of the Act of 1950 empowers the court to give relief to any party who applies, on the ground of the arbitrator's lack of impartiality, for leave to revoke the arbitrator's authority or for an injunction to restrain any other party or the arbitrator from proceeding with the arbitration.

The provision in agreements for a public officer to appoint arbitrators was recognised by the courts in *Palgrave Gold Mining Co.* v. *McMillan* (1892), where Lord Hobhouse said: "It is very common in England to invest responsible public officials with the duty of appointing arbitrators under given circumstances. Such appointments should be made with integrity and impartiality."

Where there is a reference to several arbitrators, all appointments must be valid and the disputes for which each is appointed must be co-extensive. In *Davies* v. *Price* (1864), where one of three arbitrators had been appointed with only a limited authority, the award of the other two arbitrators was held to be invalid.

Reference to a sole arbitrator

There must be a valid appointment to act as sole arbitrator. Contrast *Drummond* v. *Hamer* (1942) with *Kiril Mischeff Ltd.* v. *British Doughnut Co. Ltd.* (1954)—both cases in which the reference was, by the agreement, to be to two arbitrators, one appointed by each party, and one of the parties failed to make an appointment for himself.

The arbitration agreement may provide that the reference is to be to a sole arbitrator.

When the appointed sole arbitrator dies, refuses to act or is incapable of acting, his place should be filled by another person under the provisions of the agreement. It is good practice for a nominated arbitrator to have his successor agreed to by the parties at the time of his own nomination. Similarly, where an official person has been asked to appoint the arbitrator, he should also be asked to nominate a successor. Where the parties reach deadlock, they may apply to court under section 10 of the Act of 1950 as amended by the Act of 1979.

In addition to the possibility that the arbitration agreement may provide for a reference to a sole arbitrator, there are under the Act of 1950 the following instances in which there may be a reference to a sole arbitrator:

(a) under section 6;
(b) under section 7(*b*);
(c) under section 8(3);
(d) under section 10; and
(e) under section 25(2).

(a) Section 6 of the Act provides that unless a contrary intention is expressed in an arbitration agreement, the agreement shall be deemed to include a provision that the reference is to be to a single arbitrator, if no other mode of reference is provided.

(b) By section 7, where the agreement provides that the reference shall be to two arbitrators, one to be appointed by each party, then (unless a contrary intention is expressed in the agreement) if one party fails to appoint an arbitrator for seven clear days after the other party, having appointed his own arbitrator, has served the first party with notice to make the appointment, the second party may appoint his own arbitrator to act as sole arbitrator. The appointment may be set aside by the court.

(c) Under section 8(3) at any time after the appointment of an umpire the court may, if application is made to it by any party to the reference and in spite of anything to the contrary in the arbitration agreement, order that the umpire shall enter upon the reference instead of the arbitrators and as if he were a sole arbitrator.

(d) Section 10 deals with the court's power of appointment in certain cases. A sole arbitrator might be appointed in the circumstances described in section 10(1)(*a*) or (*b*) or in section 10(2) (which was added by the Act of 1979). These circumstances are:

- (i) where the arbitration agreement provides that the reference is to be to a sole arbitrator and all the parties do not, after differences have arisen, concur in the appointment of an arbitrator;
- (ii) if an appointed arbitrator refuses to act, or is incapable of acting, or dies, and the arbitration agreement does not show that it was intended that the vacancy should not be supplied and the parties do not supply the vacancy;
- (iii) where the arbitration agreement provides for the appointment of an arbitrator by a third person (*e.g.* the holder of an office) and that person refuses to make the appointment or does not make it within the time specified in the agreement or (if not time is specified) within a reasonable time.

Before making the application to the court the party making the application must serve a written notice on the other party (in situations (i) and (ii)) or on the third person (in situation (iii)) and then allow seven clear days to elapse.

(e) By section 25(2) where the authority of an arbitrator or arbitrators is revoked by leave of the court, or a sole arbitrator or all the arbitrators is or are removed by the court, then the court may, if applied to by any party to the arbitration agreement, appoint a person to act as sole arbitrator in place of the person or persons removed.

Reference to two or more arbitrators

Where the parties desire to postpone the appointment of arbitrators until the disputes actually arise, there is sometimes a preference for each party to appoint his own arbitrator, and also to provide for the appointment of a third party to decide between such arbitrators should they dispute among themselves. The third party may be appointed as an additional arbitrator, or as an umpire. In the latter instance, the umpire is usually appointed by the two arbitrators.

A third arbitrator is distinct from an umpire. The former sits with the other arbitrators and has an equal voice with them in the reference. But where an umpire sits with arbitrators (as he may do) he does not take any part in the proceedings until the arbitrators fail to agree. And if they publish an award, the umpire may never be called.

Two changes made by the Act of 1979 should be noted:

(1) The original provision in section 8(1) of the Act of 1950 was that unless there was an express contrary intention, an arbitration agreement which provided for the reference to be to two arbitrators was deemed to include a provision that the two arbitrators should appoint an umpire immediately after they were themselves appointed. This could involve unnecessary formality if the two arbitrators agreed on their award, though there can be circumstances in which it is prudent for an umpire to be appointed before it becomes clear that the two arbitrators are to disagree on their award. Section 8(1), as amended by the Act of 1979, takes account of these factors. It provides that unless there is an express contrary intention an arbitration agreement which provides for the reference to be to two arbitrators is deemed to include a provision that the two arbitrators *may* appoint an umpire at any time after they are themselves appointed and *must* do so forthwith if they cannot agree.

(2) Section 9 of the Act of 1950 originally included the provision that where the reference was to three arbitrators, one appointed by each party and the third appointed by the two arbitrators appointed by the parties, the arbitration agreement took effect as if it provided for the appointment of an umpire and not for the appointment of a third arbitrator. That provision was open to the criticism that it defeated what would usually be the intention of the parties: if the parties agreed that there were to be three arbitrators, there was no good reason why they should be required to have instead only two arbitrators and an umpire. The original provision was therefore removed by the Act of 1979, and section 9 of the Act of 1950 now simply provides that (unless there is an express contrary intention in the arbitration agreement) where there is a reference to three arbitrators, the award of any two of the arbitrators is to be binding.

By section 7(*a*) of the Act of 1950, where the arbitration agreement provides for the reference to be to two arbitrators, one appointed by each party, then (unless a contrary intention is expressed in the agreement) if either of the appointed arbitrators refuses to act, or is incapable of acting, or dies, the party who appointed him may appoint a new arbitrator in his place. For the further provision in section 7, applicable where one party fails to appoint his arbitrator, either originally, or by way of substitution where a vacancy occurs in one of the circumstances mentioned, see page 37, above.

Under section 10(1) of the Act the court has power in certain cases to appoint an arbitrator, umpire or third arbitrator on the application of one of the parties, provided written notice has been served on the person concerned and seven clear days have elapsed after service of the notice; see also page 41, below.

Where two arbitrators are required to appoint an umpire or a third arbitrator, they must exercise their will and judgment and not make the appointment merely by chance (*e.g.* by tossing a coin or drawing lots). If, however, the two arbitrators by exercising their will and judgment chose two or more persons each of whom they agree to be a fit and proper person and then draw lots to settle which one of those selected is to be appointed, the appointment is good (*Neale* v. *Ledger* (1812)).

Reference to a fluctuating body

There is nothing to prevent a valid reference to a fluctuating body, *i.e.* a class of persons who may vary from time to time, and the reference will be treated as being to the members of that body or class when the dispute comes up for decision. See *Rathven Parish* v. *Elgin Parish* (1875): "The Society of Inspectors of Poor for Scotland" were held by the House of Lords to be proper arbitrators, although an unincorporated and fluctuating body. See also *Re Keighley, Maxsted & Co. and Durant & Co.* (1893) (committee of the London Corn Trade Association appointing five of their number for the hearing of any appeal).

Appointment by the Court

The court has powers under section 10 of the Act of 1950, as amended by the Act of 1979, to appoint arbitrators and umpires in certain cases. There are further powers of appointment under section 25 where an arbitrator or umpire has been removed by the court or has had his authority revoked by the court.

The court has no general power to appoint: all cases in which appointments are made must be within the statutory provisions.

The court will not make an appointment where the arbitration agreement provides a method by which appointments are to be made and that method has not been invoked (*Re Wilson & Son* and *Eastern Counties Navigation Co.* (1892) and *Finzel, Berry & Co.* v. *Eastcheap Dried Fruit Co.* (1962)).

Section 10

The court's powers under section 10 as amended arise where there is:

(a) failure in the appointment of a sole arbitrator;
(b) failure of an appointed arbitrator to act;
(c) failure in the appointment of an umpire or third arbitrator; and
(d) failure of an umpire or third arbitrator to act.

(a) *Failure in the appointment of a sole arbitrator*

The court may appoint a sole arbitrator under section 10(1)(*a*) provided:

(i) there is a valid arbitration agreement providing that the reference be to a sole arbitrator; and
(ii) differences have arisen: and
(iii) all the parties do not concur in the appointment of an arbitrator.

As regards (i), the provision for reference to a sole arbitrator need not be an express term in the arbitration agreement, because section 6 of the Act of 1950 provides that unless a contrary intention is expressed in the agreement, every arbitration agreement is deemed, if no other mode of reference is provided, to include a provision that the reference be to a sole arbitrator.

The court's power to appoint a sole arbitrator may also be exercised under section 10(2) (a provision added by the Act of 1979) in the situation where the arbitration agreement provides for the appointment to be made by a third person (*i.e.* a person other than one of the parties), such as the holder of an office, and that third person fails to make the appointment within the specified time or (if no time is specified) within a reasonable time.

(b) *Failure of an appointed arbitrator to act*

The court may appoint an arbitrator under section 10(1)(*b*) if:

(i) an appointed arbitrator refuses to act, or is incapable of acting, or dies; and
(ii) the arbitration agreement does not show that it was intended that the vacancy should not be filled; and
(iii) the parties do not fill the vacancy.

As regards (i), the phrase "an appointed arbitrator" suggests that section 10(1)(*b*) would not apply to the situation where two arbitrators are appointed one by each party, but only to the situation where there is a sole arbitrator. This view is confirmed by the concluding words of section 10, which are to the effect that the court's appointee is to have the same powers as if he had been appointed "by consent of all parties." Where there is a reference to two arbitrators, one appointed by each party, an application might be made under section 13(3) for removal by the court on the ground of failure to proceed with all reasonable speed, and if one of the two arbitrators were removed, the court would then have power under section 25(1) to appoint an arbitrator in place of the one removed.

Section 10(1)(*b*) is applicable only on refusal, incapacity or death of the appointed arbitrator: mere neglect of an arbitrator to act is not covered by this provision, but a remedy might again be sought under sections 13(3) and 25(1).

(c) *Failure in the appointment of an umpire or third arbitrator*

The court may appoint an umpire or third arbitrator under section 10(1)(*c*) where:

(i) the parties or two arbitrators are required or are at liberty to appoint an umpire or third arbitrator; and
(ii) they do not appoint him.

The original provision of the Act of 1950 (s.10(1)(*c*)) did not cover the situation where the parties or two arbitrators were *required* to appoint a third arbitrator; the amendment was made by the Act of 1979.

Section 10(2) gives the court power to appoint "an arbitrator or umpire" where the third person who was intended to make the appointment has failed to do so. The provision, which was new in 1979, does not specifically mention a third arbitrator.

(d) *Failure of an umpire or third arbitrator to act*

The court's power to appoint an umpire or third arbitrator is under section 10(1)(*d*). The requirements are the same, *mutatis mutandis*, as those of section 10(1)(*b*) applicable where there is failure of an appointed arbitrator to act (see p. 41, above).

Before an application can be made under section 10 for a court appointment of an arbitrator, umpire or third arbitrator, the party seeking the appointment must serve on the other party or on the arbitrators or on the third person as the case may be a written notice to appoint; it is only if an appointment is not made within seven clear days after the service of the notice that the remedy of applying to the court is open.

According to the judgment of the Court of Appeal in *Tritonia Shipping Inc.* v. *South Nelson Forest Products* (1966) the court has a discretion to appoint or refuse to appoint under section 10. In the earlier case of *Re Eyre and Leicester Corporation* (1892) the Court of Appeal had held that "may appoint" in the corresponding provision of the Act of 1889 meant "must appoint" and therefore that the court could exercise no discretion in deciding whether to appoint or refuse to appoint.

In *Abu Dhabi Gas Liquefaction Co. Ltd.* v. *Eastern Bechtel Corporation and Another* and *Eastern Bechtel Corporation and Another* v. *Ishikawajima-Harima Heavy Industries Ltd.* (1982) the Court of Appeal held that under section 10 the court had power to appoint the same arbitrator in two arbitrations between different parties to a building contract (*i.e.* between employers and main contractors on the one hand and between the main contractors and the subcontractors on the other hand). The judgment of the Court of Appeal is contradictory of the view which previously governed commercial practice, *viz.* that a tripartite arbitration required the express consent of the third party.

Section 25

The court's powers to appoint arbitrators or an umpire under section 25 arise where the court has removed one or more arbitrators or an umpire or where the authority of an arbitrator or arbitrators or umpire is revoked by leave of the court. There are two distinct provisions:

(a) Where an arbitrator who is not a sole arbitrator, or where two or more arbitrators who are not all the arbitrators, or where an umpire who has not entered on the reference is or are removed by the court, any party to the arbitration agreement may apply to the court for the court to appoint a person or persons in place of the person or persons removed (s.25(1)).

(b) Where the authority of an arbitrator or arbitrators or umpire is revoked by leave of the court or where a sole arbitrator or all the arbitrators or an umpire who has entered on the reference is or are removed by the court, any party to the arbitration agreement may apply to the court for the court to appoint a person to act as sole arbitrator in place of the person or persons removed (s.25(2)).

Revocation of Authority and Removal

The unwillingness of a party to arbitrate may be based on his objections to the arbitrator and not necessarily to arbitration itself as a means of settling disputes. The party may therefore seek to revoke the arbitrator's authority or to have the arbitrator removed, while leaving open the possibility of having another arbitrator appointed to conduct the arbitration.

The parties themselves may agree to revoke their arbitration agreement (and consequently the arbitrator's authority which arises out of it) or they may agree to remove one or more of their arbitrators. In the absence of such agreement between the parties recourse may be had to one or more of the statutory provisions relating to revocation of authority and removal, namely those in sections 1, 2, 7, 13(3), 23(1), 24(1) and (2) and 25 of the Act of 1950.

Section 1

Section 1 provides that an arbitrator's authority is, unless a contrary intention is expressed in the arbitration agreement, irrevocable except by leave of the court.

This provision leaves open two possibilities for revocation.

First, it enables the parties, by an express provision, to exclude the section, the result being that the common law rule of revocation by one of the parties would then prevail.

Secondly, the arbitrator's authority may be revoked by leave of the court. Decided cases establish that the court's discretion to revoke is to be used cautiously and sparingly and only in exceptional circumstances, because the parties have chosen arbitration as the method of settling their disputes and it would be contrary to justice to permit one party to get rid of arbitration on the mere ground that he found that the case was going against him.

Examples of circumstances in which the court may grant leave to revoke are:

(a) where the arbitrator exceeds or refuses the jurisdiction which has been conferred on him by the parties (*Re Lord Gerard and London & North Western Ry* (1895) (arbitrator accepting evidence which he ought to have rejected));
(b) where the arbitrator is guilty of such misconduct as would be a ground for setting aside his award if the arbitration were allowed to continue (*European & American S.S. Co. v. Crosskey & Co.* (1860) (two arbitrators appointing the umpire by lot));
(c) where the arbitrator is disqualified (*e.g.* because he does not have the special qualifications required by the arbitration agreement or where he has a disqualifying interest);
(d) where injustice is being done and no other remedy is available to prevent it.

The time at which an application for leave to revoke is made is a consideration which the court will take into account: if the application is made at an early stage of the arbitration proceedings, the court is more likely to grant leave to revoke (*Re Lord Gerard and London & North Western Ry., above.*)

Section 2

The authority of an arbitrator is not revoked by the death of any party by whom he was appointed (s.2(2)), but this does not affect the operation of any rule of law by which the death would extinguish any right of action with which the arbitration may be concerned (s.2(3)).

Section 7

Section 7 relates to an arbitration agreement under which the reference is to be to two arbitrators, one to be appointed by each party. The section provides that, unless a contrary intention is expressed in the arbitration agreement, then:

(*a*) if either of the appointed arbitrators refuses to act, or is incapable of acting, or dies, the party who appointed him may appoint a new arbitrator in his place; and

(*b*) if one party fails to appoint an arbitrator, either originally, or by way of substitution under (*a*), for seven clear days after the other party, having appointed his arbitrator, has served the party in default with notice to make the appointment, the party who has appointed an arbitrator may appoint that arbitrator to act as sole arbitrator.

The court has, however, a discretion to set aside any appointment made under section 7(*a*) or (*b*).

Section 13(3)

Any party to a reference may apply to the court for the removal of an arbitrator or umpire who fails to use all reasonable dispatch in entering on and proceeding with the reference and making an award.

An arbitrator or umpire who is removed under this provision is not entitled to receive any remuneration for his services.

The phrase "proceeding with the reference" includes, in a case where two arbitrators are unable to agree, giving notice of that fact to the parties and to the umpire.

Section 23(1)

Section 23(1) provides that where an arbitrator or umpire has misconducted himself or the proceedings, the court may remove him.

"Misconduct" in relation to arbitrators has a wide meaning: it covers mistaken conduct as well as wilful misconduct and corruption; it includes everything which makes the proceedings contrary to natural justice. There is copious case law on the topic, *e.g.*:

In *Veritas Shipping Corporation* v. *Anglo-Canadian Cement Ltd.* (1966) the managing director of a party to the arbitration signed a letter appointing himself as that party's arbitrator. He was held to have misconducted himself in doing so and was removed under section 23(1).

In *Thomas Borthwick (Glasgow) Ltd.* v. *Faure Fairclough Ltd.* (1968) there were circumstances in which the Board of Appeal of a trade association was held to have acted unfairly in not allowing a party the oppportunity to adduce further evidence. Donaldson J. said:

> "What is complained of here—I venture to think that the same can be said of all allegations of misconduct by arbitrators—is that the Board was in breach of its duty to act fairly and to be seen to act fairly. This is not to say that the Board intended to be unfair or was aware that it might appear to have acted unfairly."

In *Gunter Henck* v. *Andre & Cie. S.A.* (1970), in which a similar body was held not to have misconducted itself, Mocatta J. said:

> "Although the language . . . used, namely, 'That the Court of Appeal misconducted itself' is necessary language for the purposes of seeking to set aside an award, that language sometimes refers to conduct which the ordinary man in the street would call reprehensible and, indeed, misconduct, and in other cases to conduct which is only misconduct in the eyes of the law and in no way reflects adversely upon the bona fides or care or conscientiousness or fair-mindedness of the arbitral tribunal in question."

Section 24(1)

Section 24(1) empowers the court to give relief where the arbitrator provided for in the agreement may not be impartial. The provision is that where the parties have agreed that disputes arising in the future between them are to be referred to an arbitrator named or designated in the agreement, and after a dispute has arisen any party applies, on the ground that the arbitrator is not or may not be impartial, for leave to revoke his authority or for an injunction to restrain any other party or the arbitrator from proceeding with the arbitration, then it is not a ground for refusing the application that the applicant at the time when he made the agreement knew, or ought to have known, that the arbitrator, on account of his relation towards any other party to the agreement or of his connection with the subject, might not be capable of impartiality.

Where the court has power under section 24(1) to give leave to revoke the authority of an arbitrator, the court may refuse to stay any action which is brought by a party in breach of the arbitration agreement (s. 24(3)).

Section 24(2)

Section 24(2) relates to the position where the dispute involves the question whether a party has been guilty of fraud. The provision is that where an agreement between any parties provides that disputes which may arise in the future between them are to be referred to arbitration and the dispute which arises involves the question of fraud, the court has power to order that the agreement shall cease to have effect and power to give leave to revoke the authority of any arbitrator or umpire appointed under the agreement; the purpose of the provision is to enable the question of fraud to be decided by the court itself.

By section 3(3) of the Act of 1979, where there is a foreign element in the arbitration (*e.g.* if the proceedings are to be in a state other than the United Kingdom or one of the parties is not resident in the United Kingdom) and the parties have entered into an "exclusion agreement" (excluding the right of appeal to the court on a question of law), section 24(2) of the Act of 1950 does not apply, *i.e.* the question of fraud will require to be decided by the arbitrator.

Where the court has power under section 24(2) to order that an arbitration agreement shall cease to have effect or to give leave to revoke the authority of an arbitrator or umpire, the court may refuse to stay any action which is brought by a party in breach of the arbitration agreement (s.24(3)).

Section 25

Section 25 is concerned with powers which the court may exercise after it has removed an arbitrator or umpire or has granted leave for the revocation of their authority. The court's power to appoint a substitute arbitrator or umpire or to appoint a sole arbitrator has been already noted (p. 43, above). A further power is the power to order that a *Scott* v. *Avery* clause (see p. 22, above) in the agreement shall cease to have effect if the court has ordered that the agreement itself is to cease to have effect (s.25(4)).

REMUNERATION

The arbitrator may tax the costs of the award, *i.e.* he may fix his own remuneration in his award. When he does this, and the amount of his fees is paid when a party takes up the award, that amount cannot be looked at by a taxing master. The only exceptions to this rule are:

(a) when the procedure under section 19 of the Act is adopted (*viz.* application is made to the court to order an arbitrator, who refuses to deliver his award except on payment of fees, to deliver his award); or
(b) that the court may set aside the award on the ground of misconduct because the arbitrator's fees are excessive; for the arbitrator should fix his own remuneration on a reasonable scale (*Wilkie* v. *Scottish Aviation* (1956)).

In commercial arbitrations it is agreed that when an arbitrator is appointed there is an implied promise to pay him on a reasonable scale (*Brown* v. *Llandovery Terra Cotta Co.* (1909)).

When a fee is not fixed in an award, then it may be taxed as between party and party, even if one party has already paid the fee demanded by the arbitrator (*Llandrindod Wells Water Co.* v. *Hawksley* (1904)).

The arbitrator's remuneration is generally fixed at the outset of the case, which is by far the best course. When the award fixes the arbitrator's fees, they should be separate from all other costs in the award (*Re Gilbert & Wright* (1904)). Generally, in practice an arbitrator notifies the parties when the award is ready to be taken up on the payment of his fees, and he states the amount in his notice. He has a lien on his award, and the submission documents which are in his possession, and may retain them until his fee has been paid, but he may not retain documents put in as evidence at the hearing (*Re Coombs* (1850); *Ponsford* v. *Swaine* (1861)). When the party who takes up the award is the successful party, and is not liable for costs in it, he can recover the amounts, including the arbitrator's fees, from the unsuccessful party, if, as is usual, that party is ordered to pay costs. If, however, the fees are excessive, he can recover only a reasonable sum, and may sue the arbitrator for the balance (*Barnes* v. *Hayward* (1857)).

An arbitrator who is removed by the court for failing to use all reasonable dispatch in entering on and proceeding with the reference and making an award is not entitled to receive any remuneration for his services (s.13(3)).

Further Reading: *Russell on Arbitration*, Chaps. 7, 8, 9, 10 and 18.

Chapter 4

PROCEDURE PRIOR TO THE HEARING

	page		page
Notification to arbitrator of appointment	50	Discovery and inspection of documents	53
First duties of arbitrator	51	Inspection of property and things by arbitrator and parties	53
The preliminary meeting	52		
Points of claim and defence	52		
Particulars of claim or of counterclaim	53	Fixing time and place for hearing	54
Amendments	53	Proceeding *ex parte*	55

NOTIFICATION TO ARBITRATOR OF APPOINTMENT

THE first step in any arbitration proceedings is to notify an arbitrator that he has been appointed in a dispute, and the parties or their solicitors, should write to him to ask if he will accept the office. The notification, in the case of an arbitrator nominated by one of the professional bodies, would come from the particular institution. The documents which give him authority to act are then sent to the arbitrator for his signature. As soon as this formality is completed, the arbitration agreement is sent to him. See *Iossifoglu* v. *Coumantaros and Others* (1941), in which arbitrators were held to have entered upon the reference as soon as they had accepted their appointment and had communicated with each other about the reference. When an arbitrator is appointed by the court during an action, the order is served on him by the court.

The following are the principal ways in which the authority of an arbitrator can arise:

(a) by actual submission in a separate and independent document, which sets out the parties, recites the disputes and invests the arbitrator with his powers;

(b) by an agreement to refer, which means that a nominated arbitrator may be referred to in a clause in a contract, or that some other person or body may be called upon to nominate him;

(c) by reference after action has been brought by the parties, and in such action the parties have agreed to refer certain matters to arbitration; the court will make such an order;

(d) by statutory arbitration where the arbitrator is appointed in pursuance of a general or special Act of Parliament; the appointment must be in accordance with the terms of the Act; where these matters are not provided for in the particular Act, the Act of 1950 applies, except for the provisions in section 31(2) (see *post*, Appendix 1).

Acceptance of the office is necessary to perfect the arbitrator's appointment, as it has been held to be so in the analogous case of the appointment of an umpire (*Ringland* v. *Lowndes* (1864)). The dictum of Byles J. in this case was approved in *Tradax Export S.A.* v. *Volkswagenwerk A.G.* (1970); and the court approved the statement on this matter in *Russell on Arbitration, viz.* "it would seem to be only reasonable that an appointment should not be considered effective until the person appointed has agreed either expressly or tactitly to exercise the functions of the office" (20th ed. (1982), p. 251).

First Duties of Arbitrator

The arbitrator must first see that his appointment is in order; he must see if the submission and agreement require him to possess any special qualifications, and at the same time make sure that he has the authority to decide the dispute before him. In other words, the arbitrator at an early stage should make quite sure that he ought to go on with the arbitration or otherwise. If it becomes clear to him that he has no jurisdiction, he could take the view that he should not hold a hearing at all See *Christopher Brown Ltd.* v. *Genossenschaft Oesterreichischer, etc.* (1954). It should be noted that where two arbitrators are in the position of advocates, one for each party, an award of an umpire may be set aside on the ground that he has decided a matter in excess of his jurisdiction, without the consent of the mover's arbitrator (*Kawasaki Kisen Kaisha Ltd.* v. *Government of Ceylon* (1962)). Thus an arbitrator should go further than merely making a formal examination of the documents sent to him at the opening stages of the reference: he should obtain the clearest conception possible of the intention of the parties, and the actual matters in dispute. Several of these matters may also be discussed in a preliminary meeting. But it should be noted that only the disputes which arise out of a particular contract may be included in the reference, since it has been held that consideration, by an arbitrator or umpire, of contracts extraneous to the reference, constitutes misconduct on his part. See *Walford, Baker & Co.* v. *Macfie & Sons* (1915) (arbitrator looking at an earlier contract between the parties as well as the contract which gave rise to the dispute); "*Agroexport*" *Entreprise D'Etat, etc.* v. *N.V. Goorden Import Cy. S.A.* (1956) (arbitrators relying on second analysis for which the contract made no provision). Note that the latter case was distinguished in *W.N. Lindsay & Co.* v. *European Grain & Shipping Agency Ltd.* (1963) (very clear words required to exclude evidence which is normally admissible).

The Preliminary Meeting

It is customary, and it is good practice, for an arbitrator to hold a preliminary meeting with the parties before he holds the actual hearing. Where there are several controversial issues at stake, there may be further meetings before the hearing proper. The proceedings at a preliminary meeting may be likened to proceedings on a summons for directions in a High Court action; the subjects discussed are generally similar, and may include applications for the following:

(a) delivery of points of claim and defence;
(b) particulars of claim or of counterclaim;
(c) discovery and inspection of documents;
(d) inspection of property and things by (1) arbitrator and (2) parties;
(e) arrangement of any matters which will shorten or facilitate the hearing;
(f) fixing time and place for hearing.

Unless the arbitration agreement excludes section 12(1) of the Act of 1950, the arbitrator will have wide powers to deal with most of these matters. See also section 12(6) for the court's power to make orders relating to these and other matters. For extension of the arbitrator's powers where his orders are not complied with, see section 5 of the Act of 1979.

Points of claim and defence

Points of claim and defence in an arbitration are similar to pleadings in an action in the courts. They serve the purpose of informing the other party of the case which he has to meet. "It is absolutely essential that the pleading, not to be embarrassing to the defendants, should state those facts which will put the defendants on their guard, and tell them what they have to meet when the case comes on for trial" (*per* Cotton L.J. in *Philipps* v. *Philipps* (1878)).

The arbitrator has a discretion as to whether he will order points of claim and defence to be delivered. If he decides to make an order he ought to fix a reasonable time within which the claim is to be delivered, and then a further reasonable time for delivery of the defence.

Particulars of claim or of counterclaim

The arbitrator has implied power to order each party to deliver particulars to explain the facts given in the claim or in the counterclaim if there is one. He must fix a time for delivery of these which is reasonable in the circumstances.

Amendments

After the pleadings have been delivered by each party to the reference, the arbitrator at his discretion may allow or refuse amendments to such pleadings (*Re Crighton and Law Car and General Insurance Corporation Ltd.* (1910)). But under no circumstances may the arbitrator make any alterations in the arbitration agreement himself. To do so would be to introduce a fresh dispute as an amendment. In practice, leave to amend is allowed at any time prior to the close of the hearing, and the party who seeks leave to amend, and is granted it, is made to pay costs occasioned thereby.

In dealing with amendments generally, the arbitrator should follow the principles of the courts, in which the main principle is that amendments can be made provided there is no grave or manifest injustice.

Discovery and inspection of documents

The arbitrator's power to order discovery and inspection of documents is subject to the usual rules as to privilege, *i.e.* there are certain documents which need not be disclosed by the party in whose possession they are (*e.g.* communications between solicitor and client). However, since arbitration proceedings are private, confidentiality is less likely to be a ground for refusing discovery than it would be in litigation; see *Mitchell Construction Kinnear Moodie Group* v. *East Anglia Regional Hospital Board* (1971) in which the arbitrator ordered disclosure of the personal files of the claimants' employees.

Documents are generally "discovered" at the office of the solicitor who acts on behalf of a party. The arbitrator may refuse to hear such party's evidence in such documents if he refuses discovery. See the case of *James Laing, Son & Co. (M/C) Ltd.* v. *Eastcheap Dried Fruit Co.* (1962), where arbitrators refused a party's inspection of certain documents after they had satisfied themselves that the party had copies in his possession.

Inspection of property and things by arbitrator and parties

With regard to the arbitrator's right to inspect property or view premises, it is proper that he may do so, whether or not the arbitration agreement has an express clause to that effect. As Erle C.J. said in *Munday* v. *Black* (1861), "It is a matter quite in the discretion of an arbitrator whether he will view premises or not." The arbitrator also has power, under section 12(1) of the Act of 1950, to order a party to show him any property involved in the dispute, and it may be the arbitrator's duty to make such an order, if there is an express term (*Spence* v. *Eastern Counties Ry.* (1839) (express term directing arbitrator to view premises within a certain time before proceeding with the reference)). In *The Vasso* (1983) Lloyd J. held that in a salvage arbitration where ship and cargo were in conflict as to salved value the arbitrator had power under section 12(1) to order inspection of the ship on behalf of the cargo owners.

However, although viewing premises is "real" evidence (see p. 66, below), this does not dispense with the need for evidence at the hearing, except where it is clear that the arbitrator was appointed specially for his skill and knowledge of a subject, and that it was intended that he should decide without hearing any evidence on the matter. See *London General Omnibus Co. Ltd.* v. *Lavell* (1901); but this case was distinguished in *Buckingham* v. *Daily News Ltd.* (1956), in which a judge was held entitled to rely on his own impressions formed when he viewed the premises in the case. See also the Scottish case *Johnston* v. *Cheape* (1817) (arbiter appointed for skill and knowledge held entitled to refuse statement of certain facts brought before him by one of the parties).

Fixing time and place for hearing

Unless the arbitration agreement debars him from doing so, the arbitrator has an absolute discretion in fixing the time and place of hearing. He ought, however, to use his powers with reason and for the convenience of the parties to the reference. One of the chief circumstances which he should bear in mind is the place of residence of the parties and of their witnesses.

The arbitrator should send written notices to the parties concerned in reasonable time, for if any of them are taken by surprise his award may be set aside.

The arbitrator may subsequently alter the time and place of hearing by giving reasonable notice to the parties.

A refusal to allow an adjournment (*e.g.* to enable a party to call relevant evidence) may, if combined with other breaches of duty, lead the court to conclude that the arbitrator has been guilty of misconduct (as in *Re Enoch and Zaretzky, Bock & Co.* (1910)). On the other hand, an arbitrator is not bound to grant an adjournment if the application for it is not bona fide but has been made merely for the purposes of delay.

Proceeding ex parte

Where a party is obstructive (*e.g.* by absenting himself from the hearing with a view to defeating the reference), the arbitrator may and ought to proceed *ex parte* (*i.e.* hearing only one party). Before taking this course he must give the obstructive party clear notice that he is to proceed *ex parte*; otherwise his award may be set aside. It is also prudent for the arbitrator to continue to give notices to an absent party throughout the proceedings so that the party may have the opportunity of being present at later stages if he changes his mind.

See also section 5 of the Act of 1979 (p. 34, above, and p. 59, below).

Further Reading: *Russell on Arbitration*, Chaps. 12 and 13.

CHAPTER 5

PROCEDURE AT THE HEARING

	page		page
The rules of natural justice	56	Legal adviser at the hearing	60
Private communications from parties	57	Joint arbitrators	61
		Irregularities in procedure	61
Persons entitled to be present	57	Protest against irregularities	62
Conduct of the hearing	57	Waiver of procedural objections	62
Closing the case	59		
Stamps on documents	60	Delegation of duties	64
Counsel's opinion	60		

THE RULES OF NATURAL JUSTICE

AN arbitrator is in the position of a judge after he has been selected by the parties and chosen to adjudicate on certain specific facts before him. Apart from the duties imposed on him by the Arbitration Acts of 1950 and 1979, he has the duty of acting in accordance with the essential rules of "natural justice." It is customary for the parties either to rely on the statutory and common law rules of arbitration, or to supplement them by clauses from the particular business which concerns the arbitration.

The arbitrator, unlike the judge, derives his authority from the parties to the reference, and his powers are those with which such parties have entrusted him. They may consent for him to depart from the ordinary rules of procedure, except that the agreement and the procedure derived from it must not be contrary to the fundamental principles of public policy, and thus be unenforceable (*Naumann* v. *Nathan* (1930), *per* Scrutton L.J.).

The first principle is that an arbitrator must act fairly to both parties. It makes no difference whether a lawyer or layman is selected to act in the office of arbitrator.

The arbitrator can, however, deviate from the rules of court, for he has a greater latitude than the court; provided always the principles of justice are not disregarded by him, and that he follows the rules of evidence.

The arbitrator must normally not hear one party or his witnesses unless the other party is present or represented. There is an exception to this where both parties consent to the arbitrator's proceeding in the presence of one party only. In *Drew* v. *Drew* (1855), in which evidence had been taken behind the back of one of the parties but objections to that procedure appeared to have been waived, Lord Cranworth L.C. said: "The principles of universal justice require that the person who is to be prejudiced by the evidence ought to be present to hear it taken, to suggest cross-examination or himself to cross-examine, and to be able to find evidence, if he can, that shall meet and answer it; in short, to deal with it as in the ordinary course of legal proceedings."

Private Communications from Parties

Where one of the parties to the reference communicates with the arbitrator without the knowledge of the other party, the arbitrator should refuse to hear, read or be influenced by such communications. The prudent course for the arbitrator to take is to hand over to the other party copies of any written communications and to inform the other party of any oral communications.

Persons Entitled to be Present

An arbitration is a private tribunal for the settlement of disputes, and the general public may not be admitted if there is an objection to such a course by any party to the reference.

The parties who may appear at the reference are the actual parties themselves, all persons claiming through them, and any person interested or attending on behalf of the parties. Any person who assists a party in presenting his case may also attend, *e.g.* a shorthand writer, or an assessor, and such parties should not be excluded without good grounds, or the award may be set aside. Thus in *Haigh* v. *Haigh* (1861), where one of the parties desired to have his son present because the son was versed in the accounts of the business, and the arbitrator excluded the son and also a shorthand writer, the award was set aside.

Conduct of the Hearing

The arbitrator must conduct the hearing in accordance with the arbitration agreement, but he has full power to decide how the case shall be heard, and what course of civil procedure shall be followed. The usual practice is to follow the procedure of an ordinary action in the courts. The plaintiff in such an action corresponds to the claimant in an arbitration, and a defendant corresponds to a respondent.

The parties may conduct their own case, or be represented by counsel or solicitors. The arbitrator could not object to counsel or solicitors appearing unless expressly, or by implication, agreed to in the submission, for the award may otherwise be set aside. See *F.E. Hookway & Co. Ltd.* v. *Alfred Isaacs & Sons and Others* (1954). When it is the intention of a party to be represented by counsel at the hearing, he must give notice of his intention to the other party, in sufficient time for the other party to brief counsel also. If the arbitrator refuses to adjourn the hearing so that such counsel cannot appear, it may amount to misconduct on his part (*Whatley* v. *Morland* (1834)).

With regard to adjournments, the arbitrator has a discretion, and if he exercises this honestly, the court will not set aside his award, even if he was in error in refusing an adjournment.

The arbitrator should take notes in a careful and meticulous manner of all the evidence given by the parties and their witnesses throughout the hearing. He may then be able to do full justice between the parties. He may compare his notes to what was said in the examination of witnesses by counsel or solicitor, and he will have the advantage of being able to refresh his memory in any proceedings which might arise subsequent to the hearing.

The arbitrator, it appears, cannot employ shorthand writers at the expense of the parties, although they may agree to their employment and a transcription of the notes being furnished to the arbitrator. He may be requested by the parties to make an order in his award as to how the cost of this clerical work shall be borne.

The cost of making shorthand notes and transcriptions of them cannot be recovered in the High Court, on taxation of costs against the party held by the arbitrator to be liable for costs, unless there is an express direction by the court.

The ordinary procedure at the hearing, as at a trial in court, is that the party upon whom the burden of proof lies in the first instance is the party who must establish his case.

It must be remembered, however, that there are some matters which need not be proved at all, *e.g.* the law of England, public statutes, private statutes since 1850, official seals, and certain facts so well known that the court or arbitrator takes judicial notice of them without proof.

The following is the ordinary procedure at the hearing:

1. The claimant (or his advocate) opens his case, and if there is a counterclaim, he will at the same time open his defence to such counterclaim.
2. The claimant calls and examines his witnesses, who may be cross-examined by the respondent.
3. If a witness is cross-examined, the claimant may re-examine him on any matter raised in cross-examination.
4. The respondent (or his advocate) opens his case.

5. The respondent calls and examines his witnesses, who may be cross-examined by the claimant.
6. If a witness is cross-examined, the respondent may re-examine him on any matter raised in cross-examination.
7. The respondent addresses the arbitrator.
8. The claimant replies.

For a discussion on evidence and on examination of witnesses see Chapter 6.

The foregoing procedure is varied when (a) the respondent has admitted the claimant's case subject to his counterclaim, when the procedure above is reversed, or (b) at the end of the claimant's case, the respondent announces that he does not intend to submit any evidence either documentary or by parole, in which case the claimant may then address the arbitrator, and the respondent is entitled to the last word, unless he puts in certain evidence through cross-examination of the witnesses of the claimant.

In examination-in-chief, a party, or his advocate, is not entitled to ask leading questions, *i.e.* those framed so as to suggest the answer required.

Every arbitrator is authorised by the nature of his office to proceed *ex parte* for good cause. It is not necessary to give him express power to do so in the agreement, and no application to court for him to do so is necessary. The arbitrator uses his own discretion in the exercise of this power. See also Chapter 4.

By section 5 of the Act of 1979, if a party to the reference fails to comply timeously with an order made by the arbitrator, the arbitrator or any party to the reference may apply to court for an order extending the arbitrator's power so that he will be entitled to continue with the reference despite the non-appearance or other default of one of the parties. An arbitrator may prefer to avail himself of this provision, because if he exercises his own discretion under the common law he is liable to be accused of misconduct.

Where the terms of the agreement do not exclude section 14 of the Act of 1950, (see Appendix 1, *post*) the arbitrator may make an interim award if he so wishes.

Closing the Case

When the arbitrator finally closes the case, he usually informs the parties that he will "now proceed to make his award" or that he "reserves his award" and will publish it in due course. He must not close the hearing and proceed to make his award without giving due notice to the parties. His award may be set aside if, after promising to hear witnesses, he makes his award without calling them, or if, after saying that he will not continue until certain documents are produced, he makes his award without giving notice to the parties that he has found inspection of the documents unnecessary. In *Re Maunder* (1883) in an arbitration between a landlord and a tenant the arbitrators and umpire on May 23 agreed upon their award, subject only to the umpire taking legal advice upon one point; about May 26 the umpire refused an application by the landlord to be heard, on the ground that the arbitration had been closed on May 23; the award was made on June 5; the umpire's refusal to hear the landlord was held to be sufficient ground for setting the award aside, since the arbitration could not have been closed until the reserved point of law had been decided.

Until the arbitrator actually makes his award, either party can apply to him to reopen the case, even if it has been formally closed, since the arbitrator has a discretion to receive further evidence.

STAMPS ON DOCUMENTS

The arbitrator is bound by the provisions of the Stamp Act 1891 and must take notice of an omission or insufficiency in the stamping on documents laid before him. He must also see that the necessary stamp duties have been paid before documents have been received in evidence. The parties to the reference cannot agree to dispense with the stamping of documents. See *Maritime Insurance Co.* v. *Assecuranz-Union von 1865* (1935).

The Act of 1891 has been amended by many later Acts, especially Finance Acts (see, *e.g.* Finance Act 1970, s.32 and Sched. 7).

COUNSEL'S OPINION

When during the course of the reference the arbitrator takes counsel's opinion or a solicitor's advice, his submission to counsel or to the solicitor should first be shown to both parties to the reference; for should the arbitrator obtain an opinion based on an erroneous statement of fact, and act upon it, the award may be set aside (*Re Hare and Milne* (1839)).

LEGAL ADVISER AT THE HEARING

Generally speaking an arbitrator should obtain the consent of the parties, should he wish to seek legal advice, especially if he is a lay arbitrator. See *Louis Dreyfus & Co.* v. *Arunachala Ayya* (1930). But when no such consent is given, the arbitrator may still seek legal advice in drawing up his award, and on his conduct of the reference (*Threlfall* v. *Fanshawe* (1850)), and for the general principles of law governing the class of case before him. But he cannot seek advice on the actual questions of law in the dispute, except that a barrister or solicitor sitting as an arbitrator may put a point of law to a learned friend (*per* Lord Denman C.J. in *Dobson* v. *Groves* (1844)).

Although the arbitrator may seek legal advice in the conduct of the reference without the consent of the parties, he is not entitled to have his legal adviser present at the hearing without such consent. See *Proctor and Others* v. *Williamson and Others* (1860). An arbitrator who is appointed to decide disputes which involve points of law, must make his own decision and not adopt as his own the decision of some legal adviser. See *Ellison* v. *Bray* (1864). As a result of such action in this case, the award was held to be that of the advising lawyer, and was set aside. But when an arbitrator consulted his own solicitor, who happened to be also solicitor to one of the parties, this was held to be improper, but not sufficient grounds for setting the award aside (*Re Underwood and Bedford and Cambridge Ry.* (1861)).

JOINT ARBITRATORS

When two arbitrators sit together, they must exercise all the powers exercised by a sole arbitrator at a hearing. For reference to two arbitrators see Chapter 3. A joint arbitrator must not consider himself as the advocate of the party who appointed him: his duty is to decide impartially between the parties.

IRREGULARITIES IN PROCEDURE

A serious irregularity not condoned by the parties may lead to the arbitrator being removed by the court, or his award being referred back to him, or even set aside. See the cases of *Haigh* v. *Haigh* (1861), *per* Turner L.J.; *Dobson* v. *Groves* (1844); and *W. Ramsden & Co.* v. *Jacobs* (1922). In all these cases irregularities were so serious as to amount to a denial of justice, and the parties continued to attend the hearing and did not waive their objections. Where there is irregularity passed over on the part of the arbitrator in the absence of a party, it cannot be set right except by the agreement of the absent party. See the remarks of Lord Denman C.J. in *Dobson* v. *Groves*, above: "The mischief was done at the time, and cannot be removed."

In the following cases, irregularities were serious enough to invalidate the arbitrator's award:

(1) when each of two arbitrators examined a witness separately and in the absence of the parties to the reference (*Re Plews and Middleton* (1845));
(2) when the arbitrator proceeded *ex parte* without sufficient justification (*Sharpe* v. *Bickerdyke* (1815));
(3) when the arbitrator heard evidence of one party only, and made his award without hearing the opponent (*Re Brook and Delcomyn* (1864));
(4) when the arbitrator heard and communicated with a party behind the back of his opponent (*Harvey* v. *Shelton* (1844)).

But with a minor irregularity, which does not affect the arbitrator's decision, the court might take a different view. See *Matson* v. *Trower* (1824). Compare *W. Ramsden & Co.* v. *Jacobs* (1922), above.

Protest against irregularities

If any irregularities in the proceedings are sanctioned by the parties to the reference and are allowed to pass by them by their continuing the proceedings, the right to object will be taken to have been waived (*Bignall* v. *Gale* (1841)). The party aggrieved by the irregularity should therefore at once protest to the arbitrator, and if the latter does not set it right, the protesting party should then apply to the court for removal of the arbitrator, or for leave to revoke the appointment. He must not wait to see whether he has been successful, or otherwise, in the reference, and then attempt to have the award set aside (*Drew* v. *Drew* (1855)); for the court will not permit a party to lie by or act in an indecisive way, so as to obtain an award, if it is in his favour, or endeavour to set it aside, if it is not. Similarly, a party is estopped from objecting after the award that an arbitrator nominated by himself is not properly qualified (*Oakland Metal Co. Ltd.* v. *Benaim (D.) & Co.* (1953)).

If a party makes a formal protest against irregularity, and continues to attend the reference, this is not waiver of his objection (*Haigh* v. *Haigh*, above). For a party to retire from the tribunal on protest would not be a very wise move, because he might find that the irregularity to which he objected might not be serious enough to set aside the award given *ex parte* by the arbitrator.

Waiver of procedural objections

"Waiver" is a term which is not strictly defined when applied to arbitration proceedings. A dictionary definition states that a person is said to waive an injury when he abandons the remedy which the law gives him for it, and may be express or implied. In *Darnley* v. *London, Chatham & Dover Ry.* (1867), Lord Chelmsford L.C. said: "A waiver must be an intentional act with knowledge"; and in *Rolland* v. *Cassidy* (1888), Lord Selborne said: "The burden of proving a case of waiver and acquiescence is upon the person who suggests it." See also dictum of Lord Cranworth in *Darnley's* case, above.

There can be no waiver without knowledge of the material facts: the party entitled to object must be aware of the irregularity. Thus in *Jungheim, Hopkins & Co.* v. *Foukelmann* (1909) the award was declared to be null and void, although the parties had appeared before the arbitrators, the plaintiffs not having become aware until after the award was made that the defendant's arbitrator was not duly qualified.

In a statutory arbitration it is competent for the parties to renounce or waive statutory provisions which are for their benefit (*Caledonian Ry.* v. *Lockhart* (1860), in which the House of Lords held that the objection that the award had been made after the time for making it had expired was an objection which could be cured by the consent of the parties).

The best way to avoid a waiver, short of quitting the arbitration entirely, is for the party to continue to attend the arbitration and conduct his case but under a protest to the arbitrator against the irregularity. This point is brought out especially in cases where the arbitrator has exceeded his authority by entering into consideration of matters not referred to him. In *Davies* v. *Price* (1864) Pollock C.B. said: "I do not see why—if an arbitrator deals with a matter beyond his jurisdiction, and the party protests, doubting the arbitrator's authority, and yet goes on to take care of his own interests as best he can, saying I am not sure that you are right—he is to be bound by the award," and in *Hamlyn* v. *Betteley* (1880) Lord Selborne L.C. said: "Where a protest is made against jurisdiction, the party protesting is not bound to retire; he may go through the whole case, subject to the protest he has made." Continuing to take part in proceedings after protest does not amount to consent (*per* Lord Ellenborough C.J. in *Holt* v. *Meddowcroft* (1816)).

It should be remembered, however, that an arbitrator is empowered to make any inquiries necessary to enable him to decide whether he has jurisdiction or not over a matter which either of the parties asks him to consider. See *Christopher Brown Ltd.* v. *Genossenschaft Oesterreichischer Waldbesitzer R. GmbH* (1954).

Also, the parties to the reference may enlarge the jurisdiction of the arbitrator from time to time, if they agree and wish to do so. For example, a parol submission may be taken to be valid (but is not within the Act) (*Westminster Chemicals and Produce Ltd.* v. *Eichholz and Loeser* (1954)). And an arbitration agreement in writing may be altered or added to by parol, and so become a parol agreement (*Thames Ironworks, etc., Co.* v. *R.* (1869)).

An objection on the ground that an umpire has not reheard the evidence may be waived by the conduct of the parties, and if such a party seeks to impeach the award made, the fact that he made no application to the umpire (before the award was made) to rehear evidence will operate as a waiver. See *Re Tunno and Bird* (1833). In *Re Salkeld and Slater* (1840), the attorney for one party insisted on the umpire hearing the oral evidence of certain witnesses, but the umpire refused, except on a matter which had not been heard by the arbitrators, and made his award. There was no waiver, and the award was set aside.

Delegation of Duties

An arbitrator, as a general rule, must not delegate his duties, unless the parties to the reference authorise him to do so, for the maxim is *delegatus non potest delegare*. "Arbitrators cannot refer their arbitrements to others, nor to an umpire; if the submission be not so, neither can they make the arbitrement in the names of themselves, and of a third person to whom no submission was made" (*Anon.* (1468)). If there are two arbitrators they may not delegate their authority to each other (*Little* v. *Newton* (1841)).

However, an arbitrator may delegate to another the performance of an act which is ministerial in character. An example would be the delegation to a surveyor to measure a particular field. What are "ministerial acts," is often difficult to decide. See *Stevenson* v. *Watson* (1879) (architect's functions in ascertaining amount due to contractor held not to be merely ministerial).

One act of delegation has been permitted from the eighteenth century and earlier, and that is when arbitrators refer costs to be taxed by taxing masters (*Lingood* v. *Eade* (1742), *per* Hardwicke L.C.).

Arbitrators who are appointed because of their special skill and knowledge of the subject-matter in the reference, and who are not required to decide by the hearing of evidence, may consult other learned persons when necessary in order to decide on the case. They may also adopt the opinions of such persons as their own. Examples are the opinions of other professional men, *e.g.* architects, valuers, and surveyors. Thus in *Hopcraft* v. *Hickman* (1824), where land surveyors appointed to value an estate took the opinion of two builders as to the value of the mansion-house (with the knowledge of the parties) and adopted it as their own, the award could not be objected to on that ground. Leach V.-C. said: "If the two arbitrators had agreed together to be bound by the opinion of the two builders whom they consulted, there would have been much weight in the objection to the award . . . But . . . the arbitrators received the opinion of the builders merely as evidence, and adopted it as their own."

Further Reading: *Russell on Arbitration*, Chaps. 12 and 13.

CHAPTER 6

EVIDENCE

	page		page
Generally	66	False evidence	71
Kinds of evidence	66	Competence of witnesses	71
Admissibility of evidence	67	Examination of witnesses	72
Arbitrator must hear all evidence	68	(a) Examination-in-chief	72
		(b) Cross-examination	73
Decision must be made on the evidence	69	(c) Re-examination	74
		Arbitrator calling witnesses	74
The taking of evidence	69	Expert witnesses	74
Attendance of witnesses	70		

GENERALLY

FOR the benefit of readers who are not qualified lawyers this chapter starts with a brief description of the different kinds of evidence before dealing with the admissibility of evidence and the taking of evidence.

The Evidence Act 1938, the Civil Evidence Act 1968 and the Civil Evidence Act 1972 apply to arbitration as well as to actions in court.

KINDS OF EVIDENCE

There are the following kinds of evidence:

(1) Oral evidence means statements made by witnesses under legal sanction.

(2) Documentary evidence means evidence by documents produced for inspection by the arbitrator. A document which tends to establish a fact in issue (see p. 67, below) is admissible in lieu of direct oral evidence, if the maker of the statement is dead, or is unable to attend the arbitration proceedings.

(3) Conclusive evidence means evidence which the court must take as full proof of a fact, and excludes any disproving evidence.

(4) Direct evidence is that of a fact actually in issue; it also means evidence of a fact seen by the witness personally.

(5) Circumstantial evidence means evidence of a fact not actually in issue, but legally relevant to a fact in issue.

(6) Real evidence means evidence supplied by material objects produced for the arbitrator's inspection, and not by information from documents or witnesses.

KINDS OF EVIDENCE

(7) Extrinsic evidence is evidence given in connection with written documents and drawn from a source outside the documents.

(8) Hearsay means evidence of a fact not actually perceived by a witness with his own senses, but proved by him to have been stated by another person. (Note sections 1–10 of the Civil Evidence Act 1968.)

(9) Indirect evidence means either hearsay or circumstantial evidence.

(10) Original evidence means evidence which has an independent probative force of its own.

(11) Derivative evidence is derived from other sources.

(12) Parol evidence is oral extrinsic evidence, when used in connection with documents.

(13) Prima facie evidence means evidence of a fact which an arbitrator must take as proof unless disproved by further evidence.

(14) Primary evidence is evidence which itself suggests that it is the best evidence, and which is required to be produced if available.

(15) Secondary evidence is evidence which itself suggests the existence of better evidence, and which is rejected if primary evidence is available.

The arbitrator will generally find himself principally concerned with evidence under heads (1),(2),(6),(8),(14) and (15), above.

The expression "facts in issue" means the facts in dispute, and on proof or disproof of which the claim or defence is based. "Facts relevant to the issue" are details of a fact in issue, or those facts which support or rebut any inference or presumption as to the existence or non-existence of a fact in issue. See also the provisions of the Evidence Act 1938 and Civil Evidence Act 1968. The later Act provides that certain out-of-court statements tending to establish relevant facts are admissible in evidence, either by agreement of the parties, or subject to certain conditions. A statement includes any representation of fact, whether made in words or otherwise, and statements made out of court by any person. Documents are defined to include not only a document in writing but any map, plan, photograph, disc, tape or film.

ADMISSIBILITY OF EVIDENCE

An arbitrator is bound by the same rules of evidence as are the courts, unless the parties to the reference have otherwise agreed. Each party must be allowed to adduce all his evidence and must be fully heard. But the arbitrator may take the evidence of a particular witness at any moment as may be convenient and expedient. He decides all questions of admissibility of the evidence before him under the rules of court. He may adjourn the reference if he is satisfied that additional evidence is of importance, but is not yet available (*Re Enoch and Zaretzky, Bock & Co.* (1910)).

In commercial arbitrations there may be an express or implied clause in the agreement to abandon the rules of evidence; the court recognises the validity of such clauses.

The arbitrator when he decides on any matter which concerns the admission of evidence must act in a strictly judicial manner. If he makes an error on the question of the admissibility of evidence, this does not of itself constitute misconduct, and his award will not be set aside on that ground. See *Hagger* v. *Baker* (1845) and *Macpherson Train & Co. Ltd.* v. *J. Milhem & Sons* (1955).

However, when an arbitrator wrongly admits evidence which goes to the root of the question submitted to him, he is guilty of legal misconduct and his award will be set aside. See *Walford, Baker & Co.* v. *Macfie & Sons* (1915), in which the arbitrator consulted a document which was not included in the contract before him and which was wholly inadmissible and went to the root of the question submitted to him. This decision was followed in *"Agroexport" Enterprise D'Etat pour le Commerce Extérieur* v. *N.V. Goorden Import Cy. S.A.* (1956).

An arbitrator may inquire into collateral matters not submitted to him, if it is strictly necessary for him to do so in order to decide rightly on the issue before him. Even if he receives evidence on matters not properly affecting the points before him, the objection merely amounts to hearing of improper evidence, and the court will not set aside his award (*Falkingham* v. *Victorian Railways Commissioners* (1900)).

Arbitrator must hear all evidence

The arbitrator should hear all the evidence material to the question which the parties have placed before him. He must do this even though he may be of opinion that sufficient evidence has been produced, for declining to receive evidence is an unwise step to take and may be fatal to his award.

If the arbitrator should make his award without having heard all the evidence, or without having allowed any party or person a reasonable opportunity of proving his case, the award may be set aside. See *Williams* v. *Wallis and Cox* (1914) (arbitrator's refusal of evidence as to condition of premises at date of tenant's entry), *Riddell* v. *Sutton* (1828) (arbitrator's rejection of evidence offered by executor to show that he had no assets to meet a demand on the testator's estate) and *Phipps* v. *Ingram* (1835) (arbitrator inspecting

ADMISSIBILITY OF EVIDENCE

the subject-matter and hearing defendant's witness but not plaintiff's witnesses).

Objections to an arbitrator's decision whether or not to receive certain evidence may be waived, and the parties having done so cannot later seek to set aside the award on the grounds of a decision contrary to the rules of evidence.

Decision must be made on the evidence

An arbitrator must decide only on the evidence before him, and not on facts obtained otherwise. He must not rely on any knowledge he has acquired in a different capacity (*Owen* v. *Nicholl* (1948) (improper use of incidental knowledge)).

When a person of expert skill and special knowledge has been appointed arbitrator by the parties, or nominated on their behalf on account of such skill, and they authorise him to use such knowledge, then this is proper. The court will presume such authority from the mere fact of his employment. In such a case, the award cannot be objected to, and will not be set aside, should the evidence tendered by the parties be insufficient to support the award, and if there is knowledge which the arbitrator himself could have supplied to make up for such insufficiency (*Wright* v. *Howson* (1888) (arbitrator experienced in cloth held justified in deciding dispute as to quality by mere inspection of samples) and *Mediterranean and Eastern Export Co.* v. *Fortress Fabrics Ltd.* (1948) (arbitrator with expert knowledge of subject-matter of a sale awarding damages for wrongful rejection of the goods though neither party had tendered evidence as to damages)).

Finally, where the expert arbitrator is authorised to use his knowledge, and is capable of deciding a point in issue because of it, he may refuse to accept additional evidence tendered by the parties on the ground that it is unnecessary, and this will not invalidate his award; but it would not be wise to rely on this practice except in trade arbitrations. See, for example, *Johnston* v. *Cheape* (1817), (p. 54, above) and *Eads* v. *Williams* (1854) (surveyors fixing rent and other terms of a coal lease without examining witnesses).

THE TAKING OF EVIDENCE

An arbitrator has power, unless the arbitration agreement expressly provides otherwise, to examine on oath or affirmation the parties and witnesses in the reference (Arbitration Act 1950, s.12(2)). He is not compelled to take evidence on oath unless the agreement stipulates that he should do so, in which case the examination must be conducted accordingly. If no objection is taken to evidence being received otherwise than on oath, when it is expressly provided for in the agreement, that is in itself a waiver of the objection. See *Ridoat* v. *Pye* (1797), *Allen* v. *Francis* (1845) and *Wakefield* v. *Llanelly Ry. and Dock Co.* (1864).

When witnesses are required to be examined on oath by an express term in the agreement, this means an oral examination, and the taking of evidence by affidavit is not sufficient. But by section 12(6)(*c*) of the Act of 1950 the court has power to order that evidence in an arbitration be given by affidavit. See *Banks* v. *Banks* (1835).

The normal procedure is to administer the oath to all witnesses before they give evidence.

A form of oath appropriate for arbitration proceedings is: "I swear by Almighty God that the evidence which I shall give touching the matters in difference in this reference shall be the truth, the whole truth, and nothing but the truth." The person taking the oath holds the New Testament, or, in the case of a Jewish person, the Old Testament, in his uplifted hand, and says or repeats after the arbitrator the words of the oath. (Oaths Act 1978, Part I (applicable to England, Wales and Northern Ireland)). In Scotland an oath is usually administered and taken with uplifted hand without the New or Old Testament, and this is permissible in any part of the United Kingdom (Oaths Act 1978, Part II (applicable to the United Kingdom)).

Further provisions in Part II of the Oaths Act 1978 are:

(1) If an oath has been administered in a manner other than that prescribed by law, the person who has taken it is nevertheless bound by it if it has been administered in such form and with such ceremonies as he may have declared to be binding.

(2) The fact that the person taking the oath had no religious belief does not affect the validity of the oath.

(3) A person who objects to being sworn is permitted to make a solemn affirmation instead of taking an oath, and a solemn affirmation has the same force and effect as an oath.

(4) The opening words of a solemn affirmation are:
"I,   do solemnly, sincerely and truly declare and affirm"
or, if the affirmation is to be in writing:
"I,   of   , do solemnly and sincerely affirm."

Attendance of Witnesses

All witnesses may be summoned by subpeona, that is by a party who sues by writ of *subpoena ad testificandum* and thus ensures at the hearing the presence of witnesses who are within the jurisdiction of the court (Act of 1950, s.12(4)). Also a master may order the issue of a writ of subpoena to compel attendance before an arbitrator of a witness who is anywhere in the United Kingdom (s.12(4)). By section 12(5) of the same Act, a master may order the writ of *habeas corpus ad testificandum* to bring a prisoner up for examination before an arbitrator or umpire. Section 12(6)(*d*) enables a witness to be examined on oath before an officer of the court or any other person. The other writ of summons under section 12(4) is the writ of *subpoena duces tecum* to compel the bringing before arbitrators or umpires of any document which could be ordered to be brought before the judge in an action. Such writs are issued either out of the Central Office of the Royal Courts of Justice in London, or at any district registry in England and Wales (R.S.C., Ord. 32, r. 11; Ord. 73, rr. 3, 4).

Wilful disobedience to a writ by a person within the jurisdiction is contempt of court, for which a person could be committed, but only if a reasonable sum is tendered for conduct money and expenses (*Re Batson, ex p. Hastie* (1894)). Should the person be outside the jurisdiction of the English courts, disobedience to an order under section 12(4) would appear to be covered by the Attendance of Witnesses Act 1854 (ss. 3, 4).

False Evidence

For a person lawfully sworn as a witness in an arbitration, to make a statement from the witness box, which is material and which he knows to be false or does not believe to be true, is perjury (Perjury Act 1911, s.1(1),(2)).

If a person manufactures false evidence with the intention to deceive and mislead an arbitrator at the reference, even though he does not bring in such evidence, such person is guilty of a misdemeanour at common law. See *R.* v. *Vreones* (1891). If the statement is made inadvertently or by mistake, and not wilfully or deliberately, such is not a misdemeanour.

Competence of Witnesses

Generally, all normal adult persons are competent to be called as witnesses, the exceptions being on the grounds of infancy, lunacy (persons of unsound mind), drunkenness and other special reasons. Such persons are considered not to be able to understand the proceedings or the nature of the oath, or to speak the truth, and give evidence in a rational manner.

Examination of Witnesses

The examination of witnesses orally consists of: (a) examination-in-chief by the party calling him; (b) cross-examination by the other party opposing him; and (c) re-examination by his own party. In all cases the parties may be represented by counsel or solicitor. The opposing party is not entitled to cross-examine a witness who is called merely to produce a document or to identify it (on a *subpoena duces tecum*).

The arbitrator may at any time permit recall of a witness for further examination-in-chief, but this course permits the right of further cross-examination, and of re-examination on the particular matters for which the witness was recalled. Should a witness, after giving evidence, subsequently become incapable, or die, his evidence remains admissible and good. Both examination-in-chief and cross-examination must be confined to the facts in issue, or to the facts relevant to the issue. The test is whether the answer to a question put to a witness will assist, aid or abet, or is pertinent to, or bears on, the point in issue.

(a) *Examination-in-chief*

Leading questions are those questions which suggest a desired or expected answer, or questions which suggest, as facts, the points at issue. They must not be asked of a witness by his own party, or own counsel, either in examination-in-chief, or re-examination, except by express permission of the arbitrator. But such questions may be put to a witness if they are merely introductory or relate to matters on which there is no dispute. Leading questions may also be put to contradict evidence already given by a witness on the other side, or for the purpose of identifying persons or things, or when it is impossible to put a question except in the manner of a leading question. It is better to obtain permission of opposing counsel, before leading questions are put in this way. It is a great art to cross-examine well, but it requires even greater skill to examine-in-chief, in order to bring out clearly just so much as is wanted, and no more. Yet counsel must not seem to suggest anything to the witness.

In no circumstances may a party, or his counsel, attack the character of a witness whom he has himself called, nor may he call evidence to discredit him. But he may call evidence to contradict him upon a fact which is material, and not merely collateral, or where the party is compelled by the law of the land to call a witness. Sometimes an arbitrator may allow a witness, who has given evidence adverse to the party calling him, to be treated as a hostile witness, and he may then be cross-examined and contradicted, and asked leading questions, but not if such a witness merely gives evidence which is unfavourable to the party calling him (*Greenough* v. *Eccles* (1859)).

A witness must always state what happened according to his own personal knowledge, and not according to what he has subsequently been told. But he is allowed to refresh his memory by reference to notes or memoranda made at the time of the event, if they were made by him, or read and recognised by him as correct immediately afterwards (*Birchall* v. *Bullough* (1896)). The opposing party is entitled to look at a document from which a witness has refreshed his memory, and to cross-examine him on it, but not on an irrelevant matter in the notes. The notes must be originals and not copies (*Burton* v. *Plummer* (1834)). Apart from statute, an arbitrator is not entitled to hear secret information (*Fowler* v. *Fowler and Sine* (1963)).

(b) *Cross-examination*

The party, or his counsel, has more freedom in cross-examination, and leading questions may be asked as frequently as desired. Neither need he confine his questions to the facts in issue, and he may attack the character and the credit of the witness, although he should be on guard when he does so. It rests with the arbitrator whether vexatious and irrelevant questions are allowed, especially where the credibility of the witness is concerned. For in this instance the facts in issue have a bearing on the matter.

The person who conducts cross-examination should test the source of knowledge, or means of recollection, or foundation of the judgment, of the witness. He may show that the witness is an interested party, that he is biased and partial and that he has made previous statements inconsistent with his present evidence.

Cross-examination should be particularly directed to that part of the examination-in-chief of the witness which is in dispute. Failure to cross-examine on this part would amount to acceptance of the evidence given therein. Any fact which the cross-examiner intends to plead should be put to the witness, in order to give him the chance to deny such fact. Care should be taken not to include any additional, or irrelevant, evidence by cross-examination on matters which the opposing party has failed to support.

There are certain questions which a witness cannot be compelled to answer, either in cross-examination or in examination-in-chief:
    (a) where any answer would incriminate the witness;
    (b) communications between husband and wife during marriage; and
    (c) communications between client and barrister or solicitor.

(c) *Re-examination*

The object of re-examination is to give witnesses a further chance to explain any inconsistencies in their previous answers. They may also state the complete truth as to previous matters referred to, but not fully dealt with, in cross-examination. A party or his counsel may not ask, when re-examining a witness, any question which did not arise out of cross-examination, except with consent. Leading questions of a party's own witness may not be asked.

Arbitrator Calling Witnesses

At any stage in the proceedings, an arbitrator may put any question to a witness, for in this respect he is acting in a judicial capacity. Nevertheless an arbitrator may not himself call a witness as to questions of fact, unless the consent of the parties is obtained. See *Re Enoch and Zaretsky, Bock & Co.* (1910), in which the Court of Appeal held that an arbitrator or umpire had no power himself to call witnesses to fact against the will of either of the parties except where a person went into the witness-box by permission of the judge as a witness for neither party. The only exception to that rule, if exception it can be called, is that when a witness has been called by a party, and has left the box, then a judge or arbitrator may recall such a witness. In *Fallon* v. *Calvert* (1960) such a witness was recalled by an Official Referee.

Expert Witnesses

The true role of the expert witness is to offer the court the best assistance he can in getting at the truth. He may, in addition to refreshing his memory by reference to notes, refer to his own previous reports, and specialist books on the subject before the arbitrator. He may do this to support his opinions, and may quote other law cases and judgments in which he gave evidence which was accepted. Nevertheless, the arbitrator may still decide what evidence an expert witness may or may not bring before him.

In *British Celanese Ltd.* v. *Courtaulds Ltd.* (1935), a patents case concerned with thread manufacturing, the House of Lords considered the function of expert witnesses and the nature of the questions which might be put to them, and held that an expert witness is entitled to give evidence as to the state of the art and the meaning of technical terms, to give an opinion whether, on a hypothetical interpretation of a specification, a skilled worker could carry it into effect, and generally to explain scientific facts, but that he cannot be asked (even as engineer or chemist) what a specification means.

In *Morton* v. *Hargreaves Motors* (1963), a claim for damages for injuries sustained in a traffic accident, the Court of Appeal held that each side should have leave to call both an engineer and a metallurgist on the defendants' undertaking to disclose their experts' reports to the plaintiff.

Another case on the exchange of reports between expert witnesses was *Dalton* v. *Clark and Fenn* (1963). The plaintiff was claiming damages from his employers for injuries sustained at work, and liability was admitted. On being informed that medical reports had not been exchanged, the judge observed that he strongly deprecated this failure; the proper course was for the plaintiff to hand over his medical reports on the terms that, if they were not agreed, he should be entitled to see the defendants' medical reports.

A case in which expert evidence was held *not* to be admissible was *English Exporters (London) Ltd.* v. *Eldonwall Ltd.* (1973): the judge held that, although an expert valuer may in evidence express his opinion on values by drawing on hearsay, he cannot give hearsay evidence as to the facts of transactions which lie outside his personal knowledge.

Further Reading: *Russell on Arbitration*, Chap. 14; Halsbury's *Laws of England* (4th ed., 1976), the title "Evidence."

CHAPTER 7

THE MAKING OF THE AWARD

	page		page
Time for making award............	76	Formal requisites....................	77
Enlargement of time	76	Substantive requisites..............	79

TIME FOR MAKING AWARD

THE arbitrator is under a duty to proceed with due diligence and reasonable dispatch in making his award. The Act of 1950 provides that, unless there is an express intention in the arbitration agreement, an award may be made at any time (s.13(1)) but that the court may remove an arbitrator who fails to use all reasonable dispatch in entering on and proceeding with the reference and making an award (s.13(3)). An award made after a summons to remove the arbitrator may still be valid (*Lewis Emanuel & Son Ltd.* v. *Sammut* (1959)). It has been held in a case that reasonable delay need not be misconduct (*Compagnie Financière pour le Commerce Extérieur S.A.* v. *Oy. Vehna A.B.* (1963)).

ENLARGEMENT OF TIME

By section 13(2) of the Act of 1950, the court may order the time for making an award to be enlarged, when there is a fixed time in an agreement. The application for enlargement of time must not be unduly delayed (*Oakland Metal Co. Ltd.* v. *Benaim (D.) & Co. Ltd.* (1953)). See R.S.C., Ord. 73, r. 3.

Even if the parties to an agreement fix a time limit, the court may order a further enlargement (*Knowles & Sons Ltd.* v. *Bolton Corporation* (1900)). However, it seems that the parties may agree that an award shall not be binding unless made within a fixed time; they thus make time of the essence of the contract (*Randell* v. *Thompson* (1876)). The Act of 1950 gives the parties an express power to provide for a revocable submission or agreement (s.1).

The court has power to enlarge the time for making an award, even though the actual award has been made after the period for making it has expired. In such a case, the award and every act done in the reference remains valid during the extended time (*Oakland Metal Co. Ltd.* v. *Benaim (D.) & Co. Ltd.* (1953)).

The power of the court to enlarge time is entirely discretionary, and will be exercised with caution. If there has been an inexcusable delay in applying for an enlargement, the court will normally refuse an order. The test is whether the time for making the award is an essential element in the submission, or is merely for the guidance of the arbitrator.

The time generally granted for an enlargement is one calendar month.

In addition to the power of the court to enlarge the time, if the allotted time has expired it may be enlarged by the consent of the parties. This consent should be in writing, but, when it has not been expressly given and the parties proceed, it will be implied. The arbitrator himself cannot extend the time fixed for the making of an award.

Formal Requisites

(a) The award must comply with the submission; otherwise it will not be valid unless the failure to comply is of an immaterial character (as in *Gatliffe* v. *Dunn* (1738)).

(b) Unless the submission states to the contrary, a parol award is valid (*Cocks* v. *Macclefield* (1562)). Where there is no provision for writing, there must be another extraneous act by the arbitrator, for if he can change his mind, there is no award.

(c) The making of an award must not be delegated to another person (*Johnson* v. *Latham* (1850)). The arbitrator, however, may employ a legal adviser to draw up the award (*Re Underwood and Bedford Ry.* (1861)).

(d) Execution: The arbitrator usually signs the award at the foot, and has his signature attested by a witness.

Where there are two or more arbitrators, it has been said to be the rule that "all should execute the award at the same time and place" (*Russell on Arbitration*, p. 235). The rule can be supported by reference to *Re Beck and Jackson* (1857), in which an award made by two out of the three arbitrators in favour of B. was challenged by J. and set aside by the court on the ground that it had not been jointly executed. However, in *European Grain and Shipping Ltd.* v. *Johnston* (1982) there were observations by Lord Denning M.R. to the effect that in view of modern developments such as the telephone and typewriter and other forms of communication the above-mentioned rule is not to be taken too literally now: provided all the arbitrators communicate together as to the content of the award, either in each other's presence or by telephone or documents, they need not all be present at one time and place to sign the award.

By section 9 of the Act of 1950, as substituted by section 6(2) of the Act of 1979, where there is a reference to three arbitrators, the award of any two of them is binding.

If the award is not executed properly, the court may remit it to the arbitrator or umpire for proper execution.

The arbitrator's powers, save for the alteration of clerical errors under section 17, entirely cease once he has executed his award; he is said to be *"functus,"* an abridgement of *"functus officio"* (literally, "having performed his duty").

(e) Two copies of the award are usually made, one original which is signed by the arbitrator, and thus delivered to the party taking it up. The other copy will be sent to the other party on request.

(f) Publication: When the agreement provides that the arbitrator shall "make and publish" his award, it becomes valid only on publication. However, the award is generally regarded as "published" when completed by the arbitrator. For the purpose of the time for setting aside, "publication" does not come about until the award is published *to the parties*.

(g) Delivery: If the agreement stipulates that the award is to be "ready to be delivered" on a fixed day, but it is not actually delivered by that day, it will still be valid. On the other hand, if there is a condition that it "shall be delivered" by a fixed day, and actual delivery does not take place, the validity is affected. If delivery to "either party" is required, the word "either" will be construed as "every," and delivery must be made to both of the parties. If, however, the requirement is that the award be delivered "to the parties or one of them," delivery to only one of them is sufficient.

It is usual for the arbitrator to retain the award until his fees have been paid by the party taking it up. This course has judicial sanction, and is correct even when the party taking up the award is not the party asked to pay costs. The party taking up the award may in that case recover from his opponent such fees as he is required to pay (*Hicks* v. *Richardson* (1797)).

(h) Stamps: No stamps are required on an award (Finance Act 1949, s.35, Sched. 8). In accordance with the case of *Blundell* v. *Brettargh* (1810), when an award is under seal, and delivered as an award, no deed stamp is required, but it would be otherwise if the award were delivered as a deed.

(i) Recitals: The award need not contain recitals (*e.g.* as to the arbitrator's authority and the proceedings in the arbitration), but although recitals are not strictly necessary, it is advisable that they be drawn up and incorporated in the award, in order to explain the award and show that the arbitrator has properly performed his duties. In *Smith* v. *Hartley* (1851) Jervis C.J. said: "By the rules of pleading, it is not necessary to set out in the declaration the terms of the reference. It is enough to state that there were matters in difference between the parties, and that the reference was of and concerning those matters. It will be presumed that the arbitrators acted within the scope of their authority; and it lies on the defendant to plead it, if they have exceeded their authority." It is for the arbitrator to exercise his discretion as to whether recitals will be incorporated, and much will depend on the complexity of the case in hand.

A false recital cannot enlarge the arbitrator's authority. Nor does it invalidate the award (*e.g. Trew* v. *Burton* (1833) (umpire's award not vitiated by mistake in the Christian name of one of the original arbitrators who had appointed the umpire)).

(j) Reasons for award: Formerly an award which contained an error on its face might be remitted or set aside by the court, and this rule made arbitrators reluctant to include reasons in their awards. The position was changed by the Arbitration Act 1979, which provides that the court has no jurisdiction to remit or set aside an award on the ground of errors of fact or law on the face of the award (s.1(1)). It was envisaged that this provision would encourage arbitrators to state reasons in their awards.

Further, the Act of 1979 empowers the court to require an arbitrator or umpire to state the reasons for his award in sufficient detail to enable the court to consider any question of law on which an appeal has been made to the court (s.1(5)). The arbitrator or umpire will normally have had some forewarning of the requirement to state reasons because the Act also provides that the court must not make an order under section 1(5) unless it is satisfied either:

(*a*) that before the award was made one of the parties gave notice to the arbitrator or umpire that a reasoned award would be required; or

(*b*) that there is some special reason why such a notice was not given (s.1(6)).

SUBSTANTIVE REQUISITES

The award, in order to be valid, must be final, certain, consistent, possible, unambiguous, uncontradictory, unconditional and unimpeachable. It must decide the matters in the submission and no more. No technical expressions are necessary, but the arbitrator should be very precise in his adjudication.

Although the court is inclined to support the validity of an award, such a presumption will not extend to the jurisdiction of the arbitrator, for the legal maxim *omnia praesumuntur rite esse acta* ("all things are presumed to have been duly done") does not apply to arbitration proceedings: in *Christopher Brown Ltd.* v. *Genossenschaft Oesterreichischer Waldbesitzer R. GmbH* (1954) Devlin J. (as he then was) said:

> "The principle *omnia praesumuntur rite esse acta* does not apply to proceedings of arbitration tribunals or, indeed, to the proceedings of inferior tribunals of any sort. There is no presumption that merely because an award has been made it is a valid award. It has to be proved by the party who sues upon it that it was made by the arbitrators within the terms of their authority, that is, with jurisdiction. Jurisdiction has to be proved affirmatively."

(a) An arbitrator can make *only one final award*, unless he has some special authority. By section 14 of the Act of 1950, he may make an interim award, unless the arbitration agreement expresses a contrary intention. An interim award may be final as to some of the claims in the dispute. Generally it decides issues of a party's liability to pay, and the actual amount to be paid is settled afterwards.

(b) Whether an arbitrator may make a *declaration* in his award as to the rights of the parties (*i.e.* may make a "declaratory award") must depend on the nature of the dispute and on the conditions of the arbitration agreement. When parties require a decision which will bind them in future disputes over the same matter, they must submit a general question, and not only the particular dispute in issue. The arbitrator must take care if it is not clear that the general question is submitted to him otherwise than as arising in the particular case: he should try to obtain the written consent of both parties to the submission of the general question, for an oral amendment of the arbitration agreement takes the reference in part outside the Act of 1950.

(c) The award must be *final*; otherwise it will be remitted to the arbitrator or set aside. It must be the final ruling on all matters which require determination: the exclusion of merely one of such matters will make the award totally bad. The submission, however, may not require the arbitrator to decide all the matters in dispute: it may be so worded as to give the arbitrator a discretion to decide one or more of the matters in dispute without deciding all.

No objections on the ground of lack of finality can be made if the question unanswered relates to a matter which is not in dispute, nor can there be objections to an award if the arbitrator

SUBSTANTIVE REQUISITES

determines all questions brought to his notice although there may be others in the submission.

It is permissible for an arbitrator to award one general sum in respect of all money claims submitted, unless the submission provides otherwise. If the submission is ambiguous it is preferable that the award should contain separate adjudications on each claim.

Where an arbitrator omits to give necessary directions in his award, the award is not final.

If the arbitration agreement requires that there be only a single award, it must be a complete instrument in itself and not, for instance, two awards each deciding part of the matters submitted.

An award may be put in the alternative and still qualify as final (*e.g.* if the award directs one of two things to be done and the first is impossible and the second is possible).

The arbitrator must not reserve any judicial authority on the matters submitted. Where it seems likely that, having received the arbitrator's determination of one matter, the parties will agree as to other matters, the arbitrator should make only an interim award. An instance of such a situation is where the arbitrator decides a question of liability and the parties themselves then agree as to the amount of damages. Equally, an arbitrator must not delegate judicial authority by awarding that the parties must abide by the award of another person. However, the arbitrator may make a valid reservation for a further ministerial act to be done by himself or by another person at any time—even after the time for making the award has expired.

(d) An award must be *certain, i.e.* such that no reasonable doubt can arise upon its face as to the meaning of the arbitrator who drafted it or as to the duties imposed by it upon the parties. If there is any doubt as to whether the award has decided the dispute or the question referred, the award will be invalid.

If the arbitrator does not specify a sum of money but gives a rule for computing the amount, the award is sufficiently certain, in accordance with the maxim *id certum est quod certum reddi potest* ("that which can be made certain is certain").

The arbitrator must also be precise in all his directions to the parties to do any act whatsoever.

(e) The award must be *consistent* in all its parts and not ambiguous or contradictory.

(f) The award must be *legal and capable of performance*.

(g) The award may be made in a foreign currency (*Jugoslavenska Oceanska Plovidba* v. *Castle Investment Co. Inc.* (*The Kozara*) (1974)). The appropriate foreign currency is that which best expresses the claimant's loss, *i.e.* usually the currency of the claimant's business (*Services Europe Atlantique Sud (SEAS)* v. *Stockholms Rederiaktiebolag Svea* (*The Despina R.*, *The Folias*) (1979)).

Further Reading: *Russell on Arbitration*, Chaps. 16 and 17.

CHAPTER 8

PROCEEDINGS SUBSEQUENT TO THE AWARD

	page		page
Effect of award	83	Appeal under arbitration agreement	90
Award does not transfer property	84	Defence to action on award or action for declaration	90
Award as evidence	84	Remission or setting aside	90
Interest in awards	84	Appeal to court under Arbitration Act 1979	92
Enforcement of award	86	(1) Judicial review of award	92
Enforcement under section 26	86	(2) Determination of preliminary point of law	95
Enforcement of award by action	88	(3) Exclusion agreements	96
Challenge of award	90		

Effect of Award

THE award is a final judgment on all matters referred unless the arbitration agreement expressly provides otherwise (as it would do if the award were an interim award). Section 16 of the Act of 1950 enacts what was formerly a principle of the common law—the award is final and binding on the parties to the arbitration agreement and the persons claiming under them.

Strangers to the arbitration agreement are not bound by the award, unless there is agreement to the contrary.

Once the arbitrator has made his final award, he cannot re-open it. He can only alter it if it is remitted to him by the court, except that:

(*a*) he has power, unless a contrary intention is expressed in the arbitration agreement, to correct any clerical mistake or error arising from an accidental slip or omission (s.17); and

(*b*) if the award has made no provision as to costs, a party to the reference may, within 14 days of the publication of the award or such further time as the court may direct, apply to the arbitrator for an order as to costs and the arbitrator must then, after hearing any party who desires to be heard, amend his award by adding to it a direction as to costs (s.18(4)).

The court itself cannot amend or alter an award: all that it can do is to set it aside or remit it to the arbitrator. The court has, however, power to interpret an ambiguous award and declare its true meaning (R.S.C., Ord. 15, r. 16).

Only the questions actually referred are concluded by the award.

Award does not Transfer Property

Real property or personalty cannot be transferred by an award. The parties, however, may be directed (where the arbitrator has such power) to execute conveyances or otherwise make a transfer of the property in dispute. It is also possible that the parties agree that the award shall determine any legal rights in the land which is in dispute between them. Further, an award made under statute will have the effect of transferring property if the statute so provides.

Award as Evidence

An award which is valid in every respect is conclusive evidence of the facts found by the arbitrator, and evidence cannot be given to contradict it, so long as it remains unimpeached.

An award is not admissible as evidence in criminal proceedings.

An award has an effect only upon the parties to it and is not admissible in evidence against a stranger. In certain circumstances it may be evidence in favour of a stranger (*Shelling* v. *Farmer* 1726), a case in which an award under which S. had received compensation from F.'s employers was held to be good evidence on behalf of F. in an action brought by S. against F. for damages).

The arbitrator may give his award as evidence in an action brought by an unsuccessful party to the reference for the recovery of his property, if the property has been deposited with the arbitrator in the meantime (*Gunton* v. *Nurse* (1821)).

Where an award is tendered as evidence, the opposite party may destroy its effect by a reply which offers evidence to the contrary (*e.g.* evidence impeaching the validity of the award on the ground that the arbitrator did not decide all the matters referred).

The court is entitled to examine any documents which accompany and form part of an award, *e.g.* the pleadings "provided they have been so referred to by the arbitrator as to incorporate them into the award" (*per* Willis J. in *Belsfield Court Construction Co. Ltd.* v. *Pywell* (1970)).

Interest in Awards

A distinction is made between the power to award interest for the period before the making of the award and the power to award interest for the period after the making of the award. Only the second is provided for by the Act of 1950 (s.20.)

The right of arbitrators to award interest for the period before the making of the award is derived from the rule that arbitrators have the powers of the courts in the matter of awarding interest. Thus in *Chandris* v. *Isbrandtsen-Moller Co. Inc.* (1951), where an arbitrator awarded to a shipowner against the charterers of a vessel £2,137.10s. as demurrage and the question was whether the arbitrator had also jurisdiction to award interest of £170 on that sum, the Court of Appeal held that it was an implied term of the submission that the arbitrator should decide the dispute according to the existing law of contract, that that law included the provisions of the Law Reform (Miscellaneous Provisions) Act 1934, section 3(1) of which gave a court power to award interest on debt or damages, and that, therefore, the arbitrator had power to award interest.

Section 3(1) of the Law Reform (Miscellaneous Provisions) Act 1934 provides:

> "In any proceedings tried in any court of record for the recovery of any debt or damages, the court may, if it thinks fit, order that there shall be included in the sum for which judgment is given interest at such rate as it thinks fit on the whole or any part of the debt or damages for the whole or any part of the period between the date when the cause of action arose and the date of the judgment."

Because of the words "the sum for which judgment is given" this provision has been criticised for having created "the indefensible absurdity that a defendant may delay payment for years but will, if he pays the principal sum at the last moment, escape all liability for interest albeit that, if he waited a day longer, interest for the full period at a realistic rate might be and probably would be awarded against him" (*per* Parker J. in *Tehno-Impex* v. *Gebr. van Weelde Scheepvaartkantoor B.V.* (1981)).

In the *Tehno-Impex* case demurrage had been paid late, but before the commencement of the arbitration, and the question was whether the arbitrator had been right in refusing the shipowners' claim for interest on the demurrage payments. The Court of Appeal, allowing an appeal from the judgment of Parker J., held that since the shipowners' claim could have been brought in the Admiralty Court instead of in the Commercial Court, and since the Admiralty Court did have jurisdiction to award as damages interest for non-payment of money due at a particular date, the arbitrator was entitled to invoke that jurisdiction and award damages corresponding to the interest claimed.

As regards interest for the period after the making of an award, section 20 of the Act of 1950 provides that "a sum directed to be paid by an award shall, unless the award otherwise directs, carry interest as from the date of the award and at the same rate as a judgment debt." The interpretation placed on this section by the House of Lords in *Timber Shipping Co. S.A.* v. *London & Overseas Freighters Ltd.* (1972) was that an arbitration award carries interest at the same rate as a judgment debt unless the arbitrator directs that it is to carry no interest at all, and that the section does not empower an arbitrator to fix whatever rate of interest he chooses. The arbitrator had awarded a capital sum as payable by charterers to shipowners for hire of a vessel under a time charterparty and had directed that interest at 8 per cent. should run on that sum from a specified date in the past until payment. At the time of the award the rate of interest on a judgment debt was only 4 per cent., and the Court of Appeal set aside the part of the award which directed interest at the higher rate of 8 per cent. to be paid from the date of the award until payment, that part being held to be separable from the part which awarded interest at 8 per cent. up to the date of the award. The rate of interest on a judgment debt is alterable by statutory instruments ("Judgment Debts (Rate of Interest) Orders"). The rate of interest applicable is the rate fixed by the Order in force at the date of the award and does not thereafter fluctuate (*Rocco Giuseppe & Figli* v. *Tradax Export S.A.* (1983)).

Enforcement of Award

The method of enforcing an award depends upon whether the submission has excluded the provisions of the Act of 1950 or not. Where, as is generally the case, the Act of 1950 has not been excluded, enforcement under section 26 of the Act is open. Apart from that section an award may be enforced by an action in court.

Enforcement under section 26

Section 26 as amended by the Administration of Justice Act 1977 consists of three subsections: subsection (1) provides for applications to the High Court; subsection (2) for applications to a county court; and subsection (3) provides that an application to the High Court precludes an application to a county court and vice versa.

By section 26(1) an award on an arbitration agreement may, by leave of the High Court, be enforced in the same manner as a

ENFORCEMENT OF AWARD

judgment or order to the same effect and, where such leave is given, judgment may be entered in terms of the award.

This summary mode of enforcement is *not* available in the following cases:

(1) where the submission and the agreement are not in writing, for there is then no "arbitration agreement" within the meaning of Part I of the Act (s.32);

(2) where the award is merely declaratory (*e.g.* where it only fixes the amount to be paid and does not adjudicate on the liability to pay);

(3) where there is real ground for doubting the validity of the award; in *Middlemiss & Gould (a Firm)* v. *Hartlepool Corporation* (1972) the Court of Appeal granted leave to building contractors to enforce an award against the corporation as housing authority, although the arbitrator had not expressly dealt with a particular point raised by the corporation; the Court of Appeal disapproved of the test put forward by Scrutton L.J. in *Re Boks & Co. and Peters, Rushton & Co. Ltd.* (1919) (a case in which the award had been contested on the ground that the contract concerned unlawful dealing in palm nuts without the necessary licence); Scrutton L.J. had said that "this summary method of enforcing awards is only to be used in reasonably clear cases"; the accepted view now is that the summary method is "to be used in nearly all cases" and "leave should be given to enforce the award as a judgment unless there is real ground for doubting the validity of the award" (*per* Lord Denning M.R. in *Middlemiss* (above));

(4) where the award is a foreign award, but only in certain cases; some foreign awards may be enforced by the section 26 procedure (1950 Act, s.36(1); 1975 Act, s.3(1)), but even where that procedure is available, it is usual for foreign awards to be enforced by an action;

(5) where it is not possible for the English court to give a judgment or order "to the same effect"; thus in *Dalmia Cement Ltd.* v. *National Bank of Pakistan* (1974) where awards stated that sums were to be paid by the bank "in India," leave was refused because an English court would not ordinarily make an order requiring payment outside the jurisdiction and an order requiring the bank to pay the money in England would not be "to the same effect" as an award to pay the sum in India;

(6) where the award is statutory and must be enforced as provided by the Act of Parliament concerned (*Re Willesden Local Board and Wright* (1896)).

By section 26(2), if the amount sought to be recovered does not exceed the current limit on jurisdiction in section 40 of the County Courts Act 1959 and a county court so orders, it can be recovered (by execution issued from the county court or otherwise) as if payable under an order of that court and it is not enforceable under section 26(1).

Enforcement of award by action

The action may take different forms, according to the terms of the award (whether in writing or by parol). It may be an action to recover a sum of money, or an action for specific performance or an injunction to prevent some act being done. It is also possible to sue for a declaration that the award is binding.

Matters to be proved. The matters to be proved in an action on an award are:
(1) that a submission has been made, or there is an existing contract which contains an arbitration clause, followed by a dispute within the clause;
(2) that an arbitrator has been appointed in accordance with the arbitration agreement;
(3) that an award has been made; and
(4) that the amount awarded has not been paid or the award has not been otherwise performed.

All these matters must be proved because the legal principle *omnia praesumuntur rite esse acta* does not apply to arbitration proceedings (see *Christopher Brown Ltd.* v. *Genossenschaft Oesterreichischer Waldbesitzer R. GmbH* (p. 80, above).

Specific performance of award. If the award is for the doing of some specific act (other than paying a sum of money) and damages are not an adequate remedy, the court may decree specific performance. If the award is void in part only and the other part can be clearly separated, the court may decree specific performance of that other part (*per* McCardie J., *obiter*, in *Selby* v. *Whitbread & Co.* (1917)). Specific performance may also be granted when there has been part performance of the award (*i.e.* complete performance of his obligation by the party seeking the decree) (*Nickels* v. *Hancock* (1855)).

Specific performance will not be decreed in the following circumstances:
(1) where full relief cannot be given to both parties (*Blackett* v. *Bates* (1865));
(2) where the award and the submission together constitute an

unreasonable agreement or an agreement which is not capable of being worked out in a manner consistent with the intention of the parties (*Nickels* v. *Hancock,* above);
(3) where the parties have been guilty of laches, *i.e.* of an unwarrantable delay in seeking the remedy (*Eads* v. *Williams* (1854) (specific performance sought four years after the making of the award));
(4) where there is no part-performance and, by reason of section 4 of the Statute of Frauds, the award is not enforceable at law (*Walters* v. *Morgan* (1792) (submission not evidenced by writing so as to satisfy the Statute of Frauds)).

Defences to action on award. Where there has been misconduct or irregularity on the part of the arbitrator, the proper course is to move to have the award set aside: the defendant in an action on the award cannot plead the misconduct or irregularity as a defence; this is known as the "rule in *Thorburn* v. *Barnes*" (1867), a case in which arbitrators received documents on behalf of one of the parties without giving the other party an opportunity of being heard; Willes J. said that "insufficiency or want of hearing must be urged as a ground for setting aside the award on motion, and cannot be set up as a bar to an action upon it."
The defences available to the defendant in an action on an award are:

(1) that the time limits for enforcement laid down in sections 7 and 8 of the Limitation Act 1980 have expired (six years if the submission is not under seal, 12 years if it is under seal) (see p. 9, above);
(2) that the arbitrator's authority was revoked before the award was made (*Marsh* v. *Bulteel* (1822));
(3) that the arbitrator has exceeded his jurisdiction;
(4) that the sum awarded has already been attached by some person other than the plaintiff;
(5) that the arbitration agreement is ancillary to another contract and is no longer binding because the principal contract is at an end (*Bellshill and Mossend Co-operative Society Ltd.* v. *Dalziel Co-operative Society Ltd.* (1960) (former member of union of co-operative societies not bound by award made under rules of the union));
(6) that there has been accord and satisfaction, or that the award has been performed or otherwise satisfied.

Challenge of Award

Appeal under Arbitration Agreement

The arbitration agreement may allow an appeal to be made from an arbitrator's award to an umpire, and a further appeal to be made from the umpire to a committee or board of appeal. Arbitration involving several tiers is commonly provided for in the arbitration clauses in the standard forms of contract of the various trade and commodity associations. The party challenging an award by such procedure must strictly observe the rules subject to which the appeal is available, *e.g.* he is usually bound to give notice of appeal within a specified time and he may be required to deposit with the secretary of the association the amount of the disputed award (*Amalgamated Metal Corporation* v. *Khoon Seng Co. Ltd.* (1977)).

Defence to Action on Award or Action for Declaration

Where the ground of objection to an award is that the whole arbitration is a nullity or that the arbitrator has exceeded his jurisdiction (*e.g.* because he is disqualified by interest or otherwise or because he has purported to act after his removal or to decide matters beyond the scope of the reference), the award may be challenged by one party putting forward the ground of objection as a defence to an action brought by the other party to enforce the award. Alternatively the first party may take the initiative by bringing an action for a declaration that the award is a nullity.

Remission or Setting Aside

The court has statutory power to remit or set aside an award under sections 22 and 23 respectively of the Act of 1950.

Section 22 provides that the court may from time to time remit the matters referred, or any of them, to the reconsideration of the arbitrator or umpire, and that, where an award is remitted, the arbitrator or umpire must, unless the order otherwise directs, make his award within three months after the date of the order.

At common law there was no power to remit.

The statutory provisions on setting aside an award in section 23 are that where an arbitrator or umpire has misconducted himself or the proceedings, or an arbitration or award has been improperly procured, the court may set the award aside, and that where an application is made to set aside an award, the court may order that any money made payable by the award shall be brought into court or otherwise secured until the application is determined.

At common law the court has an inherent power to set an award aside.

The vital distinction between remission and setting aside is that in the case of the latter procedure the whole arbitration is made null and void, with the result that the parties are back at the beginning again, whereas in the case of remission the door is still open for the arbitration proceedings, after reconsideration and rectification, to be brought to a satisfactory conclusion.

In other respects remission and setting aside have many common features. Both the power to remit and the power to set aside are discretionary; the grounds on which they may be exercised are substantially the same and include a mistake in expression admitted by the arbitrator, misconduct of the arbitrator and the need to consider additional material evidence discovered since the making of the award, but there is no exhaustive list of grounds (*Universal Cargo Carriers Corporation* v. *Citati* (1957)). In the exercise of its discretion the court may refuse to interefere with an award even where there is a ground on which an award would usually be remitted or set aside: decided cases are merely illustrative of how the court has exercised its discretion in each particular case. Remission is appropriate where the fault is one of omission or where the arbitrator's misconduct has been coupled with a complete absence of dishonest motive. On the other hand, setting aside would be the appropriate remedy where justice demanded it (*e.g.* if the arbitrator had been guilty of fraud or might not approach the question with a fresh mind and without prejudice). Formerly it was a ground for remission or setting aside that the award was bad on its face, but this possibility was removed by section 1(1) of the Arbitration Act 1979.

A mere alleged mistake in law or in fact, whether or not it appears on the face of the award, is no ground for remission or setting aside. The "misconduct" of an arbitrator which may be a ground for remission or setting aside extends to irregularity in the conduct of the arbitration proceedings, not necessarily involving any moral turpitude. This extended meaning of the term "misconduct," "can give a wholly misleading impression of the complaint being made against an arbitrator" (*per* Sir John Donaldson M.R., delivering the judgment of the Court of Appeal in *Moran* v. *Lloyd's* (1983), a case in which there were held to be no arguable grounds for setting an award aside). The Commercial Court Committee in its report on Arbitration in 1978 (Cmnd. 7284, para. 67) recommended that some other term be substituted for "misconducted" in section 23 since that term caused considerable offence to arbitrators.

Where an award is good as to one part and bad as to another

part and the two parts are clearly separable, the bad part may be set aside and the good part allowed to stand. If the good and bad parts are not clearly separable, the whole award will be set aside.

Appeal to Court under Arbitration Act 1979

By section 21 of the Act of 1950 an arbitrator or umpire might, and if directed by the High Court was bound to, state:

(*a*) any question of law arising in the course of the reference (the "consultative case"); or

(*b*) an award or any part of an award,

in the form of a special case for the decision of the court.

The most prominent reform made by the Act of 1979 was the abolition of the special case procedure (s.1(1)) and the introduction in its place of a strictly limited right of appeal to the court. The special case procedure had been abused by parties to an arbitration who sought merely to postpone the date at which payment would ultimately require to be made. It was also regarded with disfavour by parties to major contracts involving some foreign element (*e.g.* if one of the parties were a foreign government or government agency), for such parties disliked the possibility, which the special case procedure entailed, of having to submit to the jurisdiction of the English courts; the result was that much large-scale arbitration business was being taken to other countries, to the economic disadvantage of the United Kingdom.

The Act of 1979 included certain other reforms; these have already been noted at appropriate points in this book. The major provisions of the Act relate to:

(1) the judicial review of arbitration awards—section 1 of the Act;

(2) the determination of a preliminary point of law by the court (corresponding to the former "consultative case")—section 2 of the Act; and

(3) the extent to which the parties can contract out of the statutory provisions in (1) and (2), above, by the making of an "exclusion agreement"—sections 3 and 4 of the Act.

(1) *Judicial review of award*

Subject to the restrictions to be mentioned, an appeal lies to the High Court on any question of law arising out of an award made on an "arbitration agreement" as defined by section 32 of the Act of 1950 (see 1979 Act, s.7(1)). On the determination of the appeal, the High Court may by order:

CHALLENGE OF AWARD

(*a*) confirm, vary or set aside the award; or
(*b*) remit the award to the reconsideration of the arbitrator or umpire together with the court's opinion on the question of law which was the subject of the appeal.

Where the award is remitted under paragraph (*b*), above, the arbitrator or umpire must, unless the order otherwise directs, make his award within three months after the date of the order (s.1(2)).

An appeal cannot be made unless either all the parties to the reference consent or one of the parties applies to the court and the court grants leave for the appeal to be made (s.1(3)). One of the parties is likely to be reasonably content with the award, and so will not consent to an appeal being made. Hence the first hurdle for the party wishing to appeal is normally to persuade the court to grant leave for the appeal to be brought. The High Court's decision to grant or refuse this leave cannot itself be taken on appeal to the Court of Appeal unless the High Court gives leave for such an appeal (s.1(6A), added by the Supreme Court Act 1981 to close a loophole revealed by the first case to reach the courts on section 1—*Pioneer Shipping Ltd. and Another* v. *B.T.P. Tioxide Ltd.* (*The Nema*) (1980)).

The High Court must not grant leave for an appeal to be brought unless it considers that, having regard to all the circumstances, the determination of the question of law concerned could substantially affect the rights of one or more of the parties to the arbitration agreement; and the court may make any leave which it gives conditional upon the applicant complying with such conditions as it considers appropriate (*e.g.* the applicant might be required to pay the whole or part of the claim into court or into a joint account, or to provide security for the amount of the award) (s.1(4)).

If it appears to the High Court that the award does not or does not sufficiently set out the reasons for the award, the court may order the arbitrator or umpire concerned to state the reasons for his award in sufficient detail to enable the court to consider any question of law arising out of the award (s.1(5)). To protect an arbitrator from being ordered to state reasons perhaps long after he has completed his duties on a case, the Act provides that where an award is made without any reason being given, the High Court must not make an order under subsection (5), above, unless it is satisfied either:

(*a*) that before the award was made one of the parties to the reference gave notice to the arbitrator or umpire that a reasoned award would be required; or

(b) that there is some special reason why such a notice was not given (s.1(6)).

Once the High Court has decided an appeal, the possibility of a further appeal against that decision to the Court of Appeal is still more severely restricted. Such an appeal cannot be brought unless:

(a) the High Court or the Court of Appeal gives leave; *and*
(b) the High Court certifies that the question of law either is one of general public importance or is one which for some other special reason should be considered by the Court of Appeal (s.1(7)).

Soon after the passing of the Act of 1979 significant differences of opinion emerged in the courts as to the considerations which should influence a judge in deciding how to exercise his discretion when leave was sought to appeal to the High Court. Authoritative guidance was given by Lord Diplock in the House of Lords in *The Nema* (above). The case arose out of a charterparty by which the *Nema* had been chartered for several consecutive voyages for the carriage of cargo from Sorel in Canada to ports in Europe. A strike broke out in Sorel and the question was whether the charterparty had been frustrated. The arbitrator decided that the whole charterparty had been frustrated. On appeal the judge reversed that decision, but his judgment was in turn reversed by the Court of Appeal. The House of Lords dismissed the charterers' appeal, and so the ultimate result was that the arbitrator's award was restored.

Lord Diplock emphasised that it had been Parliament's intention to promote finality in awards; judicial interference with an award was only justified if it was shown that the arbitrator had misdirected himself in law or had reached a decision which no reasonable arbitrator could have reached; in particular, in the case of "one-off" clauses or contracts (of which *The Nema* was an instance) the judge ought usually to exercise his discretion as to granting or refusing leave by refusing leave unless it was apparent from the award itself that the arbitrator had obviously ascribed the wrong meaning to the clause or contract; the award in *The Nema* had not been obviously wrong, and the judge had therefore been wrong in granting the charterers leave to appeal from the award. Lord Diplock added that there could be cases where the events relied on as amounting to frustration were not "one-off" events but were such as to affect similar transactions between many other commerical persons (*e.g.* the closing of the Suez Canal, the United States soya bean embargo, and the war between Iraq and Iran); in such cases, for the sake of uniformity, it might be proper for a judge to exercise his discretion by giving leave to appeal if he thought that the arbitrator's conclusion, though not to be stigmatised as one which no reasonable person could have reached, was not right. Where the question of law was the interpretation of a standard form contract, leave should not be given, Lord Diplock observed, unless the judge considered that a strong prima facie case had been made out that the arbitrator had been wrong in his interpretation.

Lord Diplock's guidelines have been considered in several later cases. One of these later cases was *International Sea Tankers Inc. v. Hemisphere Shipping Co. Ltd.* (*The Wenjiang*) (1982). This was not a "one-off" case, since *The Wenjiang* was one of some 60 vessels which had been trapped in the River Shatt as a result of the Iraq-Iran war and there had at the date of the case been at least four arbitrations which had fixed different dates as the date of frustration. The Court of Appeal held that the judge in this case had been right to give leave to appeal on the question of the date of frustration.

(2) *Determination of preliminary point of law*

Section 2 of the Act of 1979 enables the decision of the court to be obtained on a question of law arising in the course of the reference, *i.e.* before the award has been made. The restrictions are such as to indicate that this procedure will be seldom followed.

The application is made to the High Court by any of the parties to the reference, either:

(*a*) with the consent of an arbitrator who has entered on the reference or, if an umpire has entered on the reference, with his consent; or
(*b*) with the consent of all the other parties (s.2(1)).

The High Court must not entertain an application under (*a*) above, unless it is satisfied that:

(*a*) the determination of the application might produce substantial savings in costs to the parties; and
(*b*) the question is one in respect of which leave to appeal would be likely to be given under section 1 of the Act (s.2(2)).

If the High Court decides to entertain an application no appeal from that decision can be made to the Court of Appeal unless the High Court gives leave for such an appeal (s.2(2A), added by the Supreme Court Act 1981).

Once the High Court has given its decision on the question of law, an appeal to the Court of Appeal cannot be made except under the same restrictions as apply to such an appeal under section 1(s.2(3)).

The first application to come before the Court of Appeal under section 2 was *Babanaft International Co. S.A.* v. *Avant Petroleum Inc.* (1982), which was particularly concerned with subsection (3). The preliminary point of law was whether the shipowners' claim for detention of the vessel *The Oltenia* was time-barred. The judge held that it might be time-barred (depending on whether some documents not produced were available). He granted a certificate under section 2(3)(*b*) ("that the question of law . . . either is one of general public importance or is one which for some other special reason should be considered by the Court of Appeal"), but refused leave to appeal. This led the owners to apply to the Court of Appeal for leave to appeal. The Court of Appeal, holding that the case involved a "one-off" clause and that it was very far from apparent that the judge's decision was obviously wrong, refused leave to appeal.

(3) *Exclusion agreements*

An exclusion agreement is one which excludes the right of appeal against an award under section 1 and/or the right of applying to court for the determination of a preliminary point of law under section 2. It must be in writing (s.3(1)).

The legal efficacy of an exclusion agreement depends on whether the arbitration agreement is:

(a) domestic; or
(b) non-domestic and within one of three special categories; or
(c) non-domestic and outwith all of the three special categories.

The domestic or non-domestic character of an arbitration agreement is determined once and for all at the time when the arbitration agreement is made. The definition of "domestic arbitration agreement" for the purposes of the Act of 1979 is:

"an arbitration agreement which does not provide, expressly or by implication, for arbitration in a State other than the United Kingdom and to which neither—
  (*a*) an individual who is a national of, or habitually resident in, any State other than the United Kingdom, nor
  (*b*) a body corporate which is incorporated in, or whose central management and control is exercised in, any State other than the United Kingdom,

is a party at the time the arbitration agreement is entered into" (s.3(7)).

(a) *Domestic arbitration agreements*. To be effective the exclusion agreement must be entered into after the commencement of the arbitration (s.3(6)). The aim of this provision is to protect a party in a weak bargaining position at the time when a contract is made: he might otherwise be bullied by a stronger party into agreeing in advance of any dispute to forgo the benefits of court protection under the Act of 1979.

(b) *Non-domestic arbitration agreements within the special categories*. The three special categories are:
 (i) questions or claims falling within the Admiralty jurisdiction of the High Court;
 (ii) disputes arising out of contracts of insurance; and
 (iii) disputes arising out of "commodity contracts."

An exclusion agreement takes effect if either:
 (1) it is entered into after the commencement of the arbitration; or
 (2) the award or question relates to a contract which is expressed to be governed by a law other than English law (s.4(1)).

For the precise definition of "commodity contract" see the Arbitration (Commodity Contracts) Order 1979 (Appendix 3, *post*), made under section 4(2) of the Act.

The three special categories account for a large proportion of London arbitration business, parties are usually of more equal bargaining strength than in the case of domestic arbitrations, and it was therefore considered appropriate for exclusion agreements to have wider scope.

An exclusion agreement in relation to the special categories also excludes the operation of section 24(2) of the Act of 1950 (which empowers the High Court to intervene where a dispute involves a question of fraud) unless the agreement provides otherwise (s.3(3)).

The Act leaves open the opportunity for the removal of one or more of the special categories by statutory instrument (s. 4(3)). The effect of such removal would be that arbitrations of the type concerned would come within (c), below.

(c) *Non-domestic arbitration agreements outwith the special categories*. No restrictions are placed on the operation of exclusion agreements here (s.3(1)). The operation of section 24(2) of the Act of 1950 is similarly affected as under (b), above.

Supranational arbitrations arising out of large-scale international development contracts and also all other non-domestic arbitrations not caught by the special categories of (b), above, come under this heading.

> Further Reading: *Russell on Arbitration*, Chaps. 15, 17, 19, 20 and 21.
> Robert Gibson-Jarvie and Geoffrey Hawker, *A Guide to Commercial Arbitration under The 1979 Act* (1980, The Chartered Institute of Arbitrators).

CHAPTER 9

COSTS

	page		page
Section 18	99	Extent of arbitrator's discretion	100

It is sometimes necessary to distinguish the "costs of the reference" from the "costs of the award." The former costs include all the expenditure involved in the entire case, that is, the sum total which a party must pay in costs at an arbitration from beginning to end. The latter costs comprise the arbitrator's or umpire's remuneration and expenses only. When there is a general use of the word "costs," this means "costs of the reference."

SECTION 18

By section 18(1) of the Act of 1950, the arbitrator has full discretion as to the costs in the reference, unless the arbitration agreement has an express provision to the contrary. In this particular instance "costs" include both the costs of the award and the costs of the reference. See *Smeaton Hanscomb & Co.* v. *Sassoon I. Setty, Son & Co.* (*No. 2*) (1953). There is express power in this section for the arbitrator or umpire to direct as to the manner in which costs shall be paid, for him to "tax or settle" the amount of costs, and for him to award costs taxed as between solicitor and client, *i.e.* on the more generous "Common Fund" basis as opposed to "party and party" costs.

If an arbitrator fails to deal with costs in his award when he has a duty to do so, his award will be bad, and the court may remit or even set aside the award. As an alternative, any party, within 14 days of the publication of the award, may apply to the arbitrator for an order as to costs, and he must amend his award so as to include them (s.18(4)).

The parties to the reference are at liberty to make any arrangements as to which party shall pay costs (*Mansfield* v. *Robinson* (1928)), but a provision in an arbitration agreement that any party is to pay his own costs or any part of them is void if the agreement is for the reference of future, as distinct from existing, disputes (s.18(3)).

When the arbitrator "taxes or settles" the costs of the reference, such an assessment is part of the award and is binding unless the award is set aside.

The award need not incorporate the actual taxation of costs: by section 18(2) the High Court has jurisdiction to tax any costs directed by an award to be paid, in any case where the award does not direct otherwise (s.18(2)).

EXTENT OF ARBITRATOR'S DISCRETION

The extent of the arbitrator's discretion as to costs will vary, because different arbitration agreements give different conditions as to costs. Nevertheless, whatever discretion is given to the arbitrator, he must exercise it judicially, for it will be reviewed by the court, in the same manner as a judge's order may be reviewed on appeal (*per* Devlin J. (as he then was) in *Smeaton's* case, above, and *per* Hodson L.J. in *Perry* v. *Stopher* (1959)).

In *Lewis* v. *Haverfordwest R.D.C.* (1953) Lord Goddard L.C.J. said: "The words 'judicially exercised' . . . mean that the arbitrator must not act capriciously and must . . . show a reason connected with the case and one which the court can see is a proper reason."

In the absence of express provision in the arbitration agreement to the contrary, section 18 of the Act (see Appendix 1, *post*) gives an arbitrator the widest discretion as to costs. The court will not interfere with him merely because the court itself would have exercised such discretion differently. Neither need the arbitrator give any reasons should he decide on costs in a different manner from the usual rule that costs follow the event, *i.e.* that the unsuccessful party at the reference pays all costs. If he does give reasons, either in his award, or in an affidavit put in a case of setting the award aside, the court will not disturb his discretionary power (*Heaven & Kesterton Ltd.* v. *Sven Widaeus A/B* (1958), in which an umpire had ordered the claimants to pay the whole costs because they had recovered only a tenth of the sum claimed). Observations made by the courts in earlier cases that the mere making of an award in which a successful party has been deprived of costs, is no ground for setting aside an award, were disapproved of in *Dineen* v. *Walpole* (1969), *per* Edmund Davies L.J.

Misconduct, when used in relation to costs, is used in the wider sense. It means "misconduct" similar to that when a party applies under section 23(2) of the Act to have an award set aside.

Where there is an unusual award as to costs the rules most often looked to are those summarised by Mocatta J. in *L. Figueiredo Navegacas S.A.* v. *Reederei Richard Schroeder K.G.* (*The Erich Schroeder*) (1974). In that case arbitrators had made an award in favour of the shipowners against the charterers but had held the owners liable to pay their own costs of the reference and half of the costs of the award. The owners sought to set aside the award as to costs on the ground that the arbitrators were guilty of misconduct in making such an order. Mocatta J. held that there were no grounds for justifying a departure from the general principle that costs follow the event. The charterers had, therefore, to pay the owners' costs in the arbitration, but since the charterers had already paid the whole of the costs of the award when they took it up, no order was necessary as to the costs of the award; the award was set aside so far as it related to costs.

Mocatta J. stated five propositions:

> "First, an arbitrator, like a Judge, in dealing with costs must exercise the discretion invested in him judicially. . . . The arbitrator must not act capriciously and must, if he is going to exercise his discretion . . . , have a reason connected with the case and one which is a proper reason.
>
> Secondly, there is no need for an umpire or arbitrator, if he so exercises his discretion as to depart from the general rule, to state the reason why he does so in his award. On the other hand, in all probability, in most cases where an umpire/arbitrator does so act, it would save costs if he were to state his reasons in his award. In that event the parties would not be put to the expense of trying to ascertain what his reasons were and possibly moving the Court to set aside the award. . . .
>
> Thirdly, if the award does depart from the general rule as to costs but bears on its face no statement of the reasons supporting that departure, the party objecting to the award in that respect may bring before the Court such evidence as he can obtain as to the grounds, or lack of grounds, bearing upon the unusual exercise of discretion by the arbitrator or umpire. . . .
>
> Fourthly, the above propositions, in my judgment, apply to all categories of awards as to costs. . . .
>
> Fifthly, and finally, there is, of course, a burden of proof upon the party seeking to set aside an award in relation to the decision of an umpire or arbitrator in relation to costs, or seeking to have the award remitted so that the arbitrator or umpire may deal with the costs in a way other than that in which he originally dealt with them. . . . There must be shown to be reasons on which he could exercise his discretion in the way that he did."

Donaldson J. referred to these rules with approval when deciding *Tramountana Armadora S.A.* v. *Atlantic Shipping Co.*

S.A. (1978): the arbitrator had made an award in favour of the shipowners but, contrary to the usual rule that costs follow the event, had awarded the costs of the hearing and of the award to the charterers. The arbitrator's explanation was that the charterers had offered to pay the shipowners a much larger sum than was ultimately awarded. On the question of how an arbitrator should deal with costs where there was a "sealed offer," Donaldson J. stated the general rule as being:

> "If the claimant in the end has achieved no more than he would have achieved by accepting the offer, the continuance of the arbitration after that date has been a waste of time and money. Prima facie, the claimant should recover his costs up to the date of the offer and should be ordered to pay the respondent's costs after that date. If he has achieved more by going on, the respondent should pay the costs throughout."

The judge remitted the award to the arbitrator for him to reconsider his order for costs, emphasising, however, that it was for the arbitrator's discretion, and not for the court, to decide what new order on costs should be made.

Donaldson J. repeated his view in *Warinco A.G.* v. *Andre & Cie. S.A.* (1979) in the memorable statement: "If there is an order which on its face is unusual there is a rebuttable presumption that the arbitrators are wrong." In that case there was an unusual order as to costs, and the court was not concerned with what in fact moved the arbitrators to make such order, but solely with whether there was material upon which the arbitrators *could* have justified the order. The judge was satisfied that the order *could* have been justified and so did not interfere with it.

Further Reading: *Russell on Arbitration*, Chap. 18.

CHAPTER 10

INTRODUCTION TO SCOTS LAW OF ARBITRATION

	page		page
Terminology	103	Procedure	108
Sources	103	Time-limits and prorogation	108
The courts and arbitration	104	Enforcement of award	109
(1) Enforcement of arbitration agreement	104	Challenge of award	109
(2) Questions of law	104	(1) "Corruption, bribery, or falsehood"	109
Appointment of arbiters and oversmen	106	(2) Excess of jurisdiction	111
(1) Arbitration (Scotland) Act 1894	106	(3) Improper procedure	111
		(4) Defects in award	111
(2) Law Reform (Miscellaneous Provisions) (Scotland) Act 1980, section 17	107	Judicial references	111

THE purpose of this chapter is not to give an account of the Scots law of arbitration but merely to indicate those major respects in which it differs from English law.

TERMINOLOGY

The terms "arbiter" and "oversman" correspond in Scots law to the English terms "arbitrator" and "umpire," respectively. In Scots law an alternative term for "award" is "decree-arbitral."

SOURCES

The general Scots law of arbitration is almost wholly common law. The arbitration code now comprising Part I of the Arbitration Act 1950 does not apply to Scotland (1950 Act, s.34, as amended by Arbitration Act 1975, s.8(2)(*e*)). Nor does the Arbitration Act 1979 extend to Scotland (1979 Act, s.8(4)).

Such statutory provisions as do affect the Scots law of arbitration deal with specific aspects only and are to be found in an odd assortment of legislation—the Articles of Regulation of 1695 which were authorised by an Act of the Scottish Parliament, the Arbitration (Scotland) Act 1894 (see Appendix 4, *post*), section 3 of the Administration of Justice (Scotland) Act 1972 (see Appendix 5, *post*), and section 17 of the Law Reform (Miscellaneous Provisions) (Scotland) Act 1980.

The Courts and Arbitration

There is a marked distinction between English and Scots law in the attitude of the courts to arbitration. The supervisory role of the English courts in relation to arbitration is absent in Scots law. In particular:

(1) *Enforcement of arbitration agreement*

One of the leading provisions of the English law of arbitration is that if a party to an arbitration agreement commences court proceedings, the court *may* make an order staying these proceedings (1950 Act, s.4(1)); in Scotland the court has no such discretion: it *must* give effect to the parties' agreement to arbitrate by "sisting" the court proceedings.

Of the differing approaches in the two legal systems Lord Dunedin said in the House of Lords' case *Sanderson & Son* v. *Armour & Co. Ltd.* (1922):

> "The English common law doctrine,—eventually swept away by the Arbitration Act of 1889—that a contract to oust the jurisdiction of the Courts was against public policy and invalid, never obtained in Scotland. In the same way, the right which in England pertains to the Court under that Act to apply or not to apply the arbitration clause in its discretion never was the right of the Court in Scotland. If the parties have contracted to arbitrate, to arbitration they must go."

(2) *Questions of law*

Although an arbitrator under English law may have power to decide questions of law as well as questions of fact, his decision on questions of law is to some extent controlled by the courts: unless there is an "exclusion agreement" in operation, a party to the arbitration has, in certain circumstances, the right to appeal to the courts on a question of law arising out of an award (Arbitration Act 1979, s.1) and the courts also have jurisdiction, in certain circumstances, to determine questions of law arising in the course of a reference (Arbitration Act 1979, s.2). Before the special case procedure was abolished by the Act of 1979, a purported exclusion by agreement of the statutory provisions which became section 21 of the Act of 1950 was void and unenforceable: see *Czarnikow* v. *Roth, Schmidt & Co.* (1922), p. 21, above), in which Scrutton L.J. made his famous observation:

> [The Courts] "do not allow the agreement of private parties to oust the jurisdiction of the King's Courts. Arbitrators, unless

expressly otherwise authorised, have to apply the laws of England. . . . There must be no Alsatia in England where the King's writ does not run."

In Scots law, on the other hand, the arbiter was at common law final both on questions of fact and on questions of law and there was no right of appeal to the courts. A well-known passage is that in Lord Jeffrey's opinion in *Mitchell* v. *Cable* (1848):

"On every matter touching the merits of the case, the judgment of the arbiter is beyond our control; and beyond question or cavil. He may believe what nobody else believes, and he may disbelieve what all the world believes. He may overlook or flagrantly misapply the most ordinary principles of law; and there is no appeal for those who have chosen to subject themselves to his despotic power."

(These are extreme words when taken out of context; it should be borne in mind that Lord Jeffrey went on to explain that a decree-arbitral can stand only when the arbiter has done his duty "fairly," *i.e.* has dealt equally with both parties. In *Mitchell* v. *Cable* the arbiter was held not to have satisfied this test because he had considered proof from one party without allowing the other party a fair opportunity of bringing forward his counter-proof.)

The absence of "special case" procedure from Scots law was highlighted by *James Miller and Partners Ltd.* v. *Whitworth Street Estates (Manchester) Ltd.* (1970), in which the House of Lords held that the law governing the arbitration proceedings, as distinct from the proper law of the contract, was Scots law and that the arbiter had therefore been entitled to refuse a request from one of the parties to state his award in the form of a special case (see also p. 114, below).

Two years later the special or stated case procedure was introduced to Scotland by section 3 of the Administration of Justice (Scotland) Act 1972 (see Appendix 5, *post*). Unlike section 21 of the Act of 1950, this provision applicable to Scotland is "subject to express provision to the contrary in an agreement to refer to arbitration," *i.e.* it may be contracted out of (contrast *Czarnikow* v. *Roth, Schmidt & Co.*, above).

The provision is that the arbiter or oversman *may*, on the application of a party to the arbitration, at any stage in the arbitration state a case for the opinion of the Court of Session on any question of law arising in the arbitration, and the arbiter or oversman *must* do so if the party applies to the Court of Session and that court directs a case to be stated.

The application must be made at a "stage in the arbitration" (*e.g.* after the arbiter has issued proposed findings); it is no longer competent after the arbiter has issued his final award (*Fairlie Yacht Slip Ltd.* v. *Lumsden* (1977)).

Before April 1973 (when the provision was brought into force) stated cases in Scots law had been confined to statutory arbitrations; for example, in *Mitchell-Gill* v. *Buchan* (1921) the court held, in relation to a stated case under the Agricultural Holdings (Scotland) Act 1908, that an arbiter was not entitled to disregard the answer given by the court on the question of law.

The stated case provisions in section 3 of the Act of 1972 are still in force, despite the repeal of the corresponding provisions in section 21 of the Act of 1950.

Appointment of Arbiters and Oversmen

Statutory provisions relating to the appointment of arbiters and oversmen are:

(1) the Arbitration (Scotland) Act 1894 (see Appendix 4, *post*), and
(2) section 17 of the Law Reform (Miscellaneous Provisions) (Scotland) Act 1980.

(1) *Arbitration (Scotland) Act* 1894

This Act was passed mainly to remedy two deficiencies which had become apparent in the common law.

First, it was a principle of the common law that the appointment of an arbiter involved *delectus personae* (literally "choice of person"), and so the parties had to make a deliberate selection of a named individual and not merely agree that the arbiter would be the holder of a particular office for the time being or would be named by another person. The courts would not, as a general rule, enforce an arbitration agreement in which the arbiter was not named. There were some exceptions to the general rule (*e.g.* the arbitration agreement would be enforceable if the arbitration was necessary for the purpose of giving effect to another contract), but on the whole the common law rule had the unsatisfactory result of bringing before the courts matters which the parties had really intended should be settled by arbitration; *e.g.* an arbitration clause in a contract for the building of the Forth Railway Bridge providing that disputes were to be referred to "the engineer of the Forth Bridge Railway Company for the time being" was held to be unenforceable (*Tancred, Arrol & Co.* v. *The Steel Co. of Scotland Ltd.* (1890)).

The second deficiency was that at common law where there was a reference to two arbiters, one appointed by each side, the two arbiters had no implied power to appoint an oversman, and so if the arbiters failed to agree the result was deadlock.

The provisions of the Act are:

(a) An agreement to refer to arbitration is no longer unenforceable merely because the reference is to a person not named or to a person to be named by another, or to a person described as the holder of an office for the time being (s.1).

(b) Where there is an agreement to refer to a single arbiter and one of the parties refuses to concur in the nomination and there is no provision in the agreement to resolve the difficulty, then any party to the agreement may apply to the court for an arbiter to be appointed by the court (s.2).

(c) Where there is an agreement to refer to two arbiters and one of the parties refuses to name an arbiter and there is no provision in the agreement to resolve the difficulty, then the other party may apply to the court for an arbiter to be appointed by the court (s.3).

(d) Unless the agreement to refer provides otherwise, arbiters have power to name an oversman on whom the reference is to be devolved in the event of their differing in opinion. If the arbiters fail to agree in the nomination of an oversman, any party to the agreement may apply to the court for an oversman to be appointed (s.4).

The Act leaves a number of gaps: the court has no power to appoint an arbiter where the parties have merely agreed to refer "to arbitration" without specifying that the reference is to be to a single arbiter or to two arbiters (*M'Millan & Son Ltd.* v. *Rowan & Co.* (1903)); there is no provision corresponding to section 6 of the Act of 1950 by which in an English arbitration the reference is deemed to be to a single arbitrator if no other mode of reference is provided; there is no remedy for the situation where the clause of reference names an arbiter and he refuses to act (*British Westinghouse Electric and Manufacturing Co. Ltd.* v. *Provost, etc., of Aberdeen* (1906)).

(2) *Law Reform* (*Miscellaneous Provisions*) (*Scotland*) *Act* 1980, section 17

This section enables a Court of Session judge, if in all the circumstances he thinks fit, to accept appointment as arbiter or as oversman under an arbitration agreement where the dispute appears to him to be of a commercial character. It is a condition of his accepting appointment that the Lord President of the Court of Session has informed him that, having regard to the state of business in that court, he can be made available to do so.

The fees for the judge's services as arbiter or oversman are paid into public funds and are of an amount fixed by statutory instrument, at present £500 on appointment plus £500 for each additional day of the hearing (Appointment of Judges as Arbiters (Fees) (Scotland) Order 1980 (S.I. 1980 No. 1823)).

PROCEDURE

Where the procedure is formal, it approximates to the procedure followed in the Scottish courts.

The arbiter fixes a time within which one party must lodge written claims. He then allows a specified time within which the other party must lodge written answers. A "record" (a document setting out both sides of the dispute) may then be made up, "adjusted" and eventually "closed."

The arbiter then decides what "proof" (*i.e.* evidence) should be allowed. Sometimes it will be necessary for the arbiter to inspect premises or other property in order to inform himself of the matters in dispute, but inadequacy of inspection is not a ground on which an award may be reduced (*i.e.* set aside) by the court (*Johnson* v. *Lamb* (1981)).

The arbiter will almost always allow a hearing to both parties at the conclusion of the proof, and will often issue "proposed findings" so that the parties may have an opportunity to make final "representations" criticising the proposed findings. A further hearing may be allowed for these representations.

There are, as in England, many informal arbitrations in which both a proof and a hearing may be dispensed with and the question decided on the basis of the arbiter's personal inspection only.

The arbiter is bound to adhere to any procedure agreed on by the parties, but he usually has a wide discretion as to the procedure to be followed. The overriding principle is impartiality, which is implied in the nature of his office: he must adopt "equal and even-handed procedure towards both parties alike" (J.M. Bell, *Treatise on the Law of Arbitration in Scotland*, 2nd ed., p. 23).

TIME-LIMITS AND PROROGATION

The duration of the submission is a matter for the parties to decide.

Where the submission is a formal deed, it is usual for the arbiter to be given power to decide the dispute "between this and the . . . day of . . . next to come." If the blanks are not filled up, the submission is regarded as lasting (on the authority of Lord Bankton as applied in *Earl of Dunmore* v. *M'Inturner* (1829)) for a year and a day.

Where there is no reference to any time-limit the submission lasts for the 20-year prescriptive period.

Where the submission expressly fixes a time-limit without conferring on the arbiter power to extend the time, the submission automatically falls on the expiry of the specified time, unless the parties by express agreement or by their actings extend its duration.

It is usual practice to confer on the arbiter a power of "prorogation," *i.e.* a power to extend the duration of the submission. Such a power requires to be exercised before the fixed time has expired and before the submission has devolved on the oversman. An arbiter has no implied power of prorogation except, possibly, in ancillary submissions (*i.e.* submissions provided for by arbitration clauses in associated contracts) (Irons and Melville, *Treatise on the Law of Arbitration in Scotland*, p. 135).

In the absence of agreement to the contrary, a submission terminates on the death of either of the parties.

Enforcement of Award

An award may be enforced by action. Alternatively, if the arbitration agreement contains a consent to registration of the award in the Books of Council and Session for execution and the award is so registered, the award may be enforced by summary diligence.

Challenge of Award

An award may be set aside by an action of reduction brought in the Court of Session, but only on limited grounds, *viz.*:

(1) "corruption, bribery, or falsehood";
(2) excess of jurisdiction;
(3) improper procedure; and
(4) defects in the award.

Partial reduction is competent but only where one part of the award is open to objection, the other part is valid and the two parts are clearly severable.

(1) *"Corruption, bribery, or falsehood"*

The phrase is quoted from the twenty-fifth Act of the Articles of Regulation of 1695. These Articles were made by Commissioners under the special sanction of an Act of the Scottish Parliament of 1693, and the twenty-fifth of them dealt with the grounds on which an arbiter's award might be challenged. It provided:

"That for the cutting off of groundless and expensive pleas and processes in time coming, the Lords of Session sustain no reduction of any decree-arbitral that shall be pronounced hereafter upon a subscribed submission, at the instance of either of the parties-submitters, upon any cause or reason whatsoever, unless that of corruption, bribery, or falsehood, to be alleged against the judges-arbitrators who pronounced the same."

The provision must be viewed in its historical context. Before 1695 the courts of law had come to allow an award to be challenged in the courts on the grounds of "iniquity" committed by an arbiter or of "enorm lesion" suffered by a party, *i.e.* on the grounds that an arbiter had made a mistake or that a party had suffered undue hardship. The result was that in practically every case an award could be reviewed upon its merits at the discretion of the court—a situation which defeated the main object of the parties in resorting to arbitration.

The aim of the twenty-fifth Article was to end the practice of review by the courts: arbiters' awards were to be final and binding on the parties and were no longer to be open to challenge merely because the arbiter had made a mistake or one party had suffered undue hardship. Corruption, bribery and falsehood on the part of the arbiter, however, were to remain grounds on which an award could be challenged in court.

If this statutory provision had been given a literal interpretation it would have prevented an award from being set aside on any ground other than corruption, bribery, or falsehood. Decided cases, however, and particularly the speech of Lord Watson in the House of Lords' case *Adams* v. *Great North of Scotland Railway Co.* (1891), established that the object for which the provisions had been made had to be looked to: the provision had never been intended to go beyond the point of putting an end to the practice of review upon the merits; other common law grounds of challenge (see (2) to (4), below) remained available.

In some cases there were attempts to extend the word "corruption" so as to include "legal corruption" or "constructive corruption," *i.e.* conduct on the part of the arbiter which was mistaken but not strictly corrupt. Lord Watson in *Adams* v. *Great North of Scotland Railway Co.* protested against this extended meaning of "corruption"; actual corruption was necessary if an award was to be set aside on the ground of the Articles of Regulation: if the arbiter's mistake was innocent, it could not be brought within the term "corruption," though it might lead to reduction of the award on one of the other grounds (2) to (4), below. below.

(2) *Excess of jurisdiction*

An award which is *ultra fines compromissi* ("beyond the bounds of the submission") may be set aside.

(3) *Improper procedure*

Failure to comply with the procedure specified by the parties would come under this heading, as well as failure to observe implied conditions of honesty and impartiality.

(4) *Defects in award*

The award should be clear in its terms, correct in its form (*e.g.* if the arbitration was started by a formal deed of submission in probative form, the award also would require to be in that form (*M'Laren* v. *Aikman* (1939))), include nothing which was not referred and exhaust all that was referred.

The mere fact that an arbiter has made no finding as to expenses is not a ground for reducing the award (*Pollich* v. *Heatley* (1910)).

JUDICIAL REFERENCES

By a judicial reference is meant the procedure by which parties to a court action agree to withdraw the decision of the whole or some of the questions raised in the action from the decision of the court and, while still formally leaving the action in court, refer these questions to an arbiter.

A judicial reference is started by the lodging with the court of a "minute" stating the agreement of the parties, and the court then, if it thinks fit, "interpones authority to the minute," *i.e.* authorises the judicial reference to proceed.

The selection of the judicial referee is a matter for the parties to decide. Like an ordinary arbiter, a judicial referee is not bound by strict court procedure.

The scope of the reference is limited to the subject-matter of the action as set out in the "record."

The decision of a judicial referee takes the form of a report to the court (not an award). The report may be challenged on the same grounds as an award in an ordinary arbitration. The court will either approve of the report and grant "decree conform," *i.e.* make a court order in conformity with the terms of the report, or set the report aside; the court has no power to amend the report.

Further Reading: Enid A. Marshall, *Scots Mercantile Law* (1983, W. Green & Son Ltd.), Chap. 12.

Enid A. Marshall, *General Principles of Scots Law* (4th ed., 1982, W. Green & Son Ltd.), pp. 64–76.

M.E.L. Weir, *A Synopsis of the Law & Practice of Arbitration in Scotland* (2nd ed., 1980, Department of Building, Heriot-Watt University).

David Alexander Guild, *The Law of Arbitration in Scotland* (1936, W. Green & Son Ltd.).

John Montgomerie Bell, *Treatise on the Law of Arbitration in Scotland* (2nd ed., 1877, T. & T. Clark).

James Campbell Irons and R.D. Melville, *Treatise on the Law of Arbitration in Scotland* (1903, William Green & Sons).

CHAPTER 11

SOME ASPECTS OF INTERNATIONAL ARBITRATION

	page		page
Proper law of the contract and law governing the arbitration proceedings......................	113	Enforcement of awards.........	118
		Arbitration Act 1979..............	119
		UNCITRAL Arbitration Rules	119
Part II of the Arbitration Act 1950................................	114	I.C.C. arbitrations..................	119
Arbitration Act 1975................	116	Arbitration (International Investment Disputes) Act 1966..	119
Recognition of arbitration agreements.....................	116		

SOME of the advantages of arbitration over litigation were mentioned in an earlier chapter (see p. 3, above). Where a foreign element is involved, arbitration is even more attractive, since an arbitration clause in the contract will enable the parties to avoid the complexities of private international law and have disputes settled by a tribunal of their own choice, with whose procedures they are perhaps familiar and with whose decision they would feel reasonably satisfied.

PROPER LAW OF THE CONTRACT AND LAW GOVERNING THE ARBITRATION PROCEEDINGS

It is appropriate for the parties to a contract involving a foreign element to insert in their contract a "choice of law" clause, specifying the "proper law" of the contract, *i.e.* the system of law by which the parties intend the contract to be governed. As a general rule the courts will give effect to the parties' intention as expressed in such a clause. Where there is no such clause, it is for the court to decide what is the "proper law" on a construction of the contract as a whole. It is quite possible for the "proper law" of the contract to be English law, though neither party is a national of this country.

It is particularly common for any arbitration clause included in the contract to stipulate that disputes are to be settled by arbitration in London. The major underlying purpose of the reforms made by the Arbitration Act 1979 was to preserve the high reputation enjoyed by London arbitration circles by removing from the English law of arbitration those provisions which were disapproved of by the nationals of other states.

The law governing the arbitration is not necessarily the same as the law governing the substance of the contract. The best-known illustration of this point is the House of Lords' decision in *James Miller and Partners Ltd.* v. *Whitworth Street Estates (Manchester) Ltd.* (1970):

The English company ("W. Ltd.") owned premises in Scotland which they wished to convert into a whisky bonded warehouse. The contract was negotiated in London and was on the standard Royal Institute of British Architects (R.I.B.A.) form. The contract provided for the settlement of disputes by arbitration, but contained no express stipulation as to the law which was to govern the contract or any arbitration proceedings under it. A dispute arose about the work of conversion, and the President of the R.I.B.A., in accordance with the arbitration clause, appointed a Glasgow architect as arbiter. He in turn appointed a Glasgow solicitor to be clerk in the arbitration, and conducted the arbitration according to Scottish procedure, Scots counsel and solicitors being employed by both parties. Some points of law emerged in the course of the arbitration, and counsel for W. Ltd. asked the arbiter to state his award in the form of a special case for the opinion of the court. The arbiter refused to do so, on the ground that the arbitration was a Scottish one and by Scots law an arbiter was not bound at the date of that case to give his award in the form of a special case.

The House of Lords held that the proper law of the contract was English law—the agreement of the parties to use the R.I.B.A. form showed that that had been their intention. The arbitration, however, was, the House held, subject to Scots law—the actings of the parties after the appointment of the arbiter sufficiently showed an agreement that the arbitration proceedings should be governed by Scots law. The arbiter could, therefore, not be required to state a special case.

("Special case" procedure was introduced to Scots law by section 3 of the Administration of Justice (Scotland) Act 1972 (see p. 105, above, and Appendix 5, *post*).

Part II of the Arbitration Act 1950

Part II of the Act of 1950 is concerned with the enforcement in the United Kingdom of certain foreign awards. Unlike Part I of the Act, Part II is not restricted to England but extends, with certain modifications, to the whole of the United Kingdom (ss.41, 42).

The provisions of Part II are to be read along with the First and Second Schedules to the Act, which comprise, respectively, the Geneva Protocol on Arbitration Clauses signed on behalf of the

United Kingdom in 1923 and the Geneva Convention on the Execution of Foreign Arbitral Awards signed on behalf of the United Kingdom in 1927.

The Protocol declares that the States which are parties to it ("the Contracting States") recognise the validity of arbitration agreements made between parties who are subject to the jurisdiction of different Contracting States, whether or not the arbitration takes place in a country to whose jurisdiction none of the parties is subject. The arbitral procedure is governed by the will of the parties and by the law of the country in whose territory the arbitration takes place. Each Contracting State undertakes to ensure the execution by its authorities and in accordance with its national laws of arbitral awards made in its own territory. Where there is a valid arbitration agreement capable of being carried into effect, the courts of the Contracting Parties *must*, on the application of a party to the arbitration agreement, refer the dispute to the arbitrators unless the agreement or the arbitration cannot proceed or becomes inoperative.

The Convention of 1927 provides that in the territories of the parties to the Convention ("the High Contracting Parties"), an arbitral award made under an agreement covered by the Protocol is recognised as binding and must be enforced in accordance with the rules of procedure of the territory where the award is relied upon, provided the award has been made in a territory of one of the High Contracting Parties and between persons who are subject to the jurisdiction of one of the High Contracting Parties. To obtain recognition or enforcement certain conditions must be fulfilled, the one which has caused most difficulty being the condition that the recognition or enforcement must not be contrary to the public policy or *to the principles of the law* of the country in which it is sought to be relied upon (Article 1).

The Geneva instruments, incorporated into the law of the United Kingdom by Part II of the Act of 1950, became operative only where reciprocal provisions were made between the two States concerned. A "foreign award" for the purposes of Part II of the Act is, by section 35(1), one which is made:

(a) in pursuance of an arbitration agreement to which the Geneva Protocol applies; and
(b) between persons who are subject to the jurisdiction of Powers with which the United Kingdom has made reciprocal provisions and which have been declared by Order in Council to be parties to the Geneva Convention; and
(c) in a territory in respect of which the United Kingdom has made reciprocal provisions and which has been declared by

Order in Council to be a territory to which the Geneva Convention applies.

For Orders in Council made under section 35(1) and listing Powers which are parties to the Geneva Convention and territories to which the Geneva Convention applies see the Arbitration (Foreign Awards) Order 1978 (S.I. 1978 No. 186) and part of the Arbitration (Foreign Awards) Order 1979 (S.I. 1979 No. 304) (Appendices 7 and 8, respectively, *post*).

Section 36(1) provides that a foreign award may be enforced in England either by action or by the summary procedure of section 26 of the Act (see p. 86, above). Similarly in Scotland a foreign award may be enforced either by action or (if the arbitration agreeement contains consent to registration of the award in the Books of Council and Session for execution and the award is so registered) by summary diligence (s.41(3)).

Arbitration Act 1975

The Arbitration Act 1975, which extends to the whole of the United Kingdom, was passed to give effect to the "New York Convention," *i.e.* to the Convention on the Recognition and Enforcement of Foreign Arbitral Awards adopted by the United Nations Conference on International Commercial Arbitration in 1958.

In the New York Convention there is no requirement of reciprocity: Article I states that the Convention applies to the recognition and enforcement of arbitral awards made in the territory of a State other than the State where the recognition and enforcement of the awards are sought and that it also applies to arbitral awards not considered as domestic awards in the State where their recognition and enforcement are sought. It is, however, open to a State, when acceding to the Convention, to declare that it will apply the Convention only to awards made in the territory of another Contracting State—an exception which will become less significant as more States accede to the Convention.

Recognition of arbitration agreements

Article II provides that each Contracting State must recognise written arbitration agreements, and that where there is such an agreement the court of a Contracting State *must*, at the request of one of the parties, refer the parties to arbitration, unless it finds that the agreement is null and void, inoperative or incapable of being performed.

The Article is given the force of law in the United Kingdom by the provisions in section 1 of the Act of 1975. Section 1 applies to any arbitration agreement which is not a "domestic arbitration agreement," and that term is defined as:

> "an arbitration agreement which does not provide, expressly or by implication, for arbitration in a State other than the United Kingdom and to which neither—
>
> (a) an individual who is a national of, or habitually resident in, any State other than the United Kingdom; nor
>
> (b) a body corporate which is incorporated in, or whose central management and control is exercised in, any State other than the United Kingdom,
>
> is a party *at the time the proceedings are commenced*" (s.1(2), (4)). (The words in italics distinguish this definition of "domestic arbitration agreement" from the definition contained in the Arbitration Act 1979 (see p. 96, above).

The stay of proceedings which is provided for in section 1(1) is a "mandatory" (compulsory) stay (unlike the stay at the court's discretion in section 4(1) of the Act of 1950 applicable to domestic arbitration agreements). In the not inconsiderable number of cases which have come to court on the Act of 1975 since it was passed, the mandatory nature of the stay provisions has been repeatedly emphasised. On the other hand, the provisions do not authorise the stay of an action for payment of bills of exchange (*Nova (Jersey) Knit Ltd.* v. *Kammgarn Spinnerei GmbH* (1977)) or a claim for freight (*A/S Gunnstein & Co. K/S* v. *Jensen, Krebs and Nielsen (The Alpha Nord)* (1977)) and *Cleobulos Shipping Co. Ltd.* v. *Intertanker Ltd.* (1982)).

The application for a stay under section 1(1) of the Act of 1975 must, like an application under section 4(1), be made by the party "at any time after appearance, and before delivering any pleadings or taking any other steps in the proceedings" (see p. 26, above).

The remainder of section 1(1), however, differs from section 4(1) of the Act of 1950: "the court, unless satisfied that the arbitration agreement is null and void, inoperative or incapable of being performed or that there is not in fact any dispute between the parties with regard to the matter agreed to be referred, shall make an order staying the proceedings." In *The Rena K.* (1979) the possibility that one of the parties to the arbitration agreement would lack the financial resources to satisfy the award was held not to make the agreement "incapable of being performed," and so a stay was granted. Similarly in *Janos Paczy* v. *Haendler &*

Natermann GmbH (1981) the alleged impecuniosity of the plaintiff (who had been granted legal aid, with a nil contribution) and his consequent inability to make a deposit as was required if arbitration proceedings were to be instituted was held not to make the agreement "incapable of being performed," and a stay of the proceedings, first imposed, but later lifted, by the judge, was restored by the Court of Appeal. Buckley L.J. said:"The agreement only becomes incapable of performance in my view if the circumstances are such that it could no longer be performed, even if both parties were ready, able and willing to perform it. Impecuniosity is not, I think, a circumstance of that kind." *Associated Bulk Carriers Ltd.* v. *Koch Shipping Inc.* (1977) illustrates the interpretation of the words "there is not in fact any dispute between the parties": the plaintiff who was suing for wrongful repudiation by the defendant of a charterparty had his action stayed, although he had all the merits on his side and the defendant was merely seeking to procure delay in the payment of a substantial sum.

Enforcement of awards

Article III of the Convention requires each Contracting State to recognise arbitral awards as binding and to enforce them in accordance with the rules of procedure of the territory where the award is relied upon, under conditions laid down in other Articles of the Convention.

There are specified circumstances in which recognition and enforcement of an award may be refused, *e.g.* where the recognition or enforcement of the award would be contrary to the public policy of the country (Article V) (but the phrase "contrary to the principles of the law" of the country has been avoided in this Convention).

A further provision of the Convention is noteworthy: the Geneva Protocol and the Geneva Convention are to cease to have effect between Contracting States on their becoming bound by the New York Convention (Article VII). It is envisaged that in time the New York Convention will totally supersede the Geneva instruments. This is expressed in the Act of 1975 by the provision in section 2 that where a Convention award would also be a foreign award within the meaning of Part II of the Act of 1950, that Part II is not to apply to it.

The provisions in the Act of 1975 relating to enforcement are restricted to enforcement of a "Convention award," defined as "an award made in pursuance of an arbitration agreement in the territory of a State, other than the United Kingdom, which is a party to the New York Convention" (ss. 3–7).

ARBITRATION ACT 1975

The States which are parties to the New York Convention are listed in Schedule 2 to the Arbitration (Foreign Awards) Order 1979 (see Appendix 8, *post*).

The Act of 1975 provides that a Convention award is enforceable in England either by action or under section 26 of the Act of 1950 and in Scotland either by action or (if duly registered for execution) by summary diligence (s.3).

Arbitration Act 1979

For the provisions of this Act relating to non-domestic arbitration agreements, see p. 97, above.

UNCITRAL Arbitration Rules

These Rules were published by the United Nations Commission on International Trade Law in 1976. They are widely used as a model, *e.g.* they have been adopted by the London Court of Arbitration, which holds a pre-eminent position in the field of international arbitration.

The Rules are not embodied in any international convention and they do not have the force of law in any State. Their applicability depends on the agreement of the parties or adoption by an organisation providing arbitration services.

I.C.C. Arbitrations

The International Chamber of Commerce, with its administrative centre in Paris, has a commanding position amongst the numerous bodies which provide arbitration services to businessmen engaged in international trade. It has its own Court of Arbitration and its own code of rules.

Arbitration (International Investment Disputes) Act 1966

This Act gave effect in the United Kingdom to the Convention on the Settlement of Investment Disputes between States and Nationals of Other States.

The Convention provided for the formation of an International Centre for Settlement of Investment Disputes at the principal office of the Bank of Washington. The Centre makes available to Contracting States and foreign investors who are nationals of other Contracting States facilities for the settlement, on a voluntary basis, of investment disputes in accordance with rules laid down in the Convention.

The Convention is set out in a Schedule to the Act.

Further Reading: *Schmitthoff's Export Trade,* 7th ed. by Clive M. Schmitthoff (1980), Stevens & Sons), Chap. 26.

The Hon. Mr. Justice Kerr, *International Arbitration v. Litigation* [1980] J.B.L. 164–180.

Clive M. Schmitthoff and Others (Eds.), *International Commercial Arbitration* (loose-leaf volumes) (1974– , Oceana Publications Inc.).

Russell on Arbitration, Appendix 4 (the text of the New York Convention).

TABLE OF APPENDICES

	page
1. Arbitration Act 1950	123
2. Arbitration Act 1979	141
3. The Arbitration (Commodity Contracts) Order 1979	148
4. Arbitration (Scotland) Act 1894	151
5. Administration of Justice (Scotland) Act 1972	153
6. Arbitration Act 1975	154
7. The Arbitration (Foreign Awards) Order 1978	158
8. The Arbitration (Foreign Awards) Order 1979	162

Appendix 1

ARBITRATION ACT 1950

(14 Geo. 6, c. 27)

Arrangement of Sections

Part I

General Provisions as to Arbitration

Effect of Arbitration Agreements, &c.

SECTION
1. Authority of arbitrators and umpires to be irrevocable.
2. Death of party.
3. Bankruptcy.
4. Staying court proceedings where there is submission to arbitration.
5. Reference of interpleader issues to arbitration.

Arbitrators and Umpires

6. When reference is to a single arbitrator.
7. Power of parties in certain cases to supply vacancy.
8. Umpires.
9. Agreements for reference to three arbitrators.
10. Power of court in certain cases to appoint an arbitrator or umpire.
11. Reference to official referee.

Conduct of Proceedings, Witnesses, &c.

12. Conduct of proceedings, witnesses, &c.

Provisions as to Awards

13. Time for making award.
14. Interim awards.
15. Specific performance.
16. Awards to be final.
17. Power to correct slips.

Costs, Fees and Interest

18. Costs.
19. Taxation of arbitrator's or umpire's fees.
20. Interest on awards.

Special Cases, Remission and Setting aside of Awards, &c.

21. Statement of case.
22. Power to remit award.
23. Removal of arbitrator and setting aside of award.
24. Power of court to give relief where arbitrator is not impartial or the dispute involves question of fraud.
25. Power of court where arbitrator is removed or authority of arbitrator is revoked.

Enforcement of Award

26. Enforcement of award.

Miscellaneous

27. Power of court to extend time for commencing arbitration proceedings.
28. Terms as to costs, &c.
29. Extension of s.496 of the Merchant Shipping Act 1894.
30. Crown to be bound.
31. Application of Part I to statutory arbitrations.
32. Meaning of "arbitration agreement."
33. Operation of Part I.
34. Extent of Part I.

Part II

Enforcement of certain Foreign Awards

35. Awards to which Part II applies.
36. Effect of foreign awards.
37. Conditions for enforcement of foreign awards.
38. Evidence.
39. Meaning of "final award."
40. Saving for other rights, &c.
41. Application of Part II to Scotland.
42. Application of Part II to Northern Ireland.
43. Saving for pending proceedings.

Part III

General

44. Short title, commencement and repeal.

SCHEDULES:

First Schedule.—Protocol on Arbitration Clauses signed on behalf of His Majesty at a Meeting of the Assembly of the League of Nations held on the twenty-fourth day of September, nineteen hundred and twenty-three.

Second Schedule.—Convention on the Execution of Foreign Arbitral Awards signed at Geneva on behalf of His Majesty on the twenty-sixth day of September, nineteen hundred and twenty-seven.

[The Schedules are not reproduced here]

An Act to consolidate the Arbitration Acts 1889 to 1934.

[28th July 1950]

Part I

General Provisions as to Arbitration

Effect of Arbitration Agreements, &c.

Authority of arbitrators and umpires to be irrevocable

1. The authority of an arbitrator or umpire appointed by or by virtue of an arbitration agreement shall, unless a contrary intention is expressed in the agreement, be irrevocable except by leave of the High Court or a judge thereof.

Death of party

2.—(1) An arbitration agreement shall not be discharged by the death of any party thereto, either as respects the deceased or any other party, but shall in such an event be enforceable by or against the personal representative of the deceased.

(2) The authority of an arbitrator shall not be revoked by the death of any party by whom he was appointed.

(3) Nothing in this section shall be taken to affect the operation of any enactment or rule of law by virtue of which any right of action is extinguished by the death of a person.

Bankruptcy

3.—(1) Where it is provided by a term in a contract to which a bankrupt is a party that any differences arising thereout or in connection therewith shall be referred to arbitration, the said term shall, if the trustee in bankruptcy adopts the contract, be enforceable by or against him so far as relates to any such differences.

(2) Where a person who has been adjudged bankrupt had, before the commencement of the bankruptcy, become a party to an arbitration agreement, and any matter to which the agreement applies requires to be determined in connection with or for the purposes of the bankruptcy proceedings, then, if the case is one to which subsection (1) of this section does not apply, any other party to the agreement or, with the consent of the committee of inspection, the trustee in bankruptcy, may apply to the court having jurisdiction in the bankruptcy proceedings for an order directing that the matter in question shall be referred to arbitration in

accordance with the agreement, and that court may, if it is of opinion that, having regard to all the circumstances of the case, the matter ought to be determined by arbitration, make an order accordingly.

Staying court proceedings where there is submission to arbitration

4.—(1) If any party to an arbitration agreement, or any person claiming through or under him, commences any legal proceedings in any court against any other party to the agreement, or any person claiming through or under him, in respect of any matter agreed to be referred, any party to those legal proceedings may at any time after appearance, and before delivering any pleadings or taking any other steps in the proceedings, apply to that court to stay the proceedings, and that court or a judge thereof, if satisfied that there is no sufficient reason why the matter should not be referred in accordance with the agreement, and that the applicant was, at the time when the proceedings were commenced, and still remains, ready and willing to do all things necessary to the proper conduct of the arbitration, may make an order staying the proceedings.

(2) . . . .[1]

Reference of interpleader issues to arbitration

5. Where relief by way of interpleader is granted and it appears to the High Court that the claims in question are matters to which an arbitration agreement, to which the claimants are parties, applies, the High Court may direct the issue between the claimants to be determined in accordance with the agreement.

Arbitrators and Umpires

When reference is to a single arbitrator

6. Unless a contrary intention is expressed therein, every arbitration agreement shall, if no other mode of reference is provided, be deemed to include a provision that the reference shall be to a single arbitrator.

Power of parties in certain cases to supply vacancy

7. Where an arbitration agreement provides that the reference shall be to two arbitrators, one to be appointed by each party, then, unless a contrary intention is expressed therein—

 (*a*) if either of the appointed arbitrators refuses to act, or is incapable of acting, or dies, the party who appointed him may appoint a new arbitrator in his place;
 (*b*) if, on such a reference, one party fails to appoint an arbitrator, either originally, or by way of substitution as aforesaid, for seven clear days after the other party, having appointed his arbitrator,

---

[1] Repealed by Arbitration Act 1975, s.8(2)(*a*).

has served the party making default with notice to make the appointment, the party who has appointed an arbitrator may appoint that arbitrator to act as sole arbitrator in the reference and his award shall be binding on both parties as if he had been appointed by consent:

Provided that the High Court or a judge thereof may set aside any appointment made in pursuance of this section.

Umpires

8.—(1)[2] Unless a contrary intention is expressed therein, every arbitration agreement shall, where the reference is to two arbitrators, be deemed to include a provision that the two arbitrators may appoint an umpire at any time after they are themselves appointed and shall do so forthwith if they cannot agree.

(2) Unless a contrary intention is expressed therein, every arbitration agreement shall, where such a provision is applicable to the reference, be deemed to include a provision that if the arbitrators have delivered to any party to the arbitration agreement, or to the umpire, a notice in writing stating that they cannot agree, the umpire may forthwith enter on the reference in lieu of the arbitrators.

(3) At any time after the appointment of an umpire, however appointed, the High Court may, on the application of any party to the reference and notwithstanding anything to the contrary in the arbitration agreement, order that the umpire shall enter upon the reference in lieu of the arbitrators and as if he were a sole arbitrator.

Majority award of three arbitrators

9.[3] Unless the contrary intention is expressed in the arbitration agreement, in any case where there is a reference to three arbitrators, the award of any two of the arbitrators shall be binding.

Power of court in certain cases to appoint an arbitrator or umpire

10.[4]—(1) In any of the following cases—

(a) where an arbitration agreement provides that the reference shall be to a single arbitrator, and all the parties do not, after differences have arisen, concur in the appointment of an arbitrator;

(b) if an appointed arbitrator refuses to act, or is incapable of acting, or dies, and the arbitration agreement does not show that it was intended that the vacancy should not be supplied and the parties do not supply the vacancy;

(c) where the parties or two arbitrators are required or are at liberty to appoint an umpire or third arbitrator and do not appoint him;

---

[2] As amended by Arbitration Act 1979, s.6(1).
[3] Substituted by Arbitration Act 1979, s.6(2).
[4] As amended by Arbitration Act 1979, ss.6(3)(4), 8(3)(a).

(*d*) where an appointed umpire or third arbitrator refuses to act, or is incapable of acting, or dies, and the arbitration agreement does not show that it was intended that the vacancy should not be supplied, and the parties or arbitrators do not supply the vacancy;

any party may serve the other parties or the arbitrators, as the case may be, with a written notice to appoint or, as the case may be, concur in appointing, an arbitrator, umpire or third arbitrator, and if the appointment is not made within seven clear days after the service of the notice, the High Court or a judge thereof may, on application by the party who gave the notice, appoint an arbitrator, umpire or third arbitrator who shall have the like powers to act in the reference and make an award as if he had been appointed by consent of all parties.

(2) In any case where—

(*a*) an arbitration agreement provides for the appointment of an arbitrator or umpire by a person who is neither one of the parties nor an existing arbitrator (whether the provision applies directly or in default of agreement by the parties or otherwise), and
(*b*) that person refuses to make the appointment or does not make it within the time specified in the agreement or, if no time is so specified, within a reasonable time,

any party to the agreement may serve the person in question with a written notice to appoint an arbitrator or umpire and, if the appointment is not made within seven clear days after the service of the notice, the High Court or a judge thereof may, on the application of the party who gave the notice, appoint an arbitrator or umpire who shall have the like powers to act in the reference and make an award as if he had been appointed in accordance with the terms of the agreement.

Reference to official referee

11. Where an arbitration agreement provides that the reference shall be to an official referee, any official referee to whom application is made shall, subject to any order of the High Court or a judge thereof as to transfer or otherwise, hear and determine the matters agreed to be referred.

Conduct of Proceedings, Witnesses, &c.

Conduct of proceedings, witnesses, &c.

12.—(1) Unless a contrary intention is expressed therein, every arbitration agreement shall, where such a provision is applicable to the reference, be deemed to contain a provision that the parties to the reference, and all persons claiming through them respectively, shall, subject to any legal objection, submit to be examined by the arbitrator or umpire, on oath or affirmation, in relation to the matters in dispute, and shall, subject as aforesaid, produce before the arbitrator or umpire all documents within their possession or power respectively which may be required or called for, and do all other things which during the proceedings on the reference the arbitrator or umpire may require.

(2) Unless a contrary intention is expressed therein, every arbitration agreement shall, where such a provision is applicable to the reference, be deemed to contain a provision that the witnesses on the reference shall, if the arbitrator or umpire thinks fit, be examined on oath or affirmation.

(3) An arbitrator or umpire shall, unless a contrary intention is expressed in the arbitration agreement, have power to administer oaths to, or take the affirmations of, the parties to and witnesses on a reference under the agreement.

(4) Any party to a reference under an arbitration agreement may sue out a writ of subpoena ad testificandum or a writ of subpoena duces tecum, but no person shall be compelled under any such writ to produce any document which he could not be compelled to produce on the trial of an action, and the High Court or a judge thereof may order that a writ of subpoena ad testificandum or of subpoena duces tecum shall issue to compel the attendance before an arbitrator or umpire of a witness wherever he may be within the United Kingdom.

(5) The High Court or a judge thereof may also order that a writ of habeas corpus ad testificandum shall issue to bring up a prisoner for examination before an arbitrator or umpire.

(6) The High Court shall have, for the purpose of and in relation to a reference, the same power of making orders in respect of—

(*a*) security for costs;
(*b*) discovery of documents and interrogatories;
(*c*) the giving of evidence by affidavit;
(*d*) examination on oath of any witness before an officer of the High Court or any other person, and the issue of a commission or request for the examination of a witness out of the jurisdiction;
(*e*) the preservation, interim custody or sale of any goods which are the subject matter of the reference;
(*f*) securing the amount in dispute in the reference;
(*g*) the detention, preservation or inspection of any property or thing which is the subject of the reference or as to which any question may arise therein, and authorising for any of the purposes aforesaid any persons to enter upon or into any land or building in the possession of any party to the reference, or authorising any samples to be taken or any observation to be made or experiment to be tried which may be necessary or expedient for the purpose of obtaining full information or evidence; and
(*h*) interim injunctions or the appointment of a receiver;

as it has for the purpose of and in relation to an action or matter in the High Court:

Provided that nothing in this subsection shall be taken to prejudice any power which may be vested in an arbitrator or umpire of making orders with respect to any of the matters aforesaid.

APPENDIX 1

Provisions as to Awards

Time for making award

13.—(1) Subject to the provisions of subsection (2) of section twenty-two of this Act, and anything to the contrary in the arbitration agreement, an arbitrator or umpire shall have power to make an award at any time.

(2) The time, if any, limited for making an award, whether under this Act or otherwise, may from time to time be enlarged by order of the High Court or a judge thereof, whether that time has expired or not.

(3) The High Court may, on the application of any party to a reference, remove an arbitrator or umpire who fails to use all reasonable dispatch in entering on and proceeding with the reference and making an award, and an arbitrator or umpire who is removed by the High Court under this subsection shall not be entitled to receive any remuneration in respect of his services.

For the purposes of this subsection, the expression "proceeding with a reference" includes, in a case where two arbitrators are unable to agree, giving notice of that fact to the parties and to the umpire.

Interim awards

14. Unless a contrary intention is expressed therein, every arbitration agreement shall, where such a provision is applicable to the reference, be deemed to contain a provision that the arbitrator or umpire may, if he thinks fit, make an interim award, and any reference in this Part of this Act to an award includes a reference to an interim award.

Specific performance

15. Unless a contrary intention is expressed therein, every arbitration agreement shall, where such a provision is applicable to the reference, be deemed to contain a provision that the arbitrator or umpire shall have the same power as the High Court to order specific performance of any contract other than a contract relating to land or any interest in land.

Awards to be final

16. Unless a contrary intention is expressed therein, every arbitration agreement shall, where such a provision is applicable to the reference, be deemed to contain a provision that the award to be made by the arbitrator or umpire shall be final and binding on the parties and the persons claiming under them respectively.

Power to correct slips

17. Unless a contrary intention is expressed in the arbitration agreement, the arbitrator or umpire shall have power to correct in an award any clerical mistake or error arising from any accidental slip or omission.

Costs, Fees and Interest

Costs

18.—(1) Unless a contrary intention is expressed therein, every arbitration agreement shall be deemed to include a provision that the costs of the reference and award shall be in the discretion of the arbitrator or umpire, who may direct to and by whom and in what manner those costs or any part thereof shall be paid, and may tax or settle the amount of costs to be so paid or any part thereof, and may award costs to be paid as between solicitor and client.

(2) Any costs directed by an award to be paid shall, unless the award otherwise directs, be taxable in the High Court.

(3) Any provision in an arbitration agreement to the effect that the parties or any party thereto shall in any event pay their or his own costs of the reference or award or any part thereof shall be void, and this Part of this Act shall, in the case of an arbitration agreement containing any such provision, have effect as if that provision were not contained therein:

Provided that nothing in this subsection shall invalidate such a provision when it is a part of an agreement to submit to arbitration a dispute which has arisen before the making of that agreement.

(4) If no provision is made by an award with respect to the costs of the reference, any party to the reference may, within fourteen days of the publication of the award or such further time as the High Court or a judge thereof may direct, apply to the arbitrator for an order directing by and to whom those costs shall be paid, and thereupon the arbitrator shall, after hearing any party who may desire to be heard, amend his award by adding thereto such directions as he may think proper with respect to the payment of the costs of the reference.

(5) Section sixty-nine of the Solicitors Act 1932 (which empowers a court before which any proceeding is being heard or is pending to charge property recovered or preserved in the proceeding with the payment of solicitors' costs)[4a] shall apply as if an arbitration were a proceeding in the High Court, and the High Court may make declarations and orders accordingly.

Taxation of arbitrator's or umpire's fees

19.—(1) If in any case an arbitrator or umpire refuses to deliver his award except on payment of the fees demanded by him, the High Court may, on an application for the purpose, order that the arbitrator or umpire shall deliver the award to the applicant on payment into court by the applicant of the fees demanded, and further that the fees demanded shall be taxed by the taxing officer and that out of the money paid into court there shall be paid out to the arbitrator or umpire by way of fees such sum as may be found reasonable on taxation and that the balance of the money, if any, shall be paid out to the applicant.

(2) An application for the purposes of this section may be made by any party to the reference unless the fees demanded have been fixed by a written agreement between him and the arbitrator or umpire.

[4a] Now Solicitors Act 1974, s. 73.

(3) A taxation of fees under this section may be reviewed in the same manner as a taxation of costs.

(4) The arbitrator or umpire shall be entitled to appear and be heard on any taxation or review of taxation under this section.

Interest on awards

20. A sum directed to be paid by an award shall, unless the award otherwise directs, carry interest as from the date of the award and at the same rate as a judgment debt.

Special Cases, Remissions and Setting aside of Awards, &c.

Statement of case

21. ....[5]

Power to remit award

22.—(1) In all cases of reference to arbitration the High Court or a judge thereof may from time to time remit the matters referred, or any of them, to the reconsideration of the arbitrator or umpire.

(2) Where an award is remitted, the arbitrator or umpire shall, unless the order otherwise directs, make his award within three months after the date of the order.

Removal of arbitrator and setting aside of award

23.—(1) Where an arbitrator or umpire has misconducted himself or the proceedings, the High Court may remove him.

(2) Where an arbitrator or umpire has misconducted himself or the proceedings, or an arbitration or award has been improperly procured, the High Court may set the award aside.

(3) Where an application is made to set aside an award, the High Court may order that any money made payable by the award shall be brought into court or otherwise secured pending the determination of the application.

Power of court to give relief where arbitrator is not impartial or the dispute involves question of fraud

24.—(1) Where an agreement between any parties provides that disputes which may arise in the future between them shall be referred to an arbitrator named or designated in the agreement, and after a dispute has arisen any party applies, on the ground that the arbitrator so named or designated is not or may not be impartial, for leave to revoke the authority of the arbitrator or for an injunction to restrain any other party or the arbitrator from proceeding with the arbitration, it shall not be a ground for refusing the application that the said party at the time when he

---

[5] Repealed by Arbitration Act 1979, s.8(3)(*b*).

made the agreement knew, or ought to have known, that the arbitrator, by reason of his relation towards any other party to the agreement or of his connection with the subject referred, might not be capable of impartiality.

(2)[6] Where an agreement between any parties provides that disputes which may arise in the future between them shall be referred to arbitration, and a dispute which so arises involves the question whether any such party has been guilty of fraud, the High Court shall, so far as may be necessary to enable that question to be determined by the High Court, have power to order that the agreement shall cease to have effect and power to give leave to revoke the authority of any arbitrator or umpire appointed by or by virtue of the agreement.

(3) In any case where by virtue of this section the High Court has power to order that an arbitration agreement shall cease to have effect or to give leave to revoke the authority of an arbitrator or umpire, the High Court may refuse to stay any action brought in breach of the agreement.

Power of court where arbitrator is removed or authority of arbitrator is revoked

25.—(1) Where an arbitrator (not being a sole arbitrator), or two or more arbitrators (not being all the arbitrators) or an umpire who has not entered on the reference is or are removed by the High Court, the High Court may, on the application of any party to the arbitration agreement, appoint a person or persons to act as arbitrator or arbitrators or umpire in place of the person or persons so removed.

(2) Where the authority of an arbitrator or arbitrators or umpire is revoked by leave of the High Court, or a sole arbitrator or all the arbitrators or an umpire who has entered on the reference is or are removed by the High Court, the High Court may, on the application of any party to the arbitration agreement, either—

  (a) appoint a person to act as sole arbitrator in place of the person or persons removed; or
  (b) order that the arbitration agreement shall cease to have effect with respect to the dispute referred.

(3) A person appointed under this section by the High Court as an arbitrator or umpire shall have the like power to act in the reference and to make an award as if he had been appointed in accordance with the terms of the arbitration agreement.

(4) Where it is provided (whether by means of a provision in the arbitration agreement or otherwise) that an award under an arbitration agreement shall be a condition precedent to the bringing of an action with respect to any matter to which the agreement applies, the High Court, if it orders (whether under this section or under any other enactment) that the agreement shall cease to have effect as regards any particular dispute, may further order that the provision making an award a condition precedent to

---

[6] Restricted by Arbitration Act 1979, s.3(3).

the bringing of an action shall also cease to have effect as regards that dispute.

Enforcement of award

26.[7]—(1) An award on an arbitration agreement may, by leave of the High Court or a judge thereof, be enforced in the same manner as a judgment or order to the same effect, and where leave is so given, judgment may be entered in terms of the award.

(2) If—

(*a*) the amount sought to be recovered does not exceed the current limit on jurisdiction in section 40 of the County Courts Act 1959, and

(*b*) a county court so orders,

it shall be recoverable (by execution issued from the county court or otherwise) as if payable under an order of that court and shall not be enforceable under subsection (1) above.

(3) An application to the High Court under this section shall preclude an application to a county court and an application to a county court under this section shall preclude an application to the High Court.

Miscellaneous

Power of court to extend time for commencing arbitration proceedings

27. Where the terms of an agreement to refer future disputes to arbitration provide that any claims to which the agreement applies shall be barred unless notice to appoint an arbitrator is given or an arbitrator is appointed or some other step to commence arbitration proceedings is taken within a time fixed by the agreement, and a dispute arises to which the agreement applies, the High Court, if it is of opinion that in the circumstances of the case undue hardship would otherwise be caused, and notwithstanding that the time so fixed has expired, may, on such terms, if any, as the justice of the case may require, but without prejudice to the provisions of any enactment limiting the time for the commencement of arbitration proceedings, extend the time for such period as it thinks proper.

Terms as to costs, &c.

28.[8] Any order made under this Part of this Act may be made on such terms as to costs or otherwise as the authority making the order thinks just.

Extension of s. 496 of the Merchant Shipping Act 1894

29.—(1) In subsection (3) of section four hundred and ninety-six of the Merchant Shipping Act 1894 (which requires a sum deposited with a

[7] As amended by Administration of Justice Act 1977, s.17(2).
[8] As amended by Arbitration Act 1975, s.8(2)(*b*).

wharfinger by an owner of goods to be repaid unless legal proceedings are instituted by the shipowner), the expression "legal proceedings" shall be deemed to include arbitration.

(2)[9] For the purposes of the said section four hundred and ninety-six, as amended by this section, an arbitration shall be deemed to be commenced when one party to the arbitration agreement serves on the other party or parties a notice requiring him or them to appoint or concur in appointing an arbitrator, or, where the arbitration agreement provides that the reference shall be to a person named or designated in the agreement, requiring him or them to submit the dispute to the person so named or designated.

(3)[9] Any such notice as is mentioned in subsection (2) of this section may be served either—

(a) by delivering it to the person on whom it is to be served; or
(b) by leaving it at the usual last known place of abode in England of that person; or
(c) by sending it by post in a registered letter addressed to that person at his usual or last known place of abode in England;

as well as in any other manner provided in the arbitration agreement; and where a notice is sent by post in manner prescribed by paragraph (c) of this subsection, service thereof shall, unless the contrary is proved, be deemed to have been effected at the time at which the letter would have been delivered in the ordinary course of post.

Crown to be bound

30.[10] This Part of this Act shall apply to any arbitration to which Her Majesty, either in right of the Crown or of the Duchy of Lancaster or otherwise, or the Duke of Cornwall, is a party.

Application of Part I to statutory arbitrations

31.—(1)[11] Subject to the provisions of section thirty-three of this Act, this Part of this Act, except the provisions thereof specified in subsection (2) of this section, shall apply to every arbitration under any other Act (whether pased before or after the commencement of this Act) as if the arbitration were pursuant to an arbitration agreement and as if that other Act were an arbitration agreement, except in so far as this Act is inconsistent with that other Act or with any rules or procedure authorised or recognised thereby.

(2)[12] The provisions referred to in subsection (1) of this section are subsection (1) of section two, section three, section five, subsection (3) of

---

[9] Extended by Arbitration Act 1979, s.7(2).
[10] As amended by Arbitration Act 1975, s.8(2)(c).
[11] Explained by Arbitration Act 1979, s.7(3).
[12] As amended by Arbitration Act 1975, s.8(2)(d).

section eighteen and sections twenty-four, twenty-five, twenty-seven and twenty-nine.

Meaning of "arbitration agreement"

32. In this Part of this Act, unless the context otherwise requires, the expression "arbitration agreement" means a written agreement to submit present or future differences to arbitration, whether an arbitrator is named therein or not.

Operation of Part I

33. This Part of this Act shall not affect any arbitration commenced (within the meaning of subsection (2) of section twenty-nine of this Act) before the commencement of this Act, but shall apply to an arbitration so commenced after the commencement of this Act under an agreement made before the commencement of this Act.

Extent of Part I

34.[13] None of the provisions of this Part of this Act shall extend to Scotland or Northern Ireland.

PART II

ENFORCEMENT OF CERTAIN FOREIGN AWARDS

Awards to which Part II applies

35.—(1) This Part of this Act applies to any award made after the twenty-eighth day of July, nineteen hundred and twenty-four—

(a) in pursuance of an agreement for arbitration to which the protocol set out in the First Schedule to this Act applies; and

(b) between persons of whom one is subject to the jurisdiction of some one of such Powers as His Majesty, being satisfied that reciprocal provisions have been made, may by Order in Council declare to be parties to the convention set out in the Second Schedule to this Act, and of whom the other is subject to the jurisdiction of some other of the Powers aforesaid; and

(c) in one of such territories as His Majesty, being satisfied that reciprocal provisions have been made, may by Order in Council declare to be territories to which the said convention applies;

and an award to which this Part of this Act applies is in this Part of this Act referred to as "a foreign award."

(2) His Majesty may by a subsequent Order in Council vary or revoke any Order previously made under this section.

(3) Any Order in Council under section one of the Arbitration (Foreign

---

[13] As amended by Arbitration Act 1975, s.8(2)(e).

Awards) Act 1930, which is in force at the commencement of this Act shall have effect as if it had been made under this section.

Effect of foreign awards

36.—(1) A foreign award shall, subject to the provisions of this Part of this Act, be enforceable in England either by action or in the same manner as the award of an arbitrator is enforceable by virtue of section twenty-six of this Act.

(2) Any foreign award which would be enforceable under this Part of this Act shall be treated as binding for all purposes on the persons as between whom it was made, and may accordingly be relied on by any of those persons by way of defence, set off or otherwise in any legal proceedings in England, and any references in this Part of this Act to enforcing a foreign award shall be construed as including references to relying on an award.

Conditions for enforcement of foreign awards

37.—(1) In order that a foreign award may be enforceable under this Part of this Act it must have—

- (*a*) been made in pursuance of an agreement for arbitration which was valid under the law by which it was governed;
- (*b*) been made by the tribunal provided for in the agreement or constituted in manner agreed upon by the parties;
- (*c*) been made in conformity with the law governing the arbitration procedure;
- (*d*) become final in the country in which it was made;
- (*e*) been in respect of a matter which may lawfully be referred to arbitration under the law of England;

and the enforcement thereof must not be contrary to the public policy or the law of England.

(2) Subject to the provisions of this subsection, a foreign award shall not be enforceable under this Part of this Act if the court dealing with the case is satisfied that—

- (*a*) the award has been annulled in the country in which it was made; or
- (*b*) the party against whom it is sought to enforce the award was not given notice of the arbitration proceedings in sufficient time to enable him to present his case, or was under some legal incapacity and was not properly represented; or
- (*c*) the award does not deal with all the questions referred or contains decisions on matters beyond the scope of the agreement for arbitration:

Provided that, if the award does not deal with all the questions referred, the court may, if it thinks fit, either postpone the enforcement of the award or order its enforcement subject to the giving of such security by the person seeking to enforce it as the court may think fit.

(3) If a party seeking to resist the enforcement of a foreign award

proves that there is any ground other than the non-existence of the conditions specified in paragraphs (*a*), (*b*) and (*c*) of subsection (1) of this section, or the existence of the conditions specified in paragraphs (*b*) and (*c*) of subsection (2) of this section, entitling him to contest the validity of the award, the court may, if it thinks fit, either refuse to enforce the award or adjourn the hearing until after the expiration of such period as appears to the court to be reasonably sufficient to enable that party to take the necessary steps to have the award annulled by the competent tribunal.

Evidence

38.—(1) The party seeking to enforce a foreign award must produce—

(*a*) the original award or a copy thereof duly authenticated in manner required by the law of the country in which it was made; and
(*b*) evidence proving that the award has become final; and
(*c*) such evidence as may be necessary to prove that the award is a foreign award and that the conditions mentioned in paragraphs (*a*), (*b*) and (*c*) of subsection (1) of the last foregoing section are satisfied.

(2) In any case where any document required to be produced under subsection (1) of this section is in a foreign language, it shall be the duty of the party seeking to enforce the award to produce a translation certified as correct by a diplomatic or consular agent of the country to which that party belongs, or certified as correct in such other manner as may be sufficient according to the law of England.

(3)[14] Subject to the provisions of this section, rules of court may be made under section 84 of the Supreme Court Act 1981[15] with respect to the evidence which must be furnished by a party seeking to enforce an award under this Part of this Act.

Meaning of "final award"

39. For the purposes of this Part of this Act, an award shall not be deemed final if any proceedings for the purpose of contesting the validity of the award are pending in the country in which it was made.

Saving for other rights, &c.

40. Nothing in this Part of this Act shall—

(*a*) prejudice any rights which any person would have had of enforcing in England any award or of availing himself in England of any award if neither this Part of this Act nor Part I of the Arbitration (Foreign Awards) Act 1930 had been enacted; or

---

[14] In relation to Northern Ireland, the reference to section 84 of the Supreme Court Act 1981 is replaced by a reference to section 55 of the Judicature (Northern Ireland) Act 1978 (1978 c.23, Sched. 5, Pt. II).

[15] Substituted by Supreme Court Act 1981, s.152(1) and Sched. 5.

(b) apply to any award made on an arbitration agreement governed by the law of England.

Application of Part II to Scotland

41.—(1) The following provisions of this section shall have effect for the purpose of the application of this Part of this Act to Scotland.

(2) For the references to England there shall be substituted references to Scotland.

(3) For subsection (1) of section thirty-six there shall be substituted the following subsection:—

"(1) A foreign award shall, subject to the provisions of this Part of this Act, be enforceable by action, or, if the agreement for arbitration contains consent to the registration of the award in the Books of Council and Session for execution and the award is so registered, it shall, subject as aforesaid, be enforceable by summary diligence."

(4)[16] For subsection (3) of section thirty-eight there shall be substituted the following subsection:—

"(3) The Court of Session shall, subject to the provisions of this section, have power to make provision by Act of Sederunt with respect to the evidence which must be furnished by a party seeking to enforce in Scotland an award under this Part of this Act."

Application of Part II to Northern Ireland

42.—(1) The following provisions of this section shall have effect for the purpose of the application of this Part of this Act to Northern Ireland.

(2) For the references to England there shall be substituted references to Northern Ireland.

(3) For subsection (1) of section thirty-six there shall be substituted the following subsection:—

"(1) A foreign award shall, subject to the provisions of this Part of this Act, be enforceable either by action or in the same manner as the award of an arbitrator under the provisions of the Common Law Procedure Amendment Act (Ireland) 1856 was enforceable at the date of the passing of the Arbitration (Foreign Awards) Act 1930."

(4) . . . .[17]

Saving for pending proceedings

43. . . . .[18]

---

[16] As amended by Law Reform (Miscellaneous Provisions) (Scotland) Act 1966, s.11, Sched., Pt. I.
[17] Repealed by Judicature (Northern Ireland) Act 1978, s. 122, Sched. 7, Pt. I.
[18] Repealed by Statute Law (Repeals) Act 1978, Sched. 1, Pt. I.

Part III

General

44.—(1) This Act may be cited as the Arbitration Act 1950.

(2) This Act shall come into operation on the first day of September, nineteen hundred and fifty.

(3) The Arbitration Act 1889, the Arbitration Clauses (Protocol) Act 1924, and the Arbitration Act 1934, are hereby repealed except in relation to arbitrations commenced (within the meaning of subsection (2) of section twenty-nine of this Act) before the commencement of this Act, and the Arbitration (Foreign Awards) Act 1930 is hereby repealed; and any reference in any Act or other document to any enactment hereby repealed shall be construed as including a reference to the corresponding provision of this Act.

APPENDIX 2

ARBITRATION ACT 1979

(1979 c. 42)

ARRANGEMENT OF SECTIONS

SECTION
1. Judicial review of arbitration awards.
2. Determination of preliminary point of law by court.
3. Exclusion agreements affecting rights under sections 1 and 2.
4. Exclusion agreements not to apply in certain cases.
5. Interlocutory orders.
6. Minor amendments relating to awards and appointment of arbitrators and umpires.
7. Application and interpretation of certain provisions of Part I of principal Act.
8. Short title, commencement, repeals and extent.

An Act to amend the law relating to arbitrations and for purposes connected therewith. [4th April 1979]

Judicial review of arbitration awards

1.—(1) In the Arbitration Act 1950 (in this Act referred to as "the principal Act") section 21 (statement of case for a decision of the High Court) shall cease to have effect and, without prejudice to the right of appeal conferred by subsection (2) below, the High Court shall not have jurisdiction to set aside or remit an award on an arbitration agreement on the ground of errors of fact or law on the face of the award.

(2) Subject to subsection (3) below, an appeal shall lie to the High Court on any question of law arising out of an award made on an arbitration agreement; and on the determination of such an appeal the High Court may by order—

    (*a*) confirm, vary or set aside the award; or
    (*b*) remit the award to the reconsideration of the arbitrator or umpire together with the court's opinion on the question of law which was the subject of the appeal;

and where the award is remitted under paragraph (*b*) above the arbitrator or umpire shall, unless the order otherwise directs, make his award within three months after the date of the order.

(3) An appeal under this section may be brought by any of the parties to the reference—

(*a*) with the consent of all the other parties to the reference; or

(*b*) subject to section 3 below, with the leave of the court.

(4) The High Court shall not grant leave under subsection (3)(*b*) above unless it considers that, having regard to all the circumstances, the determination of the question of law concerned could substantially affect the rights of one or more of the parties to the arbitration agreement; and the court may make any leave which it gives conditional upon the applicant complying with such conditions as it considers appropriate.

(5) Subject to subsection (6) below, if an award is made and, on an application made by any of the parties to the reference,—

(*a*) with the consent of all the other parties to the reference, or

(*b*) subject to section 3 below, with the leave of the court,

it appears to the High Court that the award does not or does not sufficiently set out the reasons for the award, the court may order the arbitrator or umpire concerned to state the reasons for his award in sufficient detail to enable the court, should an appeal be brought under this section, to consider any question of law arising out of the award.

(6) In any case where an award is made without any reason being given, the High Court shall not make an order under subsection (5) above unless it is satisfied—

(*a*) that before the award was made one of the parties to the reference gave notice to the arbitrator or umpire concerned that a reasoned award would be required; or

(*b*) that there is some special reason why such a notice was not given.

(6A)[1] Unless the High Court gives leave, no appeal shall lie to the Court of Appeal from a decision of the High Court—

(*a*) to grant or refuse leave under subsection (3)(*b*) or (5)(*b*) above; or

(*b*) to make or not to make an order under subsection (5) above.

(7) No appeal shall lie to the Court of Appeal from a decision of the High Court on an appeal under this section unless—

(*a*) the High Court or the Court of Appeal gives leave; and

(*b*) it is certified by the High Court that the question of law to which its decision relates either is one of general public importance or is one which for some other special reason should be considered by the Court of Appeal.

(8) Where the award of an arbitrator or umpire is varied on appeal, the award as varied shall have effect (except for the purposes of this section) as if it were the award of the arbitrator or umpire.

Determination of preliminary point of law by court

2.—(1) Subject to subsection (2) and section 3 below, on an application to the High Court made by any of the parties to a reference—

---

[1] Added by Supreme Court Act 1981, s.148(2).

(a) with the consent of an arbitrator who has entered on the reference or, if an umpire has entered on the reference, with his consent, or
(b) with the consent of all the other parties,

the High Court shall have jurisdiction to determine any question of law arising in the course of the reference.

(2) The High Court shall not entertain an application under subsection (1)(a) above with respect to any question of law unless it is satisfied that—

(a) the determination of the application might produce substantial savings in costs to the parties; and
(b) the question of law is one in respect of which leave to appeal would be likely to be given under section 1(3)(b) above.

(2A)[2] Unless the High Court gives leave, no appeal shall lie to the Court of Appeal from a decision of the High Court to entertain an application under subsection (1)(a) above.

(3)[3] A decision of the High Court under subsection (1) above shall be deemed to be a judgment of the court within the meaning of section 16 of the Supreme Court Act 1981 (appeals to the Court of Appeal), but no appeal shall lie from such a decision unless—

(a) the High Court or the Court of Appeal gives leave; and
(b) it is certified by the High Court that the question of law to which its decision relates either is one of general public importance or is one which for some other special reason should be considered by the Court of Appeal.

Exclusion agreements affecting rights under sections 1 and 2

3.—(1) Subject to the following provisions of this section and section 4 below—

(a) the High Court shall not, under section 1(3)(b) above, grant leave to appeal with respect to a question of law arising out of an award, and
(b) the High Court shall not, under section 1(5)(b) above, grant leave to make an application with respect to an award, and
(c) no application may be made under section 2(1)(a) above with respect to a question of law,

if the parties to the reference in question have entered into an agreement in writing (in this section referred to as an "exclusion agreement") which excludes the right of appeal under section 1 above in relation to that award or, in a case falling within paragraph (c) above, in relation to an award to which the determination of the question of law is material.

(2) An exclusion agreement may be expressed so as to relate to a particular award, to awards under a particular reference or to any other description of awards, whether arising out of the same reference or not;

---

[2] Added by Supreme Court Act 1981, s.148(3).
[3] As amended by Supreme Court Act 1981, ss.148(3), 152(1) and Sched. 5.

and an agreement may be an exclusion agreement for the purposes of this section whether it is entered into before or after the passing of this Act and whether or not it forms part of an arbitration agreement.

(3) In any case where—

(a) an arbitration agreement, other than a domestic arbitration agreement, provides for disputes between the parties to be referred to arbitration, and
(b) a dispute to which the agreement relates involves the question whether a party has been guilty of fraud, and
(c) the parties have entered into an exclusion agreement which is applicable to any award made on the reference of that dispute,

then, except in so far as the exclusion agreement otherwise provides, the High Court shall not exercise its powers under section 24(2) of the principal Act (to take steps necessary to enable the question to be determined by the High Court) in relation to that dispute.

(4) Except as provided by subsection (1) above, sections 1 and 2 above shall have effect notwithstanding anything in any agreement purporting—

(a) to prohibit or restrict access to the High Court; or
(b) to restrict the jurisdiction of that court; or
(c) to prohibit or restrict the making of a reasoned award.

(5) An exclusion agreement shall be of no effect in relation to an award made on, or a question of law arising in the course of a reference under, a statutory arbitration, that is to say, such an arbitration as is referred to in subsection (1) of section 31 of the principal Act.

(6) An exclusion agreement shall be of no effect in relation to an award made on, or a question of law arising in the course of a reference under, an arbitration agreement which is a domestic arbitration agreement unless the exclusion agreement is entered into after the commencement of the arbitration in which the award is made or, as the case may be, in which the question of law arises.

(7) In this section "domestic arbitration agreement" means an arbitration agreement which does not provide, expressly or by implication, for arbitration in a State other than the United Kingdom and to which neither—

(a) an individual who is a national of, or habitually resident in, any State other than the United Kingdom, nor
(b) a body corporate which is incorporated in, or whose central management and control is exercised in, any State other than the United Kingdom,

is a party at the time the arbitration agreement is entered into.

Exclusion agreements not to apply in certain cases

4.—(1) Subject to subsection (3) below, if an arbitration award or a question of law arising in the course of a reference relates, in whole or in part, to—

(a) a question or claim falling within the Admiralty jurisdiction of the High Court, or
(b) a dispute arising out of a contract of insurance, or
(c) a dispute arising out of a commodity contract,

an exclusion agreement shall have no effect in relation to the award or question unless either—

(i) the exclusion agreement is entered into after the commencement of the arbitration in which the award is made or, as the case may be, in which the question of law arises, or
(ii) the award or question relates to a contract which is expressed to be governed by a law other than the law of England and Wales.

(2) In subsection (1)(c) above "commodity contract" means a contract—

(a) for the sale of goods regularly dealt with on a commodity market or exchange in England or Wales which is specified for the purposes of this section by an order made by the Secretary of State; and
(b) of a description so specified.

(3) The Secretary of State may by order provide that subsection (1) above—

(a) shall cease to have effect; or
(b) subject to such conditions as may be specified in the order, shall not apply to any exclusion agreement made in relation to an arbitration award of a description so specified;

and an order under this subsection may contain such supplementary, incidental and transitional provisions as appear to the Secretary of State to be necessary or expedient.

(4) The power to make an order under subsection (2) or subsection (3) above shall be exercisable by statutory instrument which shall be subject to annulment in pursuance of a resolution of either House of Parliament.

(5) In this section "exclusion agreement" has the same meaning as in section 3 above.

Interlocutory orders

5.—(1) If any party to a reference under an arbitration agreement fails within the time specified in the order or, if no time is so specified, within a reasonable time to comply with an order made by the arbitrator or umpire in the course of the reference, then, on the application of the arbitrator or umpire or of any party to the reference, the High Court may make an order extending the powers of the arbitrator or umpire as mentioned in subsection (2) below.

(2) If an order is made by the High Court under this section, the arbitrator or umpire shall have power, to the extent and subject to any conditions specified in that order, to continue with the reference in default of appearance or of any other act by one of the parties in like manner as a

judge of the High Court might continue with proceedings in that court where a party fails to comply with an order of that court or a requirement of rules of court.

(3) Section 4(5) of the Administration of Justice Act 1970 (jurisdiction of the High Court to be exercisable by the Court of Appeal in relation to judge-arbitrators and judge-umpires) shall not apply in relation to the power of the High Court to make an order under this section, but in the case of a reference to a judge-arbitrator or judge-umpire that power shall be exercisable as in the case of any other reference to arbitration and also by the judge-arbitrator or judge-umpire himself.

(4) Anything done by a judge-arbitrator or judge-umpire in the exercise of the power conferred by subsection (3) above shall be done by him in his capacity as judge of the High Court and have effect as if done by that court.

(5) The preceding provisions of this section have effect notwithstanding anything in any agreement but do not derogate from any powers conferred on an arbitrator or umpire, whether by an arbitration agreement or otherwise.

(6) In this section "judge-arbitrator" and "judge-umpire" have the same meaning as in Schedule 3 to the Administration of Justice Act 1970.

Minor amendments relating to awards and appointment of arbitrators and umpires

6. [*These amendments are incorporated in the Arbitration Act 1950 as printed in Appendix 1.*]

Application and interpretation of certain provisions of Part I of principal Act.

7.—(1) References in the following provisions of Part I of the principal Act to that Part of that Act shall have effect as if the preceding provisions of this Act were included in that Part, namely,—

(*a*) section 14 (interim awards);
(*b*) section 28 (terms as to costs of orders);
(*c*) section 30 (Crown to be bound);
(*d*) section 31 (application to statutory arbitrations); and
(*e*) section 32 (meaning of "arbitration agreement").

(2) Subsections (2) and (3) of section 29 of the principal Act shall apply to determine when an arbitration is deemed to be commenced for the purposes of this Act.

(3) For the avoidance of doubt, it is hereby declared that the reference in subsection (1) of section 31 of the principal Act (statutory arbitrations) to arbitration under any other Act does not extend to arbitration under section 92 of the County Courts Act 1959 (cases in which proceedings are to be or may be referred to arbitration) and accordingly nothing in this Act or in Part I of the principal Act applies to arbitration under the said section 92.

Short title, commencement, repeals and extent

8.—(1) This Act may be cited as the Arbitration Act 1979.

(2) This Act shall come into operation on such day as the Secretary of State may appoint by order made by statutory instrument; and such an order—

- (*a*) may appoint different days for different provisions of this Act and for the purposes of the operation of the same provision in relation to different descriptions of arbitration agreement; and
- (*b*) may contain such supplementary, incidental and transitional provisions as appear to the Secretary of State to be necessary or expedient.

(3) In consequence of the preceding provisions of this Act, the following provisions are hereby repealed, namely—

- (*a*) in paragraph (*c*) of section 10 of the principal Act the words from "or where" to the end of the paragraph;
- (*b*) section 21 of the principal Act;
- (*c*) in paragraph 9 of Schedule 3 to the Administration of Justice Act 1970, in sub-paragraph (1) the words "21(1) and (2)" and sub-paragraph (2).

(4) This Act forms part of the law of England and Wales only.

Appendix 3

THE ARBITRATION (COMMODITY CONTRACTS) ORDER 1979

(S.I. 1979 No. 754)

Made	2nd July 1979
Laid before Parliament	9th July 1979
Coming into Operation	1st August 1979

The Secretary of State, in exercise of the powers conferred on him by section 4(2) of the Arbitration Act 1979[1] and of all other powers enabling him in that behalf, hereby makes the following Order:—

1.—(1) This Order may be cited as the Arbitration (Commodity Contracts) Order 1979 and shall come into operation on 1st August 1979.
   (2) In this Order—
   "the Act" means the Arbitration Act 1979;
   "market" means a commodity market or exchange.

2. The following markets are hereby specified for the purpose of section 4 of the Act—

(a) the markets set out in Part I of the Schedule hereto;
(b) any market in which contracts for sale are subject to the rules or regulations of one or other of the associations set out in Part II of the Schedule, whether or not the market is a market on which commodities are bought and sold at a particular place.

3. The following descriptions of contract are hereby specified for the purpose of section 4 of the Act—

(a) contracts for the sale of goods on any market specified in Article 2 of this Order;
(b) contracts for the sale of goods which are subject to arbitration rules of the London Metal Exchange or of an association set out in Part II of the Schedule hereto.

Cecil Parkinson,
Minister of State,
Department of Trade.

2nd July 1979.

---

[1] 1979 c. 42.

SCHEDULE

Part I

Markets

The London Cocoa Terminal Market
The London Coffee Terminal Market
The London Grain Futures Market
The London Metal Exchange
The London Rubber Terminal Market
The Gafta Soya Bean Meal Futures Market
The London Sugar Terminal Market
The London Vegetable Oil Terminal Market
The London Wool Terminal Market

Part II

Markets in which contracts are subject to rules or regulations of the following Associations
The Cocoa Association of London Limited
The Coffee Trade Federation
The Combined Edible Nut Trade Association
Federation of Oils, Seeds and Fats Associations Limited
The General Produce Brokers' Association of London
The Grain and Feed Trade Association Limited
The Hull Seed, Oil and Cake Association
The Liverpool Cotton Association Limited
London Jute Association
London Rice Brokers' Association
The National Federation of Fruit and Potato Trades Limited
The Rubber Trade Association of London
Skin Hide and Leather Traders Association Limited
The Sugar Association of London
The Refined Sugar Association
The Tea Brokers' Association of London
The British Wool Confederation

EXPLANATORY NOTE

(This Note is not part of the Order.)

This Order specifies commodity markets or exchanges ("markets") in England or Wales and descriptions of contracts for the purpose of section 4 of the Arbitration Act 1979 ("the Act"), which defines "commodity contract" for the purposes of agreements excluding the right of appeal under section 1 of the Act or determinations of questions of law under section 2.

The markets specified by the Order are:

(a) the markets set out in Part I of the Schedule to the Order,
(b) markets where the contracts for sale are subject to rules or regulations of an association set out in Part II of the Schedule.

The descriptions of contract specified by the Order are

(a) contracts for the sale of goods on any market specified by the Order; or
(b) contracts for the sale of goods which are subject to arbitration rules of the London Metal Exchange or of an association set out in Part II of the Schedule to the Order.

APPENDIX 4

ARBITRATION (SCOTLAND) ACT 1894

(57 & 58 Vict. c. 13)

An Act to amend the Law of Arbitration in Scotland. [3rd July 1894]

Reference to arbiter not named, &c. not to be invalid

1. . . . [1], an agreement to refer to arbitration shall not be invalid or ineffectual by reason of the reference being to a person not named, or to a person to be named by another person, or to a person merely described as the holder for the time being of any office or appointment.

On failure to concur in nomination of single arbiter, court may appoint

2. Should one of the parties to an agreement to refer to a single arbiter refuse to concur in the nomination of such arbiter, and should no provision have been made for carrying out the reference in that event, or should such provision have failed, an arbiter may be appointed by the court, on the application of any party to the agreement, and the arbiter so appointed shall have the same powers as if he had been duly nominated by all the parties.

On failure of one party to nominate arbiter, court may appoint

3. Should one of the parties to an agreement to refer to two arbiters refuse to name an arbiter, in terms of the agreement, and should no provision have been made for carrying out the reference in that event, or should such provision have failed, an arbiter may be appointed by the court, on the application of the other party, and the arbiter so appointed shall have the same powers as if he had been duly nominated by the party so refusing.

Arbiters may devolve on oversmen unless otherwise agreed

4. Unless the agreement to refer shall otherwise provide, arbiters shall have power to name an oversman on whom the reference shall be devolved in the event of their differing in opinion. Should the arbiters fail to agree in the nomination of an oversman, the court may on the application of any party to the agreement, appoint an oversman. The decision of such oversman, whether he has been named by the arbiters or appointed by the court, shall be final.

[1] Words repealed by Statute Law Revision Act 1908.

Act not to apply to certain agreements

5. This Act shall not apply to any agreement, made before its passing, to refer to an arbiter not named or to be named by another person or merely described as the holder for the time being of an office or appointment, if any party to such agreement shall, before the passing of this Act, or within six months thereafter, have intimated to the other party by writing that he declines to be bound by such agreement.

Interpretation

6.[2] For the purposes of this Act the expression "the court" shall mean any sheriff having jurisdiction or any Lord Ordinary of the Court of Session: except that where—

(*a*) any arbiter appointed is: or
(*b*) in terms of the agreement to refer to arbitration an arbiter or oversman to be appointed must be,

a Senator of the College of Justice, "the court" shall mean the Inner House of the Court of Session.

Extent of Act and short title

7. This Act shall apply to Scotland only, and may be cited as the Arbitration (Scotland) Act 1894.

---

[2] As amended by Law Reform (Miscellaneous Provisions) (Scotland) Act 1980, s.17(4).

APPENDIX 5

ADMINISTRATION OF JUSTICE (SCOTLAND) ACT 1972

(1972 c. 59)

An Act to confer extended powers on the courts in Scotland to order the inspection of documents and other property, and related matters; to enable an appeal to be taken to the House of Lords from an intercutor of the Court of Session on a motion for a new trial; to enable a case to be stated on a question of law to the Court Session in an arbitration; and to enable alterations to be made by act of sederunt in the rate of interest to be included in sheriff court decrees or extracts. [9th August 1972]

Power of arbiter to state case to Court of Session

3.—(1) Subject to express provision to the contrary in an agreement to refer to arbitration, the arbiter or oversman may, on the application of a party to the arbitration, and shall, if the Court of Session on such an application so directs, at any stage in the arbitration state a case for the opinion of that Court on any question of law arising in the arbitration.

(2) This section shall not apply to an arbitration under any enactment which confers a power to appeal to or state a case for the opinion of a court or tribunal in relation to that arbitration.

(3)[1] This section shall not apply to any form of arbitration relating to a trade dispute within the meaning of the Industrial Courts Act 1919 or relating to a trade dispute within the meaning of the Trade Union and Labour Relations Act 1974; to any other arbitration arising from a collective agreement within the meaning of the said Act of 1974; or to proceedings before the Industrial Arbitration Board.

(4) This section shall not apply in relation to an agreement to refer to arbitration made before the commencement of this Act.

5.—(1) This Act may be cited as the Administration of Justice (Scotland) Act 1972.

(2) In this Act any reference to an enactment shall be construed as a reference to that enactment as amended by or under any other enactment.

(3)[2] Sections 1 and 3 of this Act shall come into operation on such day as the Secretary of State may by order made by statutory instrument appoint, and different days may be appointed for different purposes.

(4) This Act shall extend to Scotland only.

[1] As amended by Trade Union and Labour Relations Act 1974, Sched. 3, para. 17, Sched. 5.

[2] Power fully exercised: April 2, 1973, appointed for ss. 1 and 3 by S.I. 1973 No. 339, art. 2.

APPENDIX 6

ARBITRATION ACT 1975

(1975 c. 3)

ARRANGEMENT OF SECTIONS

Effect of arbitration agreement on court proceedings

SECTION
1. Staying court proceedings where party proves arbitration agreement.

Enforcement of Convention awards
2. Replacement of former provisions.
3. Effect of Convention awards.
4. Evidence.
5. Refusal of enforcement.
6. Saving.

General

7. Interpretation.
8. Short title, repeals, commencement and extent.

An Act to give effect to the New York Convention on the Recognition and Enforcement of Foreign Arbitral Awards. [25th February 1975]

Effect of arbitration agreement on court proceedings

Staying court proceedings where party proves arbitration agreement

1.—(1) If any party to an arbitration agreement to which this section applies, or any person claiming through or under him, commences any legal proceedings in any court against any other party to the agreement, or any person claiming through or under him, in respect of any matter agreed to be referred, any party to the proceedings may at any time after appearance, and before delivering any pleadings or taking any other steps in the proceedings, apply to the court to stay the proceedings; and the court, unless satisfied that the arbitration agreement is null and void, inoperative or incapable of being performed or that there is not in fact any dispute between the parties with regard to the matter agreed to be referred, shall make an order staying the proceedings.

(2) This section applies to any arbitration agreement which is not a

domestic arbitration agreement; and neither section 4(1) of the Arbitration Act 1950 nor section 4 of the Arbitration Act (Northern Ireland) 1937 shall apply to an arbitration agreement to which this section applies.

(3) In the application of this section to Scotland, for the references to staying proceedings there shall be substituted references to sisting proceedings.

(4) In this section "domestic arbitration agreement" means an arbitration agreement which does not provide, expressly or by implication, for arbitration in a State other than the United Kingdom and to which neither—

(a) an individual who is a national of, or habitually resident in, any State other than the United Kingdom; nor
(b) a body corporate which is incorporated in, or whose central management and control is exercised in, any State other than the United Kingdom;

is a party at the time the proceedings are commenced.

Enforcement of Convention awards

Replacement of former provisions

2. Sections 3 to 6 of this Act shall have effect with respect to the enforcement of Convention awards; and where a Convention award would, but for this section, be also a foreign award within the meaning of Part II of the Arbitration Act 1950, that Part shall not apply to it.

Effect of Convention awards

3.—(1) A Convention award shall, subject to the following provisions of this Act, be enforceable—

(a) in England and Wales, either by action or in the same manner as the award of an arbitrator is enforceable by virtue of section 26 of the Arbitration Act 1950;
(b) in Scotland, either by action or, in a case where the arbitration agreement contains consent to the registration of the award in the Books of Council and Session for execution and the award is so registered, by summary diligence;
(c) in Northern Ireland, either by action or in the same manner as the award of an arbitrator is enforceable by virtue of section 16 of the Arbitration Act (Northern Ireland) 1937.

(2) Any Convention award which would be enforceable under this Act shall be treated as binding for all purposes on the persons as between whom it was made, and may accordingly be relied on by any of those persons by way of defence, set off or otherwise in any legal proceedings in the United Kingdom; and any reference in this Act to enforcing a Convention award shall be construed as including references to relying on such an award.

Evidence

4. The party seeking to enforce a Convention award must produce—

(*a*) the duly authenticated original award or a duly certified copy of it; and
(*b*) the original arbitration agreement or a duly certified copy of it; and
(*c*) where the award or agreement is in a foreign language, a translation of it certified by an official or sworn translator or by a diplomatic or consular agent.

Refusal of enforcement

5.—(1) Enforcement of a Convention award shall not be refused except in the cases mentioned in this section.

(2) Enforcement of a Convention award may be refused if the person against whom it is invoked proves—

(*a*) that a party to the arbitration agreement was (under the law applicable to him) under some incapacity; or
(*b*) that the arbitration agreement was not valid under the law to which the parties subjected it or, failing any indication thereon, under the law of the country where the award was made; or
(*c*) that he was not given proper notice of the appointment of the arbitrator or of the arbitration proceedings or was otherwise unable to present his case; or
(*d*) (subject to subsection (4) of this section) that the award deals with a difference not contemplated by or not falling within the terms of the submission to arbitration or contains decisions on matters beyond the scope of the submission to arbitration; or
(*e*) that the composition of the arbitral authority or the arbitral procedure was not in accordance with the agreement of the parties or, failing such agreement, with the law of the country where the arbitration took place; or
(*f*) that the award has not yet become binding on the parties, or has been set aside or suspended by a competent authority of the country in which, or under the law of which, it was made.

(3) Enforcement of a Convention award may also be refused if the award is in respect of a matter which is not capable of settlement by arbitration, or if it would be contrary to public policy to enforce the award.

(4) A Convention award which contains decisions on matters not submitted to arbitration may be enforced to the extent that it contains decisions on matters submitted to arbitration which can be separated from those on matters not so submitted.

(5) Where an application for the setting aside or suspension of a Convention award has been made to such a competent authority as is mentioned in subsection (2)(*f*) of this section, the court before which enforcement of the award is sought may, if it thinks fit, adjourn the proceedings and may, on the application of the party seeking to enforce the award, order the other party to give security.

Saving

6. Nothing in this Act shall prejudice any right to enforce or rely on an award otherwise than under this Act or Part II of the Arbitration Act 1950.

General

Interpretation

7.—(1) In this Act—

"arbitration agreement" means an agreement in writing (including an agreement contained in an exchange of letters or telegrams) to submit to arbitration present or future differences capable of settlement by arbitration;

"Convention award" means an award made in pursuance of an arbitration agreement in the territory of a State, other than the United Kingdom, which is a party to the New York Convention; and

"the New York Convention" means the Convention on the Recognition and Enforcement of Foreign Arbitral Awards adopted by the United Nations Conference on International Commercial Arbitration on 10th June 1958.

(2) If Her Majesty by Order in Council declares that any State specified in the Order is a party to the New York Convention the Order shall, while in force, be conclusive evidence that that State is a party to that Convention.

(3) An Order in Council under this section may be varied or revoked by a subsequent Order in Council.

Short title, repeals, commencement and extent

8.—(1) This Act may be cited as the Arbitration Act 1975.

(2) The following provisions of the Arbitration Act 1950 are hereby repealed, that is to say—

(*a*) section 4(2);
(*b*) in section 28 the proviso;
(*c*) in section 30 the words "(except the provisions of subsection (2) of section 4 thereof)";
(*d*) in section 31(2) the words "subsection (2) of section 4"; and
(*e*) in section 34 the words from the beginning to "save as aforesaid."

(3)[1] This Act shall come into operation on such date as the Secretary of State may by order made by statutory instrument appoint.

(4) This Act extends to Northern Ireland.

---

[1] Power of appointment fully exercised: December 23, 1975, appointed by S.I. 1975 No. 1662.

APPENDIX 7

THE ARBITRATION (FOREIGN AWARDS) ORDER 1978

(S.I. 1978 No. 186)

Made .... 9th February 1978
Coming into Operation .... 2nd March 1978

At the Court at Buckingham Palace, the 9th day of February 1978
Present,
The Queen's Most Excellent Majesty in Council.

Whereas a Convention on the Execution of Foreign Arbitral Awards (hereinafter called "the Geneva Convention"[1] was, on 26th September 1927, signed at Geneva on behalf of His late Majesty King George the Fifth:
And whereas it is provided by section 35(1) of the Arbitration Act 1950[2] that Part II of that Act (which provides for the enforcement of certain foreign awards under the Geneva Convention) applies to any award made after 28 July 1924—

(*a*) in pursuance of an agreement for arbitration to which the Protocol set out in the First Schedule to that Act applies; and
(*b*) between persons of whom one is subject to the jurisdiction of some one of such Powers as Her Majesty, being satisfied that reciprocal provisions have been made, may by Order in Council declare to be parties to the Geneva Convention, and of whom the other is subject to the jurisdiction of some other of the Powers aforesaid; and
(*c*) in one of such territories as Her Majesty, being satisfied that reciprocal provisions have been made, may by Order in Council declare to be territories to which the Geneva Convention applies:

And whereas Her Majesty is satisfied that reciprocal provisions have been made:
Now, therefore, Her Majesty, by and with the advice of Her Privy Council, in pursuance of the powers conferred on Her by the said Act, and of all other powers enabling Her in that behalf, is pleased to declare, and it is hereby declared, as follows:—

Citation, interpretation and commencement

1.—(1) This Order may be cited as the Arbitration (Foreign Awards) Order 1978, and shall come into operation on 2nd March 1978.

[1] Schedule 2 to the Arbitration Act 1950.
[2] 1950 c. 27.

(2) The Interpretation Act 1889[3] shall apply for the interpretation of this Order as it applies for the interpretation of an Act of Parliament and as if this Order and the Orders hereby revoked were Acts of Parliament.

Geneva Convention States

2.—(1) The Powers listed in Column 1 of Schedule 1 to this Order are parties to the Geneva Convention.

(2) The territories listed in Column 2 of the said Schedule 1 are territories to which the General Convention applies.

Revocations

3. The Orders listed in Schedule 2 to this Order are hereby revoked.

N. E. Leigh,
Clerk of the Privy Council.

SCHEDULE 1

Geneva Convention States

Column 1	Column 2
Powers party to the Geneva Convention	Territories to which the Geneva Convention applies
The United Kingdom of Great Britain and Northern Ireland	The United Kingdom of Great Britain and Northern Ireland
	Belize
	British Virgin Islands
	Cayman Islands
	Falkland Islands and Dependencies
	Gibraltar
	Hong Kong
	Montserrat
	Turks and Caicos Islands
	West Indies, Associated States (Antigua, Dominica, St. Lucia, St. Vincent, St. Christopher, Nevis and Anguilla)
Austria	Austria
Belgium	Belgium
Czechoslovakia	Czechoslovakia
Denmark	Denmark
Finland	Finland
France	France
Federal Republic of Germany	Federal Republic of Germany
German Democratic Republic	German Democratic Republic

[3] 1889 c.63.

APPENDIX 7

Column 1	Column 2
Powers party to the Geneva Convention	Territories to which the Geneva Convention applies
Greece	Greece
India	India
The Republic of Ireland	The Republic of Ireland
Israel	Israel
Italy	Italy
Japan	Japan
Kenya	Kenya
Luxembourg	Luxembourg
Mauritius	Mauritius
Netherlands	Netherlands (including the Netherland Antilles)
New Zealand	New Zealand
Pakistan	Pakistan
Portugal	Portugal
Romania	Romania
Spain	Spain
Sweden	Sweden
Switzerland	Switzerland
United Republic of Tanzania	United Republic of Tanzania
Thailand	Thailand
Yugoslavia	Yugoslavia

SCHEDULE 2

ORDERS REVOKED

Title	Reference
Arbitration (Foreign Awards) No. 4 Order 1931.	S.R. & O. 1931/1066
Arbitration (Foreign Awards) No. 1 Order 1932.	S.R. & O. 1932/674
Arbitration (Foreign Awards) No. 2 Order 1933.	S.R. & O. 1933/544
Arbitration (Foreign Awards) No. 1 Order 1938.	S.R. & O. 1938/137
Arbitration (Foreign Awards) No 1 Order 1952.	S.I. 1952/2035
Arbitration (Foreign Awards) No. 1 Order 1953.	S.I. 1953/1555

THE ARBITRATION (FOREIGN AWARDS) ORDER 1978

Title	Reference
Arbitration (Foreign Awards) No. 1 Order 1958.	S.I. 1958/1051
Arbitration (Foreign Awards) Order 1960.	S.I. 1960/436
Arbitration (Foreign Awards) (Hong Kong) Order 1965	S.I. 1965/586

EXPLANATORY NOTE

(This Note is not part of the Order.)

This Order specifies (in Schedule 1) States which are parties to the 1927 Geneva Convention on the Execution of Foreign Arbitral Awards, and which have satisfied Her Majesty that they have made reciprocal provisions. The original Orders relating to those States listed in Schedule 2 are revoked. An arbitral award made in a Geneva Convention State is enforceable in the United Kingdom under Part II of the Arbitration Act 1950 except, where the State in question is also a New York Convention State, in so far as the award is enforceable under the Arbitration Act 1975 (c.3).

APPENDIX 8

THE ARBITRATION (FOREIGN AWARDS) ORDER 1979

(S.I. 1979 No. 304)

Made .... *14th March 1979*
Coming into Operation .... *12th April 1979*

At the Court at Buckingham Palace, the 14th day of March 1979
Present,
The Queen's Most Excellent Majesty in Council.

Whereas a Convention on the Execution of Foreign Arbitral Awards (hereinafter called "the Geneva Convention"[1] was, on 26th September 1927, signed at Geneva on behalf of His late Majesty King George the Fifth:

And whereas it is provided by section 35(1) of the Arbitration Act 1950[2] that Part II of that Act (which provides for the enforcement of certain foreign awards under the Geneva Convention) applies to any award made after 28th July 1924—

(*a*) in pursuance of an agreement for arbitration to which the Protocol set out in the First Schedule to that Act applies; and

(*b*) between persons of whom one is subject to the jurisdiction of some one of such Powers as Her Majesty, being satisfied that reciprocal provisions have been made, may by Order in Council declare to be parties to the Geneva Convention, and of whom the other is subject to the jurisdiction of some other of the Powers aforesaid; and

(*c*) in one of such territories as Her Majesty, being satisfied that reciprocal provisions have been made, may by Order in Council declare to be territories to which the Geneva Convention applies:

And whereas Her Majesty is satisfied that reciprocal provisions have been made:

And whereas a Convention on the Recognition and Enforcement of Foreign Arbitral Awards (hereinafter called "the New York Convention"[3] was acceded to by the United Kingdom of Great Britain and Northern Ireland on 23rd December 1975:

And whereas it is provided by section 7(2) of the Arbitration Act 1975[4]

---

[1] Schedule 2 to the Arbitration Act 1950.
[2] 1950 c. 27.
[3] Cmnd. 1515
[4] 1975 c. 3.

THE ARBITRATION (FOREIGN AWARDS) ORDER 1979

(which Act provides for the enforcement of foreign awards under the New York Convention) that if Her Majesty by Order in Council declares that any State specified in the Order is a party to the New York Convention the Order shall, while in force, be conclusive evidence that that State is a party to that Convention:

Now, therefore, Her Majesty, by and with the advice of Her Privy Council, in pursuance of the powers conferred upon Her by the said Acts, and of all other powers enabling Her in that behalf, is pleased to declare, and it is hereby declared, as follows:

Citation and commencement

1. This Order may be cited as the Arbitration (Foreign Awards) Order 1979 and shall come into operation on 12th April 1979.

Geneva Convention State

2.—(1) The Power specified in Column 1 of Schedule 1 to this Order is a party to the Geneva Convention.

(2) The territory specified in Column 2 of the said Schedule is a territory to which the Geneva Convention applies.

New York Convention States

3. The States listed in Schedule 2 to this Order are parties to the New York Convention.

Revocation

4. The Arbitration (Foreign Awards) Order 1975[5] is hereby revoked.

N. E. Leigh,
Clerk of the Privy Council.

SCHEDULE 1

GENEVA CONVENTION STATE

Column 1	Column 2
Power party to the Geneva Convention	Territory to which the Geneva Convention applies
Grenada	Grenada

---

[5] S. I. 1975 No. 1709.

SCHEDULE 2
NEW YORK CONVENTION STATES

Australia (including all the external territories for the international relations of which Australia is responsible)
Austria
Belgium
Benin
Botswana
Bulgaria
Central African Empire
Chile
Cuba
Czechoslovakia
Denmark
Ecuador
Egypt
Finland
France (including territories of the French Republic)
Federal Republic of Germany and Berlin (West)
German Democratic Republic
Ghana
Greece
Holy See
Hungary
India
Israel
Italy
Japan
Democratic Kampuchea
Republic of Korea
Kuwait
Madagascar
Mexico
Morocco
Netherlands (including the Netherlands Antilles)
Niger
Nigeria
Norway
Philippines
Poland
Romania
South Africa
Spain
Sri Lanka
Sweden
Switzerland
Syrian Arab Republic
Thailand
Trinidad and Tobago
Tunisia
Union of Soviet Socialist Republics
United Republic of Tanzania
United States of America (including all the territories for the international relations of which the United States of America is responsible)

EXPLANATORY NOTE

(This Note is not part of the Order.)

This Order specifies (in Schedule 1) Grenada as a State which is a party to the 1927 Geneva Convention on the Execution of Foreign Arbitral Awards, and which has satisfied Her Majesty that it has made reciprocal provisions. The Order also specifies (in Schedule 2) States which are parties to the 1958 New York Convention on the Recognition and Enforcement of Foreign Arbitral Awards. Arbitral awards made in such States are enforceable in the United Kingdom under the Arbitration Act 1975. It replaces the Arbitration (Foreign Awards) Order 1975, which is revoked.

INDEX

Administration of Justice (Scotland) Act 1972, 105, 114, 153
Agents,
  arbitration agreement, party to, 15
Appeals,
  arbitration agreement, under, 90
  arbitrator incompetent, where, 36
  award, challenging, 90–98
  board of appeal, to, 90
  'consultative case', 92–98
  court, to, 1979 Act, under, 92–98
  Court of Appeal, to, 95
  enforcement of award, for, 86–90
  excluded, 96–98
  exclusion agreement, from, 92
  High Court, to, 92–94
  international arbitration, exclusion agreements, 98
  leave to, 93, 94–95
  negligence,
    immunity from suit, 5, 6–8
  preliminary point of law, on, 95–98
  question of law, on, 92–94, 95–98
  right of, Scotland, in, 105
  Scotland, in, 104–106
    grounds of, 109–111
  section 2, 95–96
  section 7, 92–95
  setting aside award. *See* Award, setting aside of.
  special case, 92
    Scotland, in, 104–106
  statement of case, 132
  umpire, to, 90
Arbitration,
  Acts, 1–2
  advantage of, 3, 113
  agreement. *See* Arbitration Agreement.
  appeal from. *See* Appeals.
  award. *See* Award.
  building contracts. *See* Building Contracts.
  certification and, 4–8. *See also* Certification.
  commencement of. *See* Limitation of Time.

Arbitration—*cont*.
  commercial, 1
    remuneration of arbitrator, 48
  commercial court, in, 35
  commodity contracts, 148–150
  consensual, 2–3
  definition, 1
    judicial inquiry, as, 4
    valuation and, 4
  England, in, 2
  ex parte proceedings, 59
  inappropriate, 30
  industrial, 1
  injustice in, 44
  international. *See* International Arbitrations.
  investment disputes, 119
  judicial inquiry, as, 4
  limitation of time. *See* Limitation of Time.
  London, in, 113
  merchant shipping, 134–135
  mutuality, 17
  null and void, where, 90, 91
  private, 57
  procedure at. *See* Procedure.
  publicity, 3
  refusal to, 24–25
  Scottish. *See* Scotland.
  statutory, 2–3, 135
    appointment of arbitrator, 50–51
    waiver of provisions, 63
  valuation and, 4–8. *See also* Valuations.
Arbitration Act 1950, 123–140
  Part II, 114–116
Arbitration Act 1975, 116, 154–157
Arbitration Act 1979, 119
Arbitration Agreement, 10, 14–34
  abandonment of, 31–34
  alteration of, 30–31
  arbitrator, by, 53
  amendment to, 30–31, 53
  ancillary to other agreement, 89
  appeal under, 90
  appointment of arbitrator, 35–43
  bankruptcy, after, 14–15
  certainty of terms in, 21

Arbitration Agreement—*cont.*
  choice of law clause, 113
  clauses in. *See* Arbitration Clause.
  costs, provision for, 99
  deed, as, 18
  definition of, 16, 17, 136
  domestic, 96, 97, 117
  enforcement of, 24–30. *See also*
    Enforcement of Award;
    Remedies.
    death of party, where, 31
    Scotland, in, 104, 186
  exclusion agreement, 47, 92, 96–98,
    104–105, 143–145
  frustration of, 23–24, 31–34
  incorporation of, contract, in, 18–21
  informal, 18
  inspection of property clause, 54
  international, exclusion agreements,
    98
  mutual, 17
  non-domestic, 96–98, 119
  oral, 14, 64
    enforcement of, 87
  parol, 64
  parol contract, where, 16–17
  parties to. *See* Parties.
  recognition of, internationally,
    116–118
  repudiation of, 23–24, 31–34
  revocation of, 31
  scope of, 23–24
  sensible meaning, 17–18
  signed, 16–18
  sealed, 18
  Statute of Frauds, and, 16–17, 18
  terms of, 21–23
    certainty of, 21
    conduct of hearing, 57
    implied, 21
  time limit, in, 10–13
  validity of, 26–27
    internationally, 116–118
  voidable, where, 14
  writing, in, 16
    additions to, 64
    enforcement of, 87
    recognition of, 116
Arbitration Clause. *See also*
  Arbitration Agreement.
  ambiguous, 18
  appointment of arbitrator, 35–40
  assignment of, 27
  '*Atlantic Shipping*', 22–23
  bilateral reference rights, 17

Arbitration Clause—*cont.*
  bill of lading, in, 20–21
  charterparty, in, 20–21
  choice of law, 113
  determination of, 27
  frustration of, 23–24
  Geneva Protocol on, 114–116
  incorporation of, 18–21
  mutual, 17
  repudiation of, 23–24
  scope of, 23–24
  '*Scott* v. *Avery*', 22, 48
  sub-contract, in 19–20
  validity of,
    repudiation, where, 27
  void,
    ambiguity for, 18
Arbitration (Foreign Awards) Order
  1978, 158–161
Arbitration (Foreign Awards) Order
  1979, 162–164
Arbitration (Scotland) Act 1894,
  151–152
Arbitrators, 35–49
  acceptance of office by, 51
  advocate, as, 51
  agent, as, building contracts, 4
  appointment of, 35–43, 50–54
    Act of Parliament, under, 50–51
    concurrence by parties, 25
    court, by, 38, 40, 42, 43, 127–128
    death of party, where, 45
    dispute over, 38
    failure to, 25, 42
    fluctuating body, 40
    formalities, 50
    institution, by, 36
    notice to, 25
    notification of, 50–51
    other arbitrators, by, 40
    parties, by, 35–40
    professional body, by, 50
    public officer, by, 36
    Scotland, in, 106–108
    setting aside of, 37, 45
    statutory arbitrations, in, 2
    third person, by, 38
  appointment of third party, by, 25
  arbiter, 183
  Atlantic Shipping Clause, 22–23
  authority of, 51, 56
    commencement of, 50–51
    exceeds, where, 44
    irrevocable, 44, 125
    reservation of, 81

INDEX

Arbitrators—*cont.*
  authority of—*cont.*
    revocation of, 43–48, 89
      courts' powers, 133–134
    See also powers of.
  calling of witnesses, by, 74
  capacity of, 36, 37, 40, 41, 42, 45
  commercial court, in, 35
  death of, 37, 40, 41, 42, 45
  delegation of duties by, 64–65, 77
  discretion of,
    costs, 99, 100–102
    defence, 52
    place of hearing, 54–55
    points of claim, 52
    preliminary meeting, at, 52
    Scotland, in, 108
    time of hearing, 54–55
  disqualification of, 44
  duties of,
    delegation of, 64–65, 77
    evidence, 68–69
  exceeds jurisdiction, 89
  failure to act, 41–42
  failure to appoint, 25, 42
  first duties of, 51–52
  fluctuating body of, 40
  fraud by, 91, 132–133
  functus, 78
  immunity of, 4–8
  impartiality of, 36, 46–47
  incapacity of. *See* capacity.
  incompetent, 36
  jurisdiction of, 4, 23. *See also* authority of.
  legal advice, seeking of, by, 60–61
  'ministerial acts' of, delegation of, 64
  misconduct of, 44, 46, 51, 59, 68–69, 89, 91, 132–133
    costs, over, 100–102
    late award, 76
    refusal to adjourn, 54
  negligence, immunity from, 4–5
  notice to appoint, 25, 50–51
  number of, 1, 25, 36
  oversman, 103
  powers of, 21
    appointment of umpire, 39
    awards of interest, 85
    cessation of, 78
    correction, 83
    delaying tactics, where, 34
    dismissal of action, 32
    ex parte proceedings, 59
    non-compliance with, 34

Arbitrators—*cont.*
  powers of—*cont.*
    preliminary meeting, at, 52
    revoked by court, 38
    Scotland, in, prorogation, of, 109
    See also authority of.
  protests to, irregularities, where, 62
  qualities of, 3–4
  reasonable despatch requirement, 45
  refusal to act, 37, 40, 42, 45
  removal of, 42, 43–48, 132
    court, by, 40, 133
    court's powers, 133
    fraud, where, 47
    irregular procedure, where, 61
    late award, 76
    misconduct, where, 46
    not impartial, where, 46–47
    remuneration, 49
  remuneration of, 45, 48–49
    commercial arbitration, in, 48
    removed, where, 49
    Scotland, in, 107–108
    taxation of, 131–132
  reservation of opinion, 81
  revocation of authority, 43–48
  role of, 3–4
  several, 36–37, 38–40, 61, 126–127
    execution of award, 77
    Scotland, in, 106–107
    unable to agree, 45
  sole, 36, 37–38, 107, 126
    failure to appoint, 41
  specialist, 64–65, 69
  suing of, 49
  third arbitrator, failure to act, 42–43
  third party, 38–39
  See also Umpires.
Arenson v. *Arenson (1977)*, 6–8
Awards, 76–83, 130
  action on, 87–89
    defences to, 89, 90
  action to enforce, time limit, 9
  ambiguous, 83–84
  amendment of, 83–84
  appeal from. *See* Appeals.
  arbitrator removed, where, 76
  binding, 83
  capable of performance, 81
  certainty of, 79–82
  challenge to,
    Scotland, in, 109–111
    See also Appeals.
  condition precedent, as, 22
  consensual and statutory, 3

168 INDEX

Awards—*cont.*
  consistent 79–82
  'Convention award,' 118
  copies of, 78
  costs of, 99. *See also* Costs.
  declaratory, 80
    enforcement of, 87
  decree-arbitral, 103
  defects in, Scotland, in, 111
  deed, as, stamp duties, 78
  delay in making, enlargement of time, 76–77
  delegation of making, 77
  delivery of, 78
  effect of, 83–84
    New York Convention, 155
  enforcement of, 86–90, 134
    action, by, 88
    international arbitration, 118–119, 136–140
    New York Convention, 154–157
    matters to be proved, 88
    Scotland, in, 109
    specific performance, 88–89
    time limits for, 89
  enlargement of time for, 76–77
  error in, power to correct, 130
  evidence, as, 84
  execution of, 77
    improper, 78
  final, 79–83, 130
    meaning of, international arbitration, 138
  foreign, enforcement of, 87, 114–116
  See also international; International Arbitration.
  foreign currency, in, 81–82
  formal requisites for, 77–79
  interest after, 86
  interest in, 84–86
  interest on, 132
  interim, 80, 81, 83, 130
  international, effect of, 137
    Orders, 158–164
  judicial review of, 92–94, 141–142
  legal, 81
  legal advisor, drawn up by, 77
  lien by arbitrator, on, 48
  majority award, 127
  making of, 76–83
    delegation, 77
    formal requisites, 77–79
    interest after, 86
    procedure, 59–60
    time of, 130

Awards—*cont.*
  misconduct, 90
  non-compliance with, defences to, 89
  objections to, waiver of, 80–81
  parol, 77, 89
  possible, 79–82
  precise, 81
  procedure after, 83–98
  publication of, 78
  reasons for, statement of, 93–94
  reasons in, 79
  recitals in, 78–79
  recognition of, New York Convention, 154–157
  remission of, 91, 132
    costs, over, 102
    judicial review, on, 93
  See also setting aside of, *infra*.
  seal, under, 78
  stamp duties and, 78
  setting aside of, 24, 90–92
    arbitrator's misconduct, 44
    common law, at, 91
    costs award, over, 99
      burden of proof, 100, 102
    evidence wrongly admitted, 68–69
    irregular procedure, where, 62
    misconduct of arbitrator, 89
    no notice, where, 59–60
    partial, 91–92
    parties excluded, where, 57
    Scotland, in, 109–111
    ultra fires compromissi, 111
    statutory provisions, 132
  several arbitrators, where, 77, 78
  single, 81
  special case, 21
  specific performance of, 88–89
  statutory, enforcement of, 87
  statutory and consensual, 3
  substantive requisites, 79–82
  time limit for, 76–77
    remission, after, 93
  time of, 76, 130
    enlargement of, 76–77
  transfer of property and, 84
  unambiguous, 79–82
  unconditional, 79–82
  uncontradictory, 79–82
  unenforceable at law, 89
  unimpeachable, 79–82
  validity of, 87
    evidence, in, 84
    formalities, 77–79
    procedural irregularity, 4

INDEX

Awards—*cont.*
  variation of, 93

Bankruptcy, 14–15
  party, of, 125–126
Bremer Vulkan, 31–32
Building Contract, 5
  advantage of arbitration, 3
  arbitrator as agent, 4
  certification and, 4
  sub-contract, incorporation of terms, 18–21

Certification, 4–8
  negligence, immunity from suit, 5
Chartered Institute of Arbitrators, 36
Commodity Contracts, Order, 97, 148–150
Costs, 3, 99–102, 131, 134
  arbitrator's discretion, 100–102
  award, of, 99
  Common Fund, 99
  following event, 100, 102
  no provision for, 83
  party and party, 48, 99
  recovery of, 48–49
  reference, of, 99
  security for, 129
  settled, 99–100
  statutory provisions, 131
  taxed, 48, 99–100
  transcript of hearing, of, 58
Court,
  appointment of arbitrator,
    powers of, 38
    setting aside of, 37
  commercial, arbitration in, 35
  costs jurisdiction, 100
  declaratory judgment by, 24
  discretion of,
    appointment of arbitrator, 43
    setting aside of, 45
    revocation of arbitrator's authority, 44
  enforcement of award by, 86–90
  jurisdiction of, 21–23
  powers of, 21–23, 145–146
    appointment of arbitrators, 38, 40–45, 127–128
    award ambiguous, where, 84
    costs, over, 100
    dismissal of claim, 32
    extension of time, 134
    fraud, where, 132–133
    interference with award, 91

Court—*cont.*
  powers of—*cont.*
    removal of arbitrator, 40, 42, 133
    removal of arbitrator, after, 47–48
    revocation of arbitrator's authority, 43
  Scotland, in, appointment of arbitrators, 106–107
  stay in proceedings, 126
    international arbitration, 117–118
    mandatory, 117–118
    New York Convention, 154–155
    Scotland, in, 104
  time limit for award, 76–77
  preliminary point of law, determination of, by, 142–143
  role of, 21–23
  specific performance order, 24
  stay of proceedings, in, 25–30
    See also under Procedure.
    arbitrator not impartial, 47
    onus of proof, 26
    'step in the proceedings,' 28
Criminal Proceedings,
  award as evidence, 84
Crown,
  party, as, 135

Death,
  arbitrator, of, 37, 40–42, 45
  parties, of, 15, 31, 45, 125
  Scotland, in, 109
Decree-Arbitral, 103
Definitions,
  arbitration, 1
  arbitration agreement, 16, 17, 136
  'commodity contract', 97
  domestic arbitration agreement, 96, 117
  evidence, 66–67
  final award, (international arbitration), 138

Enforcement of Award, 86–90
  foreign awards, of, 114–116
  international arbitration, in, 114–116, 118–119, 136–140, 154–157
  conditions for, 137
  Scotland, in, 104, 106, 109
  statutory provisions, 134
Evidence, 3–4, 66–75
  additional, 69, 91
  rules of procedure, 68
  admissibility of, 52, 67–69

Evidence—*cont.*
  admissibility of—*cont.*
    error by arbitration, 68–69
    expert, 75
  affidavit, 70
  affirmation, on, 69–70
  award as, 84
  circumstantial, 66
  collateral matters, of, 68
  conclusive, 65
  criminal proceedings, in, 84
  decision made on, 69
  derivative, 67
  direct, 66
  documentary, 66
  expert witness, of, 74–75
  extrinsic, 67
  'facts in issue,' 67
  false, 71
  hearing, at, taking of, 58
  hearsay, 67
    expert evidence, 75
  husband, of, 73
  inadmissible. *See* admissibility of, *supra.*
  indirect, 67
  international arbitration, 138, 156
  medical reports, of, 75
  New York Convention, 156
  oath, on, 69–70
  oral, 66, 70
  oral extrinsic, 67
  order of, 67–68
  original, 67
  out-of-court statements, of, 67
  parol, 67
  perjured, 71
  primary, 67
  prima facie, 67
  privileged, 73–74
  procedure for taking, 69–70
  real, 54, 66
  re-examination, 74
  refusal to hear, 53
  Scotland, in, 108
  secondary, 67
  stay in proceedings, for, 30
  taking of, 69–70
  wife, of, 73
  witnesses, by. *See under* Procedure.
Exclusion Agreements, 47, 95–98. *See also under* Arbitration Agreement.

Geneva Convention, 118
  foreign awards Orders, 158–164

Geneva Convention—*cont.*
  states participating, 159–160
Geneva Protocol, 114–116

Hague-Visby Rules,
  time limits, extension of, 13
Hannah Blumenthal, 33–34
Hearing,
  adjournment of, 54–55
  conduct of, 57–59
  costs of. *See* Costs.
  preliminary meeting to, 52–55
  procedure, at, 56–65. *See also* Procedure.
  time and place of, 54–55
    alteration, 54
  transcript of, 58

Injunction,
  arbitration, against, 32. *See also under* Remedies.
International Arbitrations, 2, 113–119
  advantages of, 113
  appeals from, 98
  awards, effect of, 137
  choice of law, 113
  Convention on investment disputes, 119
  effect of awards, New York Convention, 155
  enforcement of award, 114–116, 118–119, 135–140, 154–157
    conditions for, 137
    New York Convention, 116
  evidence in, 138
    New York Convention, 156
  exclusion agreements, 98
  foreign awards orders, 158–164
  Geneva Convention, 116, 118
    states participating, 159–160
  Geneva Protocol, 114–116, 118
  High Contracting Parties, 115
  International Chamber of Commerce, 119
  investment disputes, 119
  law governing, 113–114
  New York Convention, 116, 118, 154–157
    states participating, 164
  Order in Council, 115–116
  reciprocity principle, 114, 115, 116
  recognition of agreements, 116–118
  recognition of awards, New York Convention, 154–157

INDEX

International Arbitration,
  Scotland. *See under* Scotland.
  stay in proceedings, 117
  UNCITRAL rules, 119
International Chamber of Commerce, 119

Judicial References, Scotland, in, 111
Judicial review, award, of, 92–94
  Scotland, in, 109–111
  statutory provisions, 141–142

Law,
  appeal on question of, 95–98
  contract governing, 114
  governing arbitration, 114
  preliminary point of, determination by court, 142–143
  question of, 3
  Scotland, in, 104–105
Limitation of Time, 8–13
  actions to enforce awards, for, 9
  arbitration agreement, by, 10–13
  '*Atlantic Shipping*' clause, 22–23
  award, making of, for, 76–77
  'cause of action', 9, 10
  commencement of arbitration, 9
  disability, where, 9
  exclusion of, 9
  extension of, 9
    arbitration agreement, from, 10
    charterparties, 10–13
    courts' powers, 134
    'undue hardship,' 10–13
      principles of, 12
  statutory, 8–10
  Scotland, in, 108–109

Natural Justice, rules of, 56–57
Negligence,
  immunity from suit,
    arbitrator, of, 4–5
    public policy, 6
New York Convention, 116, 118, 154–157
  states participating, 164
Northern Ireland,
  statutory provision, 139

Official Referee, 5, 74, 128
Order in Council, 115–116
Oversman, 103

Parties,
  administrators, 15

Parties—*cont.*
  agents, 15
  appearance of, 57
  appointment of arbitrator, by, 35–40
  assignee of contract, 27
  bankrupt, 14, 125–126
  capacity of, 14–16
  companies, 15
  claimant,
    plaintiff, as, 57
  corporations, 15
  costs, payment by, 100
  death of, 15, 31, 45, 125
  fraud by, 47
  executors, 15
  general question,
    submission of, by, 80
  guardian, as, 15
  'High Contracting Parties,' 115
  joint interest, where, 16
  minors, 14
  partners, 16
  personal representatives, as, 27, 31
  representation, of, 57–58
  respondent, claimant, as, 57
  rights of, declaration of, 80
  signatures of, 18
  solicitor, 15
  trustees, 15
  unsound mind, of, 15
Preliminary Meeting. *See under* Procedure.
Procedure, 56–65
  adjournment of hearing, 54–55
    refusal to allow, 54
  affidavit evidence, 70
  alteration of agreement, 31
  amendments to pleadings, 31, 53
  appeals. *See* Appeals.
  appointment of arbitrator,
    court, by, 38, 40
    failure to, 42
    other arbitrators, by, 40
  appointment of umpire, for, 40
  arbitration agreements, leave to amend, 53
  arbitrator and, 4
  assessors, for, 57
  award,
    after, 83–98
    making of, for, 77–78
    See also Award.
  close of case, for, 59–60
  commencement of arbitration, 9, 27

Procedure—*cont.*
  commencement of arbitration—*cont.*
    courts' powers, 134
    international arbitration, 117
  commodity contracts, under, 148–150
  conduct of, 128–129
  costs, 3, 99–102. *See also* Costs.
  counsel's opinion, 60
  counterclaims, 58
    delivery of, 53
    particulars of, 52
  cross-examination, 58–59, 72, 73
  Crown, 135
  declaratory award, for, 80
  defence,
    delivery of, 52
  defendant,
    stay of proceedings by, 27
  determination by parties, 2
  discovery of documents, 52, 53
  evidence. *See* Evidence.
  ex parte proceedings, 24, 25, 55, 59.
    irregular, where, 62
    notice of, 25
  examination-in-chief, 58–59, 72–73
  examination of witness, arbitrator, by, 62
  execution of award, 77
  general question, submission by parties, 80
  habeas corpus writ, 71
  hearing, at, 56–65
    additional evidence, 68
    adjournment, 58
    arbitrator calls witnesses, 74
    burden of proof, 58
    close of case, 59–60
    conduct of, 57–59, 128–129
    costs. *See* Costs.
    counsel appearing, 57–58
    cross-examination, 58–59, 72–73
    deviation from, 56
    evidence. *See* Evidence.
    examination-in-chief, 58–59, 72–73
    fixing of time/place, 52
    irregularities in, 61–64
    private communications, 57
    public excluded, 57
    re-examination, 74
    several arbitrators, where, 61
    time and place, 54–55
    witnesses, 70–71
  inspection of property, 52, 53–54
  interest, payment of, 85–86
  interim award, for, 80, 81

Procedure—*cont.*
  interlocutory orders, 145–146
  international arbitrations, 115
  interpleader, 126
  irregularities, in, 61–64, 91
    Scotland, in, 111
  laches, guilty of, 89
  leading questions, 59
  leave to appeal, for, 93
  legal advice,
    arbitrator, for, 60–61
  limitation of time. *See* Limitation of Time.
  natural justice rules, 56–57
  objection to,
    waiver of right, 62–64
  official referee,
    reference to, 128
  Orders in Council,
    international arbitration, 115–116
  particulars of claim, 52
    delivery of, 53
  perjury, 71
  pleading,
    amendments to, 53
    delivery of, 52
  preliminary meeting, 51, 52–55
  prior to hearing, 50–55
  privileged documents, 53
  public policy and, 56
  recovery of costs between, 48–49
  re-examination, 74
  reopening of case, 60
  removal of arbitrator, for, 43–48
  representation of parties, 57–58
  right to object,
    waiver of, 62–64
  Scotland, 108, 109
  several arbitrators, where, 61
  shorthand writers, for, 57, 58
  special case, 92
    Scotland, in, 105
  stamping documents, 60
  stated case, 105
  statement of case, 132
  statutory arbitrations, in, 2
  stay of proceedings, 25–30, 126
    application for, 30
    mandatory, 117
    New York Convention, 154–155
    refusal to, 29–30
  subpoena, 70–71
  summary, 116
  taxing of costs, 48
  trustee in bankruptcy, 27

INDEX

Procedure—*cont.*
  UNCITRAL rules, 119
  witnesses, 70–71, 128–129
    award, of, 77
    called by arbitrator, 74
    character of, 72
    competence of, 71
    cross-examination, 72, 73
    examination of, 72–74
    expert, 74–75
    hostile, 72
    incrimination of, 73
    re-examination of, 74
    refreshing of memory, 73
  Scotland, 108–109

Remedies,
  abandonment of, 63
  action for declaration, defence to, 90
  appointment of arbitrator, 25
  damages, 24
    interest, as, 85–86
  declaration, 80
    Bremer Vulkan, 32
    Hannah Blumenthal, 33–34
  declaratory judgment, 24
  ex parte proceedings, 24
  indirect, 24–30
  injunction, 88
    Bremer Vulkan, 32
  injustice, for, removal of arbitrator, 44
  interlocutory orders, 145–146
  notice to concur, (appointment of arbitrator), 25
  neglect to act, arbitrator, of, 42
  recovery of monies, 88
  removal of arbitrator, 43–48
  specific performance, 24, 88–90, 130
  stay of proceedings, 25–28
  arbitrator, of 48–49
    excessive, 49
    removed, where, 49
    retention of award, by, 78
    Scotland, in, 107–108
    taxation of, 131–132
Right of Action, 10

Scotland,
  appeals. *See* challenge of award, *infra*.
  appointment of arbiter/oversman, 106–108
  arbiter, 103
    appointment of, 106–108

Scotland—*cont.*
  arbiter—*cont.*
    appointment of,
      failure to agree on, 151
    discretion of, 108
    not named, 151
    remuneration of, 107–108
    several, 107
  arbitration law, 2
  arbitrators. *See* arbiters; oversman.
  arbitration in, 103–112
  Articles of Regulation, 109–110
  challenge of award, 109, 111
  common law, 103
  powers of,
    appointment of arbiters, 106–108
  Court,
    Session, of, 153
  decree-arbitral, 103
  'decree conform,' 111
  delectus personae, 106
  enforcement of agreement, 104, 106, 109
  exclusion agreements, 104–105
  informal arbitrations in, 108
  judicial referee, 111
  judicial references in, 111
  limitation of time, 108–109
  oversman, 103
    appointment of, 106–108
    remuneration of, 107–108
    several, 107
  procedure, 108
    judicial reference, 111
    special case, 114
  proposed findings, 108
  prorogation, 108–109
  remuneration of arbiter, 107–108
  special case procedure in, 105, 114
  stated case procedure in, 105
  statutory provision, 139, 151–153
  stay in proceedings, in, 104
  twenty-fifth Article, 109–110
Scott v. *Avery* clause, 22, 48
Special Case, 21
Stamp Duties, 60
  award, for, 78
Statutory Arbitration. *See under* Arbitration.
Sutcliffe v. *Thackrah*, 5

Thorburn v. *Barnes*, 89
Time Limits. *See* Limitation of Time.
Tribunal,
  abroad, 29

Trustee,
  bankruptcy in, arbitration
    agreement, 14–15

Umpire, 1, 35–49, 127
  appointment of,
    court, by, 40–45
    lot, by, 44
  authority of,
    irrevocable, 125
    revocation of, 43
  failure to act, 42–43
  powers of, 21

Umpire—*cont.*
  remuneration of,
    taxation of, 131
  role of, 39
  third arbitrator and, 39
Umpires *See also* Arbitrators.

Valuations, 4–8
  definition, 4
  negligence,
    immunity from suit, 5

Witnesses. *See under* Procedure.